# WHY RELIGIOUS FREEDOM MATTERS FOR DEMOCRACY

Should an employee be allowed to wear a religious symbol at work? Should a religious employer be allowed to impose constraints on employees' private lives for the sake of enforcing a religious work ethos? Should an employee or service provider be allowed, on religious grounds, to refuse to work with customers of the opposite sex or of a same-sex sexual orientation? This book explores how judges decide these issues and defends a democratic approach, which is conducive to a more democratic understanding of our 'vivre ensemble'. The normative democratic approach proposed in this book is grounded on a sociological and historical analysis of two national stories of the relationships between law, religion, diversity and the State: the British (mainly English) and the French. The book then tests the democratic paradigm by looking at cases involving clashes between religious freedoms and competing rights in the workplace. Contrary to the current alternative between the 'accommodationist view', which defers to religious requests, and the 'analogous-to-secular' view, which undermines the importance of religious freedom for pluralism, this book offers a third way. It fills a gap in the literature on the relationships between law and religious freedoms and provides guidelines for judges confronted with difficult cases.

**Volume 26 in the series Hart Studies in Comparative Public Law**

I0093878

Hart Studies in Comparative Public Law

Recent titles in this series:

New Media and Freedom of Expression
Rethinking the Constitutional Foundations of the Public Sphere
*András Koltay*

Regulation in India
Design, Capacity, Performance
*Edited by Devesh Kapur and Madhav Khosla*

The Nordic Constitutions
*Edited by Helle Krunke and Björg Thorarensen*

Human Rights in the UK and the Influence of Foreign Jurisprudence
*Hélène Tyrrell*

Australian Constitutional Values
*Edited by Rosalind Dixon*

The Scope and Intensity of Substantive Review
Traversing Taggart's Rainbow
*Edited by Hanna Wilberg and Mark Elliott*

Entick v Carrington
250 Years of the Rule of Law
*Edited by Adam Tomkins and Paul Scott*

Administrative Law and Judicial Deference
*Matthew Lewans*

Soft Law and Public Authorities
Remedies and Reform
*Greg Weeks*

Legitimate Expectations in the Common Law World
*Edited by Matthew Groves and Greg Weeks*

The Dynamics of Exclusionary Constitutionalism
*Mazen Masri*

Constitutional Courts, Gay Rights and Sexual Orientation Equality
*Angioletta Sperti*

Principled Reasoning in Human Rights Adjudication
*Se-Shauna Wheatle*

Human Rights and Judicial Review in Australia and Canada
*Janina Boughey*

# Why Religious Freedom Matters for Democracy

*Comparative Reflections from Britain and France for a Democratic 'Vivre Ensemble'*

Myriam Hunter-Henin

·HART·

OXFORD · LONDON · NEW YORK · NEW DELHI · SYDNEY

HART PUBLISHING
Bloomsbury Publishing Plc
Kemp House, Chawley Park, Cumnor Hill, Oxford, OX2 9PH, UK
1385 Broadway, New York, NY 10018, USA
29 Earlsfort Terrace, Dublin 2, Ireland

HART PUBLISHING, the Hart/Stag logo, BLOOMSBURY and the Diana logo are
trademarks of Bloomsbury Publishing Plc
First published in Great Britain 2020

First published in hardback, 2020
Paperback edition, 2021

A catalogue record for this book is available from the British Library.

**Library of Congress Cataloging-in-Publication Data**

Names: Hunter-Henin, Myriam, author.

Title: Why religious freedom matters for democracy : comparative reflections from Britain
and France for a democratic 'vivre ensemble' / Myriam Hunter-Henin.

Description: Oxford ; New York Hart, 2020. | Series: Hart studies in comparative public law ;
volume 26 | Includes bibliographical references and index.

Identifiers: LCCN 2020005225 (print) | LCCN 2020005226 (ebook) |
ISBN 9781509904747 (hardcover) | ISBN 9781509904754 (Epub)

Subjects: LCSH: Freedom of religion—France. | Freedom of religion—Great Britain. | Religious
minorities—Legal status, laws, etc.—France. | Religious minorities—Legal status, laws, etc.—Great Britain.

Classification: LCC KJC5156 .H86 2020 (print) | LCC KJC5156 (ebook) | DDC 342.4108/52—dc23

LC record available at https://lccn.loc.gov/2020005225

LC ebook record available at https://lccn.loc.gov/2020005226

ISBN: HB: 978-1-50990-474-7
PB: 978-1-50994-401-9
ePDF: 978-1-50990-476-1
ePub: 978-1-50990-475-4

Typeset by Compuscript Ltd, Shannon

To find out more about our authors and books visit www.hartpublishing.co.uk. Here you will find
extracts, author information, details of forthcoming events and the option to sign up for our newsletters.

*For my two 'bookworms', Melanie and Loriane*

# Acknowledgements

WHEN I FIRST began thinking about writing this book in 2015, my ambition was to offer a novel comparative perspective on law and religion controversies in Britain and France. 2016, with the US election and the Brexit referendum in the UK, prompted me to go further and explore connections with theories of democracy. I was fortunate during these early days to have unique opportunities to test my emerging ideas. The debate at the French Conseil d'Etat on Comparative Law and Territoriality in January 2016 was the first step towards my search for law's inclusiveness. The papers I presented on religious freedom cases in the workplace at the international conference organised at Rouen University and the workshop at UCL in 2016 and 2017 respectively confirmed the importance of the employment law sphere as an area of investigation. Finally, the conference and conversations on populism at New York University in September 2017 paved the way for my democratic approach. I am therefore grateful to the convenors of these events: Horatia Muir Watt (Sciences Po, Paris); Duncan Fairgrieve (BIICL); Ronan McCrea (UCL); Valérie Parisot (Rouen University); Hélène de Courrèges (Rouen University); and Gráinne de Búrca (NYU). As my ideas matured, I benefited from discussions within the Public Law Group at UCL. I am grateful to my colleague, Silvia Suteu, for convening the sessions. Ideas also crystallise thanks to informal conversations. For these, my thanks go in particular to: Peter Cumper (Leicester University), Javier García Oliva (Manchester University), Prakash Shah (Queen Mary University) and Lucy Vickers (Oxford Brookes University).

University College London has been my home since the beginning of my career and has fostered my reflections on the book in many ways. I am particularly indebted to Ian Dennis who recruited me, Dame Hazel Genn who encouraged me to pursue research in law and religion, and Piet Eeckhout who granted me a term's research leave at the beginning and the end of the writing phase in 2018 and 2020 respectively. Throughout my career, Grand Challenges (UCL) has supported my initiatives and provided opportunities for fruitful collaborative research, including the project on 'Fundamental British Values', conducted in collaboration with the Institute of Education (UCL), which fed into chapter 3 of the book. Within Grand Challenge Justice and Equality at UCL, I am especially indebted to Ian Scott and Siobhan Morris for their unfailing enthusiasm for interdisciplinary endeavours. Long-standing gratitude is also owed to the European Institute (UCL), in particular to Uta Staiger over many years of collaboration and, more recently, to Oli Patel and Claudia Steinberg.

The book as it stands today is the result of many drafts, some of which were read and commented upon generously by the following colleagues: Oliver Gerstenberg (UCL, Laws); Julian Rivers (Bristol University, Law School); Bob Morris (UCL, The Constitution Unit); Philippe Marlière (UCL, SELCS); and George Letsas (UCL, Laws). May they all be warmly thanked for their time and feedback. I am also extremely grateful to Natalie Sedacca (UCL Laws), who combined with impeccable efficiency her own writing for her PhD and valuable editing work.

Hart has been remarkable. Maria Skrzypiec, as copy-editor, worked on the manuscript with incredible speed, precision and good humour. Emma Platt and Rosamund Jubber, from the marketing team, and Linda Staniford, as Production Editor, then took over with the same efficiency and friendly spirit.

Finally, I owe a different kind of debt to my family and friends, for their angelic patience over the two full years of writing, in 2018–20, during which the 'vivre ensemble' only existed on paper.

# Table of Contents

*Acknowledgements* ..................................................................................*vii*
*Table of Cases* ......................................................................................... *xiii*
*Table of Statutory Materials* ...................................................................*xvii*

1. Introduction ...........................................................................................1
   I.   Goals of the Book .............................................................................2
        A.   The Method of Avoidance .........................................................2
        B.   The Principle of Inclusion ........................................................3
        C.   The Principle of Revision .........................................................4
        D.   The Analogous-to-Secular View ...............................................5
        E.   The Accommodationist View ....................................................9
   II.  Summary of My Main Argument .....................................................14
        A.   Implications for Law ...............................................................15
        B.   Implications of My Argument for Theories of Democracy
             and Legal Pluralism ................................................................16
        C.   A Contextual and Comparative Approach ..............................17
   III. Structure of the Argument .............................................................19
   IV.  Conclusion .....................................................................................21


PART I
THE BROKEN *VIVRE ENSEMBLE* –
OBSERVATIONS AND SOLUTIONS

2. Contextual Analyses: Laïcité and the Democratic *Vivre Ensemble* ...........27
   I.   The Historical Layers of Laïcité: From Hostility to Tolerance
        Towards Religion ...........................................................................31
        A.   Laïcité: A Militant Form of Secularism? .................................31
        B.   Laïcité: From Militant to Separatist and Liberal Secularism .....37
        C.   Conclusion to Section I ...........................................................44
   II.  Laïcité, Common Values and Islam ................................................44
        A.   Recent Extensions of Laïcité ...................................................45
        B.   Gilles Kepel's Laïcité .............................................................49
        C.   Communautarian versus Inclusive Laïcité ...............................53
        D.   Conclusion to Section II .........................................................56
   III. Conclusion to Chapter 2 ...............................................................57

3. **Contextual Analyses: The English Experience of** *Vivre Ensemble*............58
    I. Church Establishment: An Inclusive Type of Secularism?...............60
        A. The Possibility of Church Establishment...............................61
        B. English Establishment: An Inclusive Form of Secularism .........66
        C. Conclusion to Section I.................................................69
    II. British Values, Religious Autonomy and Liberalism .......................70
        A. Religious Minorities in England.......................................71
        B. The Decline of Religious Autonomy in English Law ................74
        C. Conclusion to Section II...............................................78
    III. Conclusion to Chapter 3 ....................................................78

4. **Conceptual Framework: The Liberal Democratic Vivre Ensemble** ..........80
    I. Why Religious Freedom Matters for Democracy............................82
        A. The Dilution of Religious Freedom....................................83
        B. The Isolation of Religious Freedom ..................................92
        C. Conclusion to Section I................................................97
    II. Why Pluralism Matters for Democracy and Religious Freedom.......98
        A. Self-restraint, Religious Freedom and Pluralism....................99
        B. Pluralism, Religious Freedom and Public Reason...................104
        C. Conclusion to Section II ..............................................110
    III. Conclusion to Chapter 4 ...................................................112

PART II
CASE STUDIES: THE MENDED VIVRE ENSEMBLE

5. **Lessons from** *Achbita* .........................................................119
    I. Spheres Over Principles...................................................121
        A. The Contractual Sphere: The Non-interventionist
            Ordoliberal Baseline Argument......................................122
        B. The National Sphere: Alleged Deference to the
            Constitutional Laïque Context ......................................126
        C. Conclusion to Section I...............................................129
    II. Consistency Over Proportionality .......................................130
        A. Introductory: The *Eweida* Case .....................................130
        B. Burdens of the Consistency Argument for Religious
            Employees' Claims .....................................................132
        C. Proportionality Test Reduced Mainly to Procedural
            Consistency ...........................................................135
        D. Conclusion to Section II .............................................137
    III. Conclusion to Chapter 5 ...................................................138

6.  Beyond *Achbita*: Possible Ways Forward ............................................. 139
    I.   Laïcite: Deference Rather than Delegation .................................. 140
         A.   *Ebrahimian*: An Extensive Deference to Laïcité ..................... 141
         B.   From *Ebrahimian* to *Achbita*: From Deference to Laïcité
              to Delegation to National Authorities................................. 144
         C.   Conclusion to Section I.............................................. 146
    II.  Proportionality Rather than Autonomy.................................... 146
         A.   The Rejection of the Church Autonomy Argument
              in *Egenberger* ....................................................... 147
         B.   Guidelines from the ECtHR's Case Law............................... 152
         C.   Conclusion to Section II ............................................ 156
    III. Religious Freedom and Equality Rights .................................. 157
         A.   Balancing Private Interests in the Context of Legislative
              Ambiguities .......................................................... 159
         B.   Balancing Private Interests in a US Context ......................... 166
         C.   Conclusion to Section III ........................................... 173
    IV.  Conclusion to Chapter 6.................................................. 173
    V.   Conclusion of Part II..................................................... 174

7.  Conclusion ............................................................................. 176
    I.   For a Democratic Approach to Religious Freedom ..................... 177
         A.   Comparative Demonstration ........................................ 177
         B.   Normative Demonstration........................................... 178
    II.  Consequences of the Democratic Approach for the Courts .......... 179
         A.   Clues Relating to the Assessment of the Religious Claim .......... 179
         B.   Against Delegation to Employers.................................... 180
         C.   For a Nuanced Deference to National Traditions ................. 181
         D.   Comments on Proportionality ...................................... 181
         E.   A Word on Brexit .................................................... 182

*Appendix*.................................................................................. 185
    Table of Pathologies ................................................................. 185
    Table of Success Stories .............................................................. 187
*Index* ....................................................................................... 189

# Table of Cases

**United Kingdom / England and Wales**

Blackburn & Anor v Revenue & Customs [2013] UKFTT 525 (TC)
[2013] 10 WLUK 23 .............................................................................. 170
Bull v Hall [2013] UKSC 73 [2013] 1 WLR 3741 .............................. 20, 163–65
Exmoor Coast Boat Cruises Ltd v Revenue & Customs [2014]
UKFTT 1103 (TC) [2014] 12 WLUK 574 ........................................ 170
Hall v Bull [2012] EWCA Civ 83 [2012] 1 WLR 2514.......................... 163
Khan v Vignette Europe Ltd [2010] UKEAT 0134/09/1401 [2010]
1 WLK 169 ...................................................................................... 133
Islington LBC v Ladele UKEAT/0453/08 (2008) .................................... 160, 162
Islington London Borough Council v Ladele [2009] EWCA
Civ 1357 [2010] 1 WLR 955............................................................ 20, 158,
161–62
Lee v Ashers Baking Company Ltd & Ors (Northern Ireland)
[2018] UKSC 49 [2018] 3 WLR 1294 ............................................ 20, 157
Mandla v Dowell Lee [1983] 2 A.C. 548 [1983] 2 WLR 620.................... 85
Marshall v Graham [1907] 2 KB 112, [1907] 4 WLUK 3 [126] ................ 69
R (Amicus MSF Section) v Secretary of State for Trade and Industry
[2004] EWHC 860 [2004] 4 WLUK 430........................................ 150
R (Begum) v Governors of Denbigh High School [2006] UKHL 15
[2006] WLR 719.............................................................................. 46, 132
R (E) v Governing Body of JFS [2009] UKSC 15 [2010] 2 WLR 153 ........ 84–85
R (London Oratory School Governing Body) v. Schools Adjudicator
[2015] EWHC 1012 (Admin) [2015] 4 WLUK 285 ........................ 75
R (Steinfeld and Keidan) v Secretary of State for the International
Development [2018] UKSC 32 [2018] 3 WLR 415.......................... 159
R (Talmud Torah Machzikhei Haddass School Trust) v. Secretary
of State for Education and Science [1985] 1 WLUK 778, The Times,
12 April 1985 .................................................................................. 72
R (Williamson and others) v Secretary of State for Education and
Employment and Others [2005] UKHL 15 [2005] 2 WLR 590................ 132
Wilkinson v Kitzinger [2006] EWHC 2022 (Fam) [2006] 7 WLUK 846 ......... 164

## France

Abbé Olivier CE 19 février 1909, Recueil Lebon, n. 27355 ............................42
APREI (association du personnel relevant des établissements pour
    inadaptés), CE 22 February 2007, Grands arrêts de la
    jurisprudence administrative 294 ..................................................127–28
Avis sur le port du voile à l'école, CE 27 November 1989, (1990)
    Revue Française de Droit Administratif, 1, J Rivero ......................45
Baby Loup, Cass Ass Plén 25 June 2014 (2014) Recueil Dalloz 1386 .......124–25,
    129, 132, 143, 186
Commune d'Aix-Marseille, CE 6 April 2007, (2007) Revue française
    de droit administratif 812 ...................................................... 128
Demoiselle Marteaux, CE Opinion 3 May 2000, (2001) Revue
    française de droit administratif, 141 ............................ 43, 141–42
Dreyfus – Cour de cassation, Chambres réunies 12 July 1906 ........................41
Epoux Aoukili CE 10 mars 1995, Recueil Lebon, n° 159981 ..........................46
'Liberté d'association', Loi complétant les dispositions des articles 5
    et 7 de la loi du 1er juillet 1901 relative au contrat d'association,
    Conseil constitutionnel Décision n° 71-44 DC 16 July 1971 ......................43
Ligue des droits de l'homme et autres – association de défense des droits
    de l'homme collectif contre l'islamophobie en France, CE ordonnance
    26 August 2016, n°402742, 402777 ..................................................50
Ligue islamique du Nord et Epoux Chabou CE 27 October 1996 Recueil
    Lebon, n°170207 170208 ..........................................................46
Loi interdisant la dissimulation du visage dans l'espace public, Conseil
    Constitutionnel Décision no. 2010-613 DC 7 October 2010,
    JO 12 October 2010, 18345 ..............................................7, 24, 48, 143
Ministre de l'Education nationale, de la recherche et de la technologie
    c./ Epoux Ait Ahmed CE 20 October 1999, n° 181486 ..........................46
Narcy, CE 28 June 1963, Grands arrêts de la jurisprudence
    administrative 293 ..............................................................127–28
Tribunal Administratif Montreuil 22 November 2011, (2012)
    Droit Administratif, 163 ..........................................................47
Union régionale des syndicats CFTC de la Réunion, CE 30 March 2005
    Juris-data 264541 ................................................................ 127

## USA

Burwell v. Hobby Lobby Stores, Inc. 134 S Ct 2751 (2014) ....................20, 166
Craig v Masterpiece Cakeshop, Inc., 370 P.3d 272 ..........................20, 157
Elaine Photography v Willcock 309 P 3rd 53 N.M. 2013 ..........................157
Fraternal Order of Police Newark Lodge No. 12 v City of Newark,
    170 F3d 359 (3d Circ 1999) ........................................................88

In the matter of Todd Wathen and Mark Wathen, Nos 2011SP2488,
  2011SP2489 (Ill. Human Rights Comm.) ................................................. 157
Kim Davis, Miller v Davis No 15-5880, 2015 WL 1069 2640 6th Circ.
  Aug 26, 2015 .............................................................................................. 158
Lyng v Northwest Indian Cemetery Protective Ass'n 485 US 439,
  441–42 (1988) ............................................................................................... 90
Mozert v Hawkins County Board of Education, 827 F.2d 1058 ...... 11, 13, 93, 95
Obergefell v. Hodges 576 U. S. (2015) ........................................................ 165
Sherbert v Verner 374 US 398 (1963) ..................................................... 88–90
USSC Masterpiece Cakeshop Ltd et al v Colorado Civil Rights
  Commission et al 584 US 16-111 (2018) ........................................... 166, 170
Washington v Arlene's Flowers, 2015 WL 94248 (Wash. Super. 2015) ........... 157
Washington v Arlene Flowers, No.17-108 (US, July 14th, 2017) .................... 157

## Court of Justice of the European Union

Asma Bougnaoui v Micropole SA OJ C 151/4 14 March 2017
  (Case C-188/15) ............................................... 117, 119–20, 122, 179
Opinion of AG Sharpston, 13 July 2016 ................................. 122, 126, 133–36
IR v JQ Grand Chamber 11 September 2018 (Case C-68/17) .... 20, 140, 146–52,
                                                                155–56, 174–75, 187
Opinion of AG Wathelet, 31 May 2018 ......................................... 148–49, 151
Reinhard Prigge and Others v Deutsche Lufthansa AG [2011]
  ECR I-08003 (Case C-447/09) ................................................................. 126
Samira Achbita and Centrum voor Gelijkheid van kansen en voor
  racismebestrijding v G4S Secure Solutions 2017 3 CMLR 21
  (Case C-157/15) ................................................................. 6, 19–20, 117,
                                                                        119–75, 180–81
Opinion of AG Kokott, 31 May 2017 ......................................... 6, 120–21, 123,
                                                                  126, 131, 135–36
Vera Egenberger v Evangelisches Werk für Diakonie und Entwicklung,
  Grand Chamber 17 April 2018 (Case C-414/16) .................. 20, 140, 146–48,
                                                                  152, 156, 174–75, 187

## European Court of Human Rights

Ahmet Arslan v Turkey App no 41135/98 (ECtHR, 23 February 2010) .......... 49
Campbell and Cosans v United Kingdom Series A no 48 (1982)
  4 EHRR 293 ............................................................................................... 132
Dahlab v Switzerland App no 42393/98 (2001) V ECHR 449 ................. 46, 145
Darby v Sweden (1991) 13 EHRR 774 ......................................................... 65
Dogru v France (2009) 49 EHRR 8 ............................................................. 145

Ebrahimian v France App no 64846/11 (ECtHR Fifth Section,
   26 November 2015) ........................................................20, 140–46, 173, 175
Eweida v UK [2013] ECHR 285 ............................................................. 20, 75
Fernández Martínez v Spain App no 56030/07 (ECtHR 12 June 2014) .....20, 152
Hassan and Chaush v Bulgaria (2002) 34 EHRR 55..................................... 134
Kokkinakis v Greece Series A no 260 (1993) 17 EHRR 397 ..................2, 80–81,
   92, 103, 112
Kurtulmus v Turkey [2006] ECHR 1169..................................................... 145
Lautsi and Others v Italy (2012) 54 EHRR 3 .................................................65
Obst v Germany, App No 425/03 (ECtHR 23 September 2010) ........ 20, 152–53,
   156, 175, 187
Sahin v Turkey (2007) 44 EHRR 5 App no 47774/98 ................................... 145
SAS v France [2014] ECHR 695 ......................................7–8, 49, 55–56,
   142–43, 186
Schüth v Germany App No 1620/03 (ECtHR 23 September 2010) ...........20, 152
Siebenhaar v Germany App No 18136/02 (ECtHR 3 February 2011) .......20, 152
Travaš v Croatia App no 75581/13 (ECtHR 4 October 2016) .......... 20, 152, 155

**European Commission of Human Rights**

Ahmad v United Kingdom (1982) 4 EHRR 126 ........................................... 134
Stedman v United Kingdom (1997) 23 EHRR CD 168 ................................. 134

# Table of Statutory Materials

## United Kingdom / England and Wales

*Statutes*

Burial Act 1880 (43 & 44 Vict c 41) ................................................................66
Church of England Assembly (Powers) Act 1919 (as amended by the
    Synodical Government Measure 1969) ....................................................68
Civil Partnership Act 2004 ............................................................... 159, 164–66
Civil Partnerships, Marriages and Deaths (Registration etc) Act 2019
    s 2 .......................................................................................................... 159
Church of Scotland Act 1921 .......................................................................58
Counter-Terrorism and Security 2015 Act
    s 26 ..................................................................................................... 24, 77
Divorce and Matrimonial Causes Act 1857 (20 & 21 Vict c 85) ....................67
Education Act 1944
    s 25 ...........................................................................................................71
Education Act 1993
    s 138(2) ....................................................................................................70
Education Act 2002
    s 78 ...........................................................................................................76
Education and Inspections Act 2006 ............................................................75
Education Reform Act 1988
    s 7(1) .......................................................................................................70
Equality Act 2010 ................................................................15, 88, 182–83
    Sch 9 ...................................................................................................... 150
Excommunication Act 1813 (53 Geo III c 127) ............................................66
Jewish Relief Act 1858 (21 & 22 Vict c 49) ..................................................66
Marriage and Registration Acts 1836 (6 & 7 Wm IV cc 85 and 86) ...............66
Marriage Act 1949 .......................................................................................66
Matrimonial Causes Act 1973 ......................................................................67
Mundella Education Act 1880 .......................................................................71
Oaths Act 1888 (51 & 52 Vict c 45) .............................................................66
Priests (Ordination of Women) Measure 1993 (1993 No 2) ...........................68
Religious Disabilities Act 1846 (9 & 10 Vict c 59) ........................................66

Repeal of Test and Corporation Acts 1828 (9 Geo IV c 17) ..........................66
Roman Catholic Relief Act 1829 (10 Geo IV c 7) .......................................66
Welsh Church Act 1914 ...........................................................................58

*Statutory Instruments*

Education (Independent School Standards) (England) (Amendment)
   Regulations 2014, SI 2014/2374.................................................................76
Education (School Teachers' Appraisal) (England) Regulations 2012,
   SI 2012/115
   reg 6 ....................................................................................................76
Employment Equality (Sexual Orientation) Regulations 2003,
   SI 2003/1661
   reg 7(3) ...............................................................................................150
Teachers' Disciplinary (England) Regulations 2012, SI 2012/560
   reg 4 ....................................................................................................76

*Bills*

EU (Withdrawal) Bill, HC Bill 5, Session 2017-9, cl 2 ................................183

**France**

Loi du 20 septembre 1792 sur l'état civil (Law on civil status of
   20th September 1792)..............................................................................32
Loi du 18 Germinal An X (8 avril 1802) relative à l'organisation des cultes
   (Law on 8th April 1802 for the organisation and expression of the
   Catholic and Protestant Faith), Bulletin des Lois, an X,
   2e semestre, p13....................................................................................40
Décrets du 17 mars 1808 relatifs respectivement à l'organisation du culte,
   des institutions et des droits des Juifs (Decrees of 17th March 1808
   relating to the organisation and institutions of the Jewish Faith and
   the rights of Jews)..................................................................................40
Loi du 30 octobre 1886 sur l'organisation de l'enseignement primaire
   dite Loi Goblet (Law of 30 October 1886 on primary education).............38
La loi concernant la séparation des Églises et de l'État du 11 décembre 1905
   (Law on the Separation of Church and State of 11 December 1905),
   JO 11 December 1905, 7205 ...................................................................37
Loi n. 2004-228 du 15 mars 2004 encadrant, en application du principe
   de laïcité, le port de signes ou de tenues manifestant une appartenance
   religieuse dans les écoles, collèges et lycées publics (Law of
   15 March 2004 on religious symbols in state schools), JO
   17 March 2004, 5190 .........................................................................23, 46

Loi n. 2010-1192 du 11 octobre 2010 interdisant la dissimulation
du visage dans l'espace public (Law of 11 October 2010 banning
the covering of the face in the public sphere),
JO 12 October 2010 ................................................................7, 24, 48, 143
Loi n° 2016-1088 du 8 août 2016 relative au travail, à la modernisation du
dialogue social et à la sécurisation des parcours professionnels,
(Law of 8 August 2016 relating to the workplace, the modernization of
social dialogue and the stability of career paths) JO 9 August 2016,
n°0184 ................................................................................................ 124
Loi n.83-634 du 13 juillet 1983, as amended by Loi n.2016-483 du
20 avril 2016 relative à la déontologie et aux droits et obligations
des fonctionnaires (Law of 13 July 1983 as amended by Law of
20 April 2016 on the ethics, rights and obligations of civil servants),
JO 21 April 2016, n°0094
Art 25 ................................................................................................ 141
Art 32 ................................................................................................ 141

*Administrative regulation*

Circulaire du 15 mars 2017 relative au respect de la laïcité dans la
fonction publique (Regulation of 15 March 2017 on the respect owed
to 'laïcité' in the public service) ............................................................. 141

## Germany

Grundgesetz
Art 140 ....................................................................................................... 147
Weimar Constitution (Weimarer Verfassung WRV) on religious societies ..... 147

## Spain

Ministerial Order of 11 October 1982 on teachers of Catholic religion
and ethics in secondary educational centres, implementing
1979 Agreement between Spain and the Holy See ..................................... 154

## USA

Religious Freedom Restoration Act, Pub. L. No. 103-141, 107 Stat.
1488 (1993) (codified as amended at 42 U.S.C. §§ 2000bb–2000bb-4
(2006)) ................................................................................................167, 169
s 3 ............................................................................................................. 168

## European Union

Charter of Fundamental Rights of the European Union ...................... 120, 123,
180, 183, 185
Council Directive 2000/78/EC of 27 November 2000 Establishing
a General Framework for Equal Treatment in Employment
and Occupation ................................................................. 15, 117, 119–20,
122–23, 126–28,
137–38, 150, 182–83
Art 4(2) ......................................................................... 124, 147–48, 185


## Council of Europe

Council of Europe, 'European Convention on Human Rights –
Convention for the Protection of Human Rights and Fundamental
Freedoms – Rome, 4.XI.1950 ................................... 15, 16, 65, 83, 117, 130,
134, 136, 141, 144, 161

# 1

# *Introduction*

S HOULD AN EMPLOYEE be allowed to wear a religious symbol at work? Should the answer depend on the size and conspicuousness of the symbol, the underlying national constitutional tradition, the question of whether the employee is working in the public or private sector, the existence or absence of an applicable neutrality company policy? Should a religious employer be allowed to impose constraints on employees' private lives for the sake of enforcing a religious work ethos? Should the answer depend on the role of the employee within the organisation, on the publicity surrounding the alleged violations, on the status of the employer as a Church or ordinary employer, of the employee, as a minister or lay person, on the constitutional status of the Church, the connection with the employee's tasks and employer's activities? Should an employee or service provider be allowed, on religious grounds, to refuse to work with customers of the opposite sex or of a same-sex sexual orientation? Should the answer depend on whether access to the service is possible, at no extra cost for the customer? Should it make a difference whether the service or product refused involves a high degree of personal involvement of the provider, or whether the provision of the service implies the endorsement of views contrary to the provider's religious convictions or does not carry any message? This book explores how judges must decide these issues and defends a 'democratic approach', which insists on the normative link between religious freedom and democracy. By democracy, I understand 'an open-ended *reason-giving* process of deliberation'[1] woven into the fabric of our *vivre ensemble*. Democracy in that sense cannot be reduced to majority rules and aggregation of interests; its key features are deliberation,[2] participation on equal terms[3] and self-revision.[4] Construed by judges in a way that fosters these democratic features, religious freedoms, I submit, are valuable for believers as well as for democracy.

---

[1] A Gutmann and D Thompson, *Why Deliberative Democracy?* (Princeton University Press, 2004) 3.
[2] J Habermas, *Between Facts and Norms. Contributions to a Discourse Theory of Law and Democracy* (trs W Rehg, Polity Press, 1998) (1st edn, Massachusetts Institute of Technology, 1996).
[3] J Cohen, *Philosophy, Politics, Democracy. Selected Essays* (Harvard University Press, 2009).
[4] RM Unger, *The Religion of the Future* (Harvard University Press, 2014) 304.

## I. GOALS OF THE BOOK

I seek to show that religious freedom is important not only as a negative liberty, to protect believers from intrusions and interferences, but also as a positive value to society, to support pluralism and equality and thereby enrich democracy. As expressed by the European Court of Human Rights:

> Freedom of thought, conscience and religion is one of the foundations of a 'democratic society' within the meaning of the Convention. It is, in its religious dimension, one of the most vital elements that go to make up the identity of believers and their conception of life, but it is also a precious asset for atheists, agnostics, sceptics and the unconcerned. The pluralism indissociable from a democratic society, which has been dearly won over the centuries, depends on it.[5]

Following the Court's statement, the book defends a dual dimension of religious freedom: a negative dimension, as a defensive liberty; and a positive dimension, as a welcome principle and source of pluralism. I thus make a conceptual argument and submit that religious freedoms are important for and within democracy as well as for believers themselves. From this conceptual position, helpful guidelines can follow for judges confronted with the abovementioned instances of clashing rights. Drawing on the renowned work of late American philosopher, John Rawls,[6] and moving beyond it, I submit that the connections between democracy, pluralism and religious freedoms ought to rely on the following: a method of avoidance; a principle of inclusion; and a principle of revision.

### A. The Method of Avoidance

The method of avoidance, to use the term coined by NYU political theory professor Stephen Holmes,[7] captures the negative dimension of religious freedom and manifests itself by a degree of separation between the state and religion.[8] The notion of separation guarantees that the state does not encroach on citizens' freedom of conscience and leaves them, in solo or collectively,[9] to

---

[5] *Kokkinakis v Greece* Series A no 260, 17 EHRR 397; *Application no 14307/88*, judgment of 25 May 1993.

[6] J Rawls, *Political Liberalism*, 2nd edn (New York, Columbia University Press, 1996).

[7] S Holmes, *Passions and Constraints. On the Theory of Liberal Democracy* (Chicago, University of Chicago Press, 1995). See further, Ch 4 of this book.

[8] On the importance of separation for secularism, see C Taylor, *A Secular Age* (Cambridge, MA, Harvard University Press, 2007). However, for a historical critique of the paradigm of separation, with a US focus, see PA Hamburger, *Separation of Church and State*, 2nd edn (Cambridge MA, Harvard University Press, 2004).

[9] I leave aside here but will examine in depth in the book how the individual and collective exercise of religious freedoms may come into conflict. See Ch 6. On this tension between individual rights and collective membership, see J Montgomery, 'The Value of Tolerance and the Tolerability of Competing Values' in R Williams and others (eds), *Social Scaffolding, Applying the Lessons of Contemporary Social Science to Health and Healthcare* (Cambridge, Cambridge University Press, 2019) 105.

practise their religion free of interference. Separation thus allows religious beliefs and freedoms to flourish and more generally allows everyone the freedom to decide how to pursue their lives, a consequence which few would disapprove of, whether for the sake of religious vitality or concerns for freedom and autonomy (or both).[10] Reciprocally, however, I will demonstrate that this separation can also benefit the state and democracy, by freeing the political sphere from intractable controversies.[11] Rather than a paradigm of separation, the method at play here is therefore more properly named 'a method of avoidance', under which the state avoids interfering with religious doctrines and practices for the sake of religious citizens and groups and avoids cluttering democratic debate with conflicting issues. Far from signalling indifference towards religion, separation between state and religion under the method of avoidance would signal respect for religion in all of its diversity, but with awareness of the deep disagreement that this (religious and non-religious) diversity potentially generates. As a standalone paradigm, however, the method of avoidance risks advantaging majority factions.

## B. The Principle of Inclusion

To avoid minority vulnerable members of society being excluded from the start from public debate and remaining locked in positions of vulnerability, the method of avoidance described above supposes that the position of non-interference is never absolute or fixed.[12] Non-interference will cease to be justified, for example, if systemic disadvantage works against minority groups and vulnerable members of society. Left to fight in the free-range competition between ideas within society, minority religious groups and views might struggle to find a place and a voice. I argue in this book that such muffling of minority voices would come at a loss both for the individuals and groups concerned (who are likely to feel disparaged) and for the political sphere. The diversity of voices that religion brings is, I submit, enriching for democratic debate. The second feature, the principle of inclusion, conveys this idea that religious freedoms are important not only for themselves, to ensure merely that religion is strong in civil society, but also for the enriching pluralism that they bring to public debate and the equality between citizens which they protect. A libertarian model of free

---

[10] On the need to protect individuals' conceptions of the good, see J Rawls, *A Theory of Justice* (Oxford, Clarendon Press, 1972); Rawls, *Political Liberalism* (n 6); R Dworkin, *Justice for Hedgehogs*, 2nd edn (Cambridge MA, Belknap Press of Harvard University Press, 2013).

[11] On the two-way approach of the principle of separation, see Gutmann and Thompson, *Why Deliberative Democracy?* (n 1).

[12] As Rawls put it, 'that certain matters are reasonably taken off the political agenda does not mean that a political conception of justice should not provide the grounds and reasons why this should be done', *Political Liberalism* (n 6) 151, in footnote.

market economy,[13] based solely on a principle of state non-interference, might well achieve the former aim,[14] of strengthening religion, but not the latter, of strengthening pluralism. That is why the principle of inclusion must complement the method of avoidance. Under the principle of inclusion, the state and its institutions will intervene as required, to ensure that vulnerable members of society play a part in political debate. Consequently, the requirement, underlined by Rawls,[15] to streamline political debate and free the political sphere from irresolvable but reasonable disagreements stemming from people's diverse 'comprehensive views',[16] as per the method of avoidance, needs to be sufficiently inclusive. This will ensure that religious citizens, and especially marginalised religious (and non-religious) citizens are not discouraged from the outset from contributing to democratic debate.[17] Finally, the principle of revision captures the ideas of fluidity and limits.

## C. The Principle of Revision

The principle of revision guarantees that religious freedoms, whilst recognising the intrinsic importance of religious commitments for believers, do not lead to an atomisation of society. Under the principle of revision, citizens are expected to review their commitments in light of the overall political framework and the horizon of a democratic *vivre ensemble*. When they fail to do so, judges will legitimately set limits to the expression or manifestation of their views and practices. Naturally, the limits themselves lead to a diversity of answers, rather than one single, legitimate answer and must also be part of the democratic dialogue. The line between 'what falls within' and 'what falls outside' the terms of legitimate diversity must therefore itself be kept under constant review, and subject to further questioning, each time a new case comes to court, each time new contestations emerge. The democratic understanding of the *vivre ensemble* is not, therefore, about pushing for adherence to core liberal *substantive values* associated with democracy (such as equality, liberty and autonomy), even though

---

[13] As developed by A Smith, *An Inquiry into the Nature and Causes of the Wealth of Nations: A Selected Edition* (K Sutherland ed, Oxford, Oxford Paperbacks, 2008) book V, ch I, pt II, art III, 309–10.

[14] See for this argument that a non-established Church and free exercise of religion led to a strengthening of religious faith in America, A de Tocqueville, *Democracy in America* (JP Mayer ed, Garden City, NY, Doubleday, 1969) 292, 295–301.

[15] I am here referring to Rawls' requirement of public reason, see Ch 4, section II below.

[16] Rawls defines comprehensive views as doctrines that address non-political life, including 'conceptions of what is of value in human life, and ideals of personal character, as well as ideals of friendship and of familial and associational relationships, and much else that is to inform our conduct' – *Political Liberalism* (n 6) 13. For further discussion, see Ch 4 of this book.

[17] I will show in Ch 4 of this book that this is possible under Rawls' inclusive conception of public reason. This is known as 'public reason revisited'.

these values undoubtedly inspire the very idea of a *vivre ensemble* and the three abovementioned features, but about *procedural* guarantees that tie pluralism, religious freedom and democracy together.

Let me underline why this democratic approach is worthwhile. It lies in contrast to two opposite views, which I call the 'analogous-to-secular' view and the 'accommodationist' view respectively, the key features of which are explained below. Contrary to the analogous-to-secular view, which struggles with the concept of religious freedom itself and its underlying implication that religion would be special,[18] the democratic approach helps understand the positive value of the concept of religious freedom: its benefits for pluralism and democratic debate. Moreover, contrary to the accommodationist view, which struggles with the notion of limits, the democratic approach helps understand why courts may impose legitimate limits on diversity and religious freedoms. By offering a third way, which overcomes the deadlocks and weaknesses of these views, this book hereby fills a gap in the literature on the relationships between law and religious freedoms and provides guidelines for judges confronted with difficult cases.

## D. The Analogous-to-Secular View

It is one of the objectives of this book to offer a counter-claim to those liberal authors who would dispense with the concept of religious freedom. For the sake of impartiality concerns, a few liberal authors have challenged the special consideration that law and political theory attach to 'religion' through the legal concept of religious freedom. Instead, they claim, equality or liberty could do the work of the concept of religious freedom.[19] Whilst possible, religious freedom in liberalism, the argument goes, would therefore not be desirable, as a legal and political theory category. In this view, dispensing with the concept would solve the epistemological problems associated with religion and guarantee fair treatment between religious and non-religious citizens. Two prominent manifestations of this approach are US law professors and constitutional theorists Christopher Eisgruber's and Lawrence Sager's work on the one hand, and Oxford political theory professor Cécile Laborde's on the other. The former insist on the equal treatment of people with diverse spiritual views, whether these be religious or secular. If it is difficult to disagree with this goal, the theoretical and practical consequences that Eisgruber and Sager draw from it leave room for debate. From a theoretical perspective,

---

[18] M Schwartzman, 'What If Religion Is Not Special?' (2012) 79 *University of Chicago Law Review* 1351.

[19] See C Eisgruber and L Sager, *Religious Freedom and the Constitution* (Cambridge, MA, Harvard University Press, 2010); C Laborde, *Liberalism's Religion* (Cambridge, MA, Harvard University Press, 2017).

Eisgruber and Sager suggest that law protects religious freedom *because* of equality concerns between secular and religious views. From a practical perspective, they conclude that law should accommodate religious freedom where an actual (or hypothetical) secular analogous interest has been or would have been similarly accommodated. Eisgruber and Sager convincingly argue[20] that if two residents, both called Ms Campbell, wanted to provide food for the homeless, in derogation to zoning laws, one because of the demands of her religious faith and the other because of her abhorrence for human suffering, it would be unfair to accommodate the religiously motivated request whilst denying the secular motivated one. However, the argument proves that the category of religious freedom should be extended to analogous deep secular commitments. It does not demonstrate that the category of religious freedom only exists to ensure equivalence between religious and secular commitments. Concretely, Eisgruber and Sager argue that their approach will avoid the divisions that discussions about religion generate. This is a valid and important consideration. As this book will argue, open-minded deliberation is key to a democratic *vivre ensemble*. However, the analogous approach risks being either under- or over-inclusive, so that instead of pacifying deliberation, it simply eliminates certain voices from the discussion.

### i. The Under-inclusion or Over-inclusion Problem of the Analogous Approach

Take the example of the *Achbita* case.[21] In that case, a Muslim employee wished to wear a headscarf at work, against a company neutrality policy, which prohibited display of beliefs in the workplace. The fact that the policy applied consistently to religious convictions as well as philosophical and political beliefs weighed strongly in favour of the employer in the proportionality assessment of the ban.[22] Consequently, the only potentially problematic difference of treatment, according to the Advocate General's Opinion on *Achbita*, was between 'employees who wish to give active expression to a particular belief ... and those who do not feel the same compulsion'.[23] In that example, an analogous approach leads to undermining the force of religious commitments. The notion that manifestation of beliefs is, in many cases, intrinsic to religious faith itself is not even considered.

Conversely, the analogous approach can be used to expand religious requests exponentially. In the US *Masterpiece Cakeshop* case, for example,[24] the analogous approach was invoked in a brief to support the baker's religious claim that

---

[20] Eisgruber and Sager, *Religious Freedom* (n 19) 11.
[21] Case C-157/15 *Samira Achbita and Centrum voor Gelijkheid van kansen en voor racismebestrijding v G4S Secure Solutions* 14 March 2017.
[22] Opinion of AG Kokott, 31 May 2017, in *Achbita* (n 21) para 53.
[23] ibid.
[24] *Masterpiece Cakeshop Ltd et al v Colorado Civil Rights Commission et al* 584 US 16-111 (2018).

he should be exempt from baking a cake for a same-sex wedding.[25] The argument was that if bakers were allowed to refuse to bake cakes endorsing anti-same-sex marriage messages, they should also be allowed to refuse to bake cakes endorsing pro-same-sex marriage messages. However, the analogy may not be entirely accurate. In the *Masterpiece Cakeshop* case, the baker had not been asked to add a message to the cake. The 'message' which allegedly violated the baker's religious beliefs merely derived from the destination of the cake as a same-sex wedding cake. My point is not that the baker in that case should (necessarily) be denied an exemption but that if he does benefit from an exemption, reasons linked to his religious commitments must be put forward to justify it. The mere fact that other bakers have benefited from exemptions on secular grounds does not suffice. In other words, the question of legitimacy (and the proper evolving terms and limits of legitimacy of our *vivre ensemble*) should not be set aside.

## ii. The Disaggregative Argument

The second trend of the analogous-to-secular view – the 'disaggregative' approach – fully recognises the interests underlying a particular exemption. Judges, confronted with difficult cases, would need to examine precisely the underlying value(s) at stake and would not be able to assume the existence of an underlying protected interest because of the 'religious' nature of the request. At first sight, the disaggregative approach would thus comply with the principle of inclusion (as law would not confer any superior status to some interests over others) as well as with the principle of revision (as discussion about the proper limits and justification of exemptions and legal solutions would not be avoided). In practice, (most of) the outcomes reached under a disaggregative approach are moreover likely to be compatible with the democratic view of religious freedom proposed in this book. Yet I suggest that there would still be a loss both in practical and democratic terms should the category of religious freedom be abandoned or construed in this way.

## iii. Potentially Lesser Protection of Religious Freedom under a Disaggregative Approach

In practical terms, the *SAS* case[26] against France, in which a Muslim French citizen challenged the French law banning the full covering of the face in public places,[27] provides an apposite illustration of the possible loss, which a

---

[25] ibid, paras 1734–40 (Gorsuch J, concurring, joined by Alito J, concurring); and at 1740 (Thomas J concurring) (indicating agreement with Gorsuch's analysis). For a convincing critique of this argument, see J Oleske, 'Free Exercise (Dis)Honesty' (2019) *Wisconsin Law Review* 689.

[26] *SAS v France* App No 43835/11 (ECtHR, 1 July 2014).

[27] Loi n. 2010-1192 interdisant la dissimulation du visage dans l'espace public of 11 October 2010, JO 12 October 2010 (Act prohibiting the full covering of the face in the public sphere).

disagreggative approach would entail for religious citizens. In that case, the applicant was a Muslim woman who at times felt the need to wear a full covering Muslim veil, depending on her spiritual mood or during periods of special religious significance.[28] She complained that the French ban unduly restricted her religious freedom to wear a veil to suit these special times of enhanced piety. Under the disaggregative approach, the applicant would have an a priori legitimate claim not, by definition, on the ground of her religious freedom but because of an integrity-protecting-commitment (IPC),[29] where integrity is defined as an ideal of congruence between one's ethical commitments and one's actions,[30] based on a person's ethical system. However, the emphasis in the concept of IPC on congruence can lead *in fine* to an – I would argue – undue curtailment of religious freedom. As Laborde writes about the *SAS* case, pointing to the applicant's own sporadic wearing of the veil, 'in such cases, the burden of uniform laws is less severe than in the case of perceived obligations'.[31] In my own approach, whilst lack of coherence might point on the facts of the case to a lack of sincerity, consistent congruence between beliefs and actions would not be a requirement. It is part of religious commitments to find expression in one's life in varied forms and intensity. Identifying a lack of consistency in religious practice does not per se prove a lack of intensity of the commitment. On the contrary, under a principle of inclusion, an openness towards the personal circumstances and motivations behind the applicant's varying practices is key, in order to properly understand and engage with the full complexity of the applicant's point of view. More profoundly, setting aside the characterisation of a claim as 'religious' would, I submit, have detrimental consequences both for religious citizens and for democracy.

### iv. Responses to the Disaggregative Approach

Psychologists have shown how religious commitments structure individual and collective identity.[32] Denying religious citizens and groups the right to phrase their claim as 'religious' leads to a distortion between legal reasoning and their feeling of identity, the way they define themselves.[33] Naturally, there may be good reasons preventing law from fully recognising individuals' and groups' feelings of identity.[34] Besides, the discrepancy between legal discourse and people's

---

[28] *SAS* (n 26) para 12.

[29] Laborde, *Liberalism's Religion* (n 19) Ch 6, 197 ff.

[30] ibid, 203.

[31] ibid, 223.

[32] For a summary, see W Marshall, 'Religion as Ideas: Religion as Identity' (1996) 7 *Journal of Contemporary Legal Issues* 385.

[33] For an argument that law should strive to respect this 'feeling of identity', see D Gutmann, *Le sentiment d'identité: étude de droit des personnes et de la famille* (The feeling of identity – study of the rights of persons and of the family) (Paris, LGDJ 2000).

[34] This is a point I will examine in more detail when I consider the requirement of public reason, in Ch 4.

own perceptions does not remove the possibility for people to express and live their identities in the background culture, nor would the category of religious freedom necessarily (in most cases) lead to greater rights for religious citizens and groups. Nonetheless, the disaggregative approach fails to show why such discrepancy should be actively introduced and encouraged. Far from guaranteeing an egalitarian approach between secular and religious citizens, the removal of the label of religion, under the disaggregative approach, favours secular citizens whose commitments will be described in the liberal secular categories that match their sense of identity. By contrast, for a religious citizen, the characterisation of her wish to wear a veil as an IPC will fail to capture the religious motivation behind her decision, creating a loss both for the claimant and for democracy. In other words, this religious motivation,[35] I submit, is also important and valuable for democratic debate. I am not suggesting that the wearing of the Muslim veil cannot also rely on cultural, psychological and social factors. My argument is that for women who feel a religious obligation to wear a veil, the characterisation of their claim as a 'religious freedom' claim is more respectful of their feeling of identity and that this dimension is enriching for democratic debate. It is also more likely to foster a willingness on the part of judges to listen to the personal reasons for wanting to wear a veil. Indeed, it is to be feared that the dialogical exercise which the category of religious freedom allows (as I will show) might seem futile if the legal question no longer explicitly revolves around considerations of the religious but can be solved in light of what might be assumed to be purely secular values. Here, finally, the argument that dispensing with the category of religious freedom would solve the abovementioned epistemological difficulties associated with the category falls down. The critics who denounce the ethnocentric and Christian understanding of what religion is in liberalism's legal concepts would no doubt voice a similar critique against the liberal secular values of liberty, equality and autonomy,[36] which absorb religious requests under a disaggregative model.

## E.　The Accommodationist View

The second contrast is with the view that I call 'the accommodationist view', embodied most representatively by Stanford constitutional law professor

---

[35] I am hereby embracing an inclusive approach of public reason, drawing upon Rawls' trajectories in 'The Idea of Public Reason Revisited' (1997), republished in *Political Liberalism*, Expanded edn (New York, Columbia University Press, 2005) 440. Contra, see R Audi, 'The Separation of Church and State and the Obligations of Citizenship' (1989) 18 *Philosophy and Public Affairs* 259, 278, arguing that citizens in political debate put forward only secular reasons, in the sense both of reasons phrased in secular terms and reasons relying on secular motivations. Audi's approach would fall foul of my principle of inclusion.

[36] See for example, denouncing the mythology and lack of neutrality of the human rights discourse, S Moyn, *The Last Utopia. Human Rights in History* (Cambridge MA, Belknap Press of Harvard University Press, 2010) 223.

Michael McConnell, which embraces a mainly negative conception of religious freedom and restricts the role of courts in adjudicating religious freedom cases to safeguarding a principle of state non-interference into religious claims. I name this view 'accommodationist' because the hands-off approach that it encourages judges to adopt, leads to deferring to religious requests and therefore to accommodating religious claims extremely generously. In this view, courts are to refrain from assessing the legitimacy of religious claims, with religious freedoms acting as shields against the gaze of judges, but this hands-off approach yields positive, accommodationist outcomes for religious citizens whose requests are likely to be granted. McConnell's aim is to defend the idea of religious freedom as 'a first freedom – both in chronological and logical priority'.[37] The principle of non-interference in religious domains, in McConnell's construction, expresses the priority of religion over spiritual issues: 'the separation of church from state is the most powerful possible refutation of the notion that the political sphere is omnicompetent'.[38] One might think that from such a premise, McConnell would go on to elaborate an argument of mutual indifference between the secular state and religion, each sovereign in its own sphere. On the contrary, however, McConnell clarifies that the principle of non-interference conveys and fosters respect for religious views, which are thereby more likely to flourish unhindered, as well as for democracy, in the interest of which it is to keep even the intolerant religious within the system. As McConnell explains:

> when particular groups are excluded from democratic participation, they become-alienated and radicalized. They do not 'get out of politics.' They engage in a different kind of politics – politics outside of the system.[39]

According to McConnell therefore, the secular state has an interest in securing religious citizens' cooperation and in protecting religious freedom in its full diversity. In suggesting that religious citizens can (should) be part of a shared constitutional framework, McConnell stands in opposition to American law professor Stanley Fish. According to Fish, there is no hope of any common ground or mutual understanding between religion and the liberal state. The devout religious person would never be able to find reasons to tolerate ideas which are outside her own religious framework, nor would the liberal state be able to find reasons to tolerate the intolerant religious devout person. Consequently, Fish writes, 'The religious person should not seek an accommodation with liberalism; he should seek to rout it from the field, to extirpate it, root and branch'.[40] The principle of non-interference, in Fish's scheme, does not

---

[37] M McConnell, 'Why Is Religious Liberty the First Freedom' (2000) 21 *Cardozo Law Review* 1243, 1244.

[38] ibid, 1247.

[39] M McConnell, 'Five Reasons to Reject the Claim That Religious Arguments Should Be Excluded from Democratic Deliberation' (1999) *Utah Law Review* 639, 650.

[40] S Fish, 'Why We Can't All Just Get Along' (1996) *First Things* 18.

convey mutual respect between the secular state and religious views but mutual alienation. Clearly, McConnell on the contrary argues that religious freedoms deserve respect and even logical prioritisation from secular courts. Reciprocally, there is a suggestion that such respect for religious freedom is more likely to encourage, in return, respect from religious citizens for the common framework. However, if it does not, if the intolerant religious citizen remains intolerant, secular courts must nonetheless, in McConnell's perspective, accommodate the intolerant views, within the limits set by criminal law.

### i. Accommodation of the Intolerant View

As an illustration of this tolerance towards the intolerant, McConnell quotes the US *Mozert* case,[41] in which a pupil's mother objected to her daughter being exposed through the school's critical reading programme to views that contradicted her religious upbringing. Contrary to the judgment made against the mother in that case, McConnell argues that the mother's claim should have been granted. Similarly, if a fundamentalist Christian complains that teaching evolution at a state school without discussing creationist objections expresses disapproval of his religious view, courts should, according to McConnell, defer to the applicant's view and include creationism in the syllabus.[42] One might infer from that 'accommodationist' perspective that religious freedom claims would also have the upper hand in all the instances of clashing rights mentioned at the start of the introduction. As the logical priority granted to religious freedom inhibits the ability of courts to impose limits on religious requests, there would be no legitimate reason for the courts to deny these religiously-motivated requests. I identify the motivation for the accommodationist position in two often connected concerns, which I classify as being either epistemological or of impartiality. The epistemological concern points to the inability of liberal laws and courts to truly understand religious normative systems. The impartiality concern underlines liberal laws and courts' bias against minority religious views.

### ii. The Epistemological and Impartiality Concerns

According to the epistemological concern, courts would never be able to fully understand or fully grasp the complexity of religious practices. McConnell points to the special transcendence of religious beliefs, to the special relationship they express between God's creatures and their Creator, to explain law's inability to reflect religious freedoms truly and accurately.[43] This inability of courts

---

[41] *Mozert v Hawkins County Board of Education*, 827 F2d 1058, 1063.

[42] M McConnell, 'Religious Freedom at a Crossroads' (1992) 59 *The University of Chicago Law Review* 115, 149.

[43] M McConnell, 'Why Protect Religious Freedom?' (2013) 123 *Yale Law Journal* 770.

to venture into religious waters is also tainted by suspicions of illegitimacy. Merging into a jurisdictional objection, the epistemological concern, the argument that law cannot understand religion, turns into an ultra vires objection, an argument that law would go beyond its remit if it did regulate religion. Religious freedom then would not only protect the religious citizen against state intrusions but, more controversially, would protect the autonomy of the spiritual domain from state interference. In that light, McConnell's accommodationist view does incorporate the notion of limit, but as a separating line between religious and secular spheres. It cannot help justify the limits which the state might legitimately impose on religious freedoms. Indeed, outside of criminal law and the limits set to avoid criminal harm caused to others, the accommodationist view suggests that state restrictions would be arbitrary.

Other authors[44] who share these epistemological concerns are willing to concede that law is able to portray majority Christian understandings of religion. However, they underline the mismatch between law and minority religions and ways of life. As the category of religious freedom would be rooted in a majoritarian Christian understanding of religion, the very framing of minority religious freedom claims into legal categories would be distortive of minority religions, and particularly of minority ways of life that do not fit well into the concept of 'religion' itself.[45] The very fact of legal intervention would impose a distortion, if not a violence, on certain communities and their members, independently of legal outcomes.[46] Without disclaiming the category of religion itself, American professor of religious studies, Winnifred Fallers Sullivan, in her tellingly entitled book *The Impossibility of Religious Freedom*, argues that liberal courts cannot genuinely apprehend minority religious traditions and lack the legitimacy to do so:

> Courts need some way of deciding what counts as religion if they are to enforce these laws. Is it possible to do this without setting up a legal hierarchy of religious orthodoxy? And who is legally and constitutionally qualified to make such judgments? Can 'lived religion' ever be protected by laws guaranteeing religious freedom? Religion and law today speak in languages largely opaque to each other. The modern religio-political arrangement has been largely, although not exclusively, indebted, theologically and phenomenologically, to protestant reflection and culture.[47]

---

[44] SN Balagangadhara, *The Heathen in his Blindness: Asia, the West and the Dynamic of Religion* (Leiden, Brill, 1994); T Asad, *Formations of the Secular: Christianity, Islam, Modernity* (Stanford, Stanford University Press, 2003); T Fitzgerald, *The Ideology of Religious Studies* (Oxford, Oxford University Press, 2005). WF Sullivan, *The Impossibility of Religious Freedom* (Princeton, Princeton University Press, 2005) 3.

[45] Balagangadhara, *The Heathen in his Blindness* (n 44). And for its implications for legal responses, see P Shah, 'Legal Responses to religious diversity (or to cultural diversity?)' in S Ferrari (ed), *Routledge Handbook of Law and Religion* (Abingdon, Routledge, 2015) 119.

[46] On the violence that the legal language imposes on the 'alien' who comes from a different system, see J Derrida, *De l'Hospitalité* ('Of Hospitality') (Paris, Calmann-Lévy, 1997) 21.

[47] Sullivan, *The Impossibility of Religious Freedom* (n 44) 3.

As a result, Sullivan concludes, while religious freedom as a political idea was arguably once a force for tolerance, it has now become a force for intolerance.

### iii. Responses to the Accommodationist View

Whilst acknowledging the difficulties in apprehending religious claims, I will point to two problematic consequences of this purely negative approach to religious freedom: the muffling of conflicting views and the ossification of religious views and communities. McConnell's illustration helps us understand the dangers of an exclusivist non-interventionist approach to religious freedom. Potential dissenting views within religious communities will have no voice. The child's own preferences and interests in the *Mozert* case[48] are simply absorbed by her mother's religious freedom claim, ironically hiding potentially conflicting religious claims from the child herself or/and her right to education. In the employment and commercial context referred to above, the potential conflicting rights of same-sex couples, for example, would similarly be ignored. In McConnell's construction, the logical priority granted to religious freedom thus undermines conflicting interests at the outset and deprives courts of justifications for setting limits to illiberal religious requests. By contrast, as I have explained,[49] the democratic approach complements the method of avoidance with principles of inclusion and revision. If courts are to retract, as per the method of avoidance, from assessing the legitimacy of religious beliefs, the principle of inclusion requires that all actors are given the opportunity to express their view and interests. Moreover, the principle of revision provides a basis for setting limits to religious freedom requests and an incentive for citizens (not just state institutions) to review the terms of legitimate diversity and their own commitments. Under the principle of revision, citizens are expected to revise their commitments and beliefs in light of contrasting views, hence accepting the horizon of a democratic *vivre ensemble*, of a constitutional overarching framework, and the obligations of reciprocity and renewal it carries. Contrary to McConnell's conclusion, therefore, the democratic approach would lead to a rejection of the mother's request in *Mozert*. However, as is hopefully beginning to emerge, the limits, which the democratic approach imposes on religious freedoms under the principle of revision, do not suggest a weakened importance of the concept of religious freedom for the sake of equality or impartiality. In that respect, the democratic approach also stands in contrast with what I have termed the analogous view.

---

[48] *Mozert* (n 41).
[49] See section I.C above.

## II. SUMMARY OF MY MAIN ARGUMENT

To sum up, against epistemological objections, I propose to demonstrate that legal adjudication and, more broadly, discussions in the public sphere about the legitimacy of particular regulations such as government or work policies may endorse a dialogical function, in which competing views are confronted and explained. Gradually, this process may thus work out a shared *vivre ensemble* (itself under constant review) compatible with individuals' and groups' own (evolving) legal and religious normative overarching framework. Against accommodationists who would allow any religious practices to flourish, I argue for a democratic *vivre ensemble* based on reciprocity in which positive rights of participation come with limits attached. Indeed, it would be inconsistent if the inclusive conception of religious freedom adopted for the sake of pluralism allowed some citizens to retreat from diversity altogether and refuse any exposure to differing views and ways of life. Against those liberals who would dissolve, disaggregate and dilute religious freedom into underlying secular values of liberty and equality, I argue that such an approach would not solve but just divert the epistemological problems associated with the category of religion and unduly undermine the importance of the religious self-definition of religious citizens. My suggestion is not that religious commitments are necessarily more intense than secular ones[50] and that law should therefore give them systematic precedence in case of conflicting rights. The argument is that the category of religion in political philosophy and of religious freedom in law matters – to ensure that legal reasoning itself is open to diversity[51] – and that religious freedom thereby invigorates democratic debate.

In other words, the main argument of the book is thus that religious freedom matters for the construction of a democratic understanding of the *vivre ensemble*. I argue that, properly construed, religious freedoms ensure a healthy pluralism, which invigorates democracy. Following the trajectory of Rawls,[52] I submit that law can maintain and deepen the connections between democracy, pluralism and religious freedom thanks to three features. The first feature is a method of avoidance, which portrays religious freedoms as negative liberties and protects them against state interference. The second, the principle of inclusion, guarantees equality and fair terms of cooperation between religious and non-religious citizens and, the third and last feature, the principle of revision, implies that the terms of legitimate diversity may be subject to limits and are constantly under

---

[50] *cf* contra, J Garvey, 'An Anti-Liberal Argument for Religious Freedom' (1996) 7 *J Contemporary Legal Issues* 275, 287, arguing that the pursuit of religious truth should be granted greater protection because the harm suffered by religious citizens who are denied the possibility to act according to their convictions would allegedly be more serious.

[51] See, pursuing that goal, H Muir Watt, 'Discours sur les méthodes du droit international privé ('Discourse on the methods of international private law') in *Collected Courses of the Hague Academy of International Law* (Vol 389) (Leiden, Koninklijke Brill NV 26, 2018). Muir Watt argues for a new theory of inter-alterity in law, based on a principle of recognition of and respect for the 'other'.

[52] Rawls, *Political Liberalism* (n 6).

review. In that light, religious freedoms not only safeguard a private sphere from state interference (under the method of avoidance); they also positively bolster rights to participation. If construed under the principles of inclusion and revision in an inclusive and open-ended manner, religious freedoms ensure that the voice of the minorities, the marginal and vulnerable members of society may be heard and contribute to the political debate. Religious freedoms would then guarantee 'the openness to the other', which liberalism has often been accused of lacking.[53]

## A. Implications for Law

From what precedes, the book reads as an argument in favour of the democratic-deepening effect of religious freedoms in liberalism and hereby joins the debates about democracy and religion in political philosophy. However, the book also offers a legal argument. Part II of the book explores the consequences for legal controversies involving religious freedom, taking the employment sphere as an area of investigation.[54] The employment sector is of particular interest for my purposes. It is where the most delicate issues of conflicting rights in horizontal relationships,[55] relationships outside of the state, between private individuals and groups, have emerged in recent times, raising difficult clashes between grounds of discrimination on the basis of religion and on the basis of equality.[56] Besides, religious freedoms in the workplace are at the centre of an intertwined layer of norms. At national legislative level, religious rights, which are entrenched in the Human Rights Act 1998 and the Equality Act 2010 in Britain and the Code du Travail (Employment Law Code) in France, are inspired and guided by two distinct complementary European frameworks: EU Council Directive 2000/78/EC of 27 November 2000 Establishing a General Framework for Equal Treatment in Employment and Occupation[57] and Article 9 of the European Convention

---

[53] The liberal ideal of tolerance would fall short of such openness given that the state remains entitled to decide who deserves tolerance and who does not. See M Nussbaum, *The New Religious Intolerance. Overcoming the Politics of Fear in an Anxious Age* (Cambridge MA, Harvard University Press, 2012).

[54] By contrast, the background for the discussions in Part I of the book is set at schools, for this is where national conceptions of religious freedom and *vivre ensemble* have been expressed most emblematically. See M Hunter-Henin (ed), *Law, Religious Freedoms and Education in Europe* (Farnham, Ashgate, 2011).

[55] See H Collins, 'The Protection of Civil Liberties in the Workplace' (2006) 69 *Modern Law Review* 619.

[56] See for example, N Tebbe, *Religious Freedom in an Egalitarian Age* (Cambridge MA, Harvard University Press, 2017); K Greenawalt, *Religion and the Constitution: volume I – Free Exercise and Fairness* (Princeton, Princeton University Press, 2006) Ch 18; S Knights, *Freedom of Religion, Minorities and the Law* (Oxford, Oxford University Press, 2007) Ch 5; R Adhar and I Leigh, *Religious Freedom in the Liberal State*, 2nd edn (Oxford, Oxford University Press, 2013) Ch 10; L Vickers, *Religious Freedom, Religious Discrimination and the Workplace*, 2nd edn (Oxford, Oxford University Press, 2016).

[57] On the influence of EU (and ECHR) law on UK discrimination law, see the rich synthesis by C O'Cinneide, 'Values, rights and Brexit – Lessons to be learnt from the slow evolution of United Kingdom discrimination law' (2017) 30 *Australian Journal of Labour Law* 1.

on Human Rights (ECHR). In scrutinising the jurisprudence of national courts and European courts on religious freedom in the workplace, the book aims to provide a method for approaching the abovementioned difficult controversies. A note must be added on the scope of my proposal. The state framework, which transpires from much of political philosophy reflection on religion and democracy on the one hand, and from the two English and French national stories, in which my demonstration is embedded on the other, is not to indicate that the state is the exclusively legitimate or inevitable framework for addressing issues of religious freedom, law or democracy.

## B. Implications of My Argument for Theories of Democracy and Legal Pluralism

It lies outside of the scope of the book to discuss theories of democracy beyond the state, whether in the European arena[58] or the polymorphous sphere of 'transnational law'[59] or 'global law'.[60] Nor does the book claim to take sides in debates over the democratic legitimacy of legal pluralism[61] within the state[62] or beyond.[63] My argument does, however, yield conclusions relevant for these discussions. First, the principles of inclusion and revision which I propose, under which the terms of legitimacy are to be constantly reviewed in debates inclusive of marginal voices, logically leans towards radical conceptions of democracy[64] and democratic experimentalism,[65] in which democratic sites are multiple[66] and democratic solutions transient.[67] Second, these principles of

---

[58] See O Gerstenberg, *Europe and its Discontents* (Oxford, Oxford University Press, 2018).

[59] C Scott, '"Transnational Law" as Proto-Concept: Three Conceptions' (2009) 10 *German Law Journal* 859; M del Mar and R Cotterrell, *Authority in Transnational Legal theory* (Cheltenham, Edward Elgar, 2016).

[60] N Walker, *Intimations of Global Law* (Cambridge, Cambridge University Press, 2015).

[61] J Griffiths, 'What is Legal Pluralism?' (1986) 24 *Journal of Legal Pluralism and Unofficial Law* 1, where legal pluralism is said to rely on a multitude of sites of legal orders.

[62] W Menski, 'Plural Worlds of Law and the Search for Living Law' (2012) *Recht Analyse als Kulturforschung* 71.

[63] P Zumbansen, 'Transnational Legal Pluralism' (2010) 1 *Transnational Legal Theory* 141; R Michaels, 'Globalisation and Law: Law Beyond the State' in R Banakar and M Travers (eds), *Theory and Method in Socio-Legal Research* (Oxford, Hart Publishing, 2013) 287; H Muir Watt, 'Globalization and Private International Law' in J Basedow and others, *Encyclopedia of Public International Law* (Cheltenham, Edward Elgar, 2017).

[64] J Cohen, *Philosophy, Politics, Democracy. Selected Essays* (Cambridge MA, Harvard University Press, 2009). Under a radical conception, democracy goes beyond majority rules and aggregation of interests, to include broader conditions of participation and deliberation.

[65] CF Sabel and WH Simon, 'Destabilization Rights: How Public Law Litigation Succeeds' (2004) 117 *Harvard Law Review* 1015; MC Dorf and C Sabel, 'A Constitution of Democratic Experimentalism' (1998) 98 *Columbia Law Review* 267.

[66] J Cohen and C Sabel, 'Directly-Deliberative Polyarchy' (1997) 3 *European Law Journal* 314.

[67] This approach allows a more dialogical and fluid view of adjudication, in which judicial decisions (whatever the outcome) offer opportunities for continued and refined deliberation on contested issues.

inclusion and revision need not be exclusively associated with the legal normative power of the state. On the contrary, my extensive analysis of European
jurisprudence (from the Court of Justice of the European Union as well as from
the European Court of Human Rights) reveal that these principles also feature,
sometimes more prominently, sometimes less, in the supra-national European
framework. Similarly, the principles of revision and inclusion provide a useful
prism through which to scrutinise the flurry of norms created by government
regulations, employment policies, ministerial advice etc. Albeit discarded by
some from the category of 'legal norms',[68] these norms have a coercive effect on
religious freedom and an impact on pluralism, which can be as powerful as that
of statutory provisions. This book will consequently consider norms at both
supra and infra-state level. In that sense, my argument does therefore recognise
the plurality of normative and democratic sites and hereby incorporates pluralism in the conception of democracy[69] and law[70] itself. Given this broad scope of
investigation, a few brief words are in order about the contextual and comparative approach I adopt.

## C. A Contextual and Comparative Approach

I adopt a contextual approach in two ways. First, the democratic paradigm
I defend (namely, a concept of religious freedom amenable to pluralism and
deepening of democracy)[71] is grounded in a sociological and historical analysis
of two national stories of the relationships between law, religion, diversity and
the state. Second, I then put the democratic paradigm to the test (so to speak)
and elaborate upon it through the detailed scrutiny of concrete cases involving
clashes between religious freedom and competing rights. This double contextual
layer has several advantages. As the functionalist methods in comparative law
have shown, such incorporation of the 'facts' in legal reasoning help the critique

---

See W Simon, 'Justice and Accountability: Activist Judging in the Light of Popular Constitutionalism
and Democratic Experimentalism' (2016) *Law, Culture, and the Humanities* 1: 'The exercise of judicial
power (would then be) more provisional and contingent than the critics allow'. And for discussions in
the European context, see Gerstenberg, *Europe and its Discontents* (n 58) fn 13.

[68] *cf* criticising the definition of law as derived from state institutions, W Twining, *General
Jurisprudence: Understanding Law from a Global Perspective* (Cambridge, Cambridge University
Press, 2009).

[69] On the idea that giving a voice to affected people is a pre-condition of law's legitimacy, see
AM Slaughter, *A New World Order* (Princeton, Princeton University Press, 2004); Muir Watt,
*Discours sur les méthodes* (n 51).

[70] See N Roughan and A Halpin, *In Pursuit of Pluralist Jurisprudence* (Cambridge, Cambridge
University Press, 2017). See also H Petersen and H Zahle (eds), *Legal Polycentricity: Consequences
of Pluralism in Law* (Dartmouth, Aldershot, 1995).

[71] On the basis of a method of avoidance and principles of inclusion and revision, see section I.C
above and Ch 4 below.

to reveal and challenge assumptions in legal reasoning which are empirically untenable.[72] The contextual approach also usefully reminds us that law is the bearer of values[73] and hence preserves us from the myth of the purely abstract nature of law.[74] To achieve this eye-opening gaze, the contextual approach I adopt draws on several disciplines and includes a comparative dimension,[75] as a subversive force[76] against concepts and ideas that one might take for granted. Thanks to this comparative lens, law is not merely the passive vehicle of the dominant narratives,[77] which insidiously shape our views, but itself a discursive phenomenon.[78] The aim of the comparative analysis I undertake of Britain and France is not, therefore, to devise a common model for both,[79] or identify the better model. The goal is to add embeddedness and sharpen the critique of legal reflections, situated in the tensions between universality and particularity. In the words of the French sociologist and political scientist Dominique Schnapper:

> One must refuse the general, the unique or the universal and choose the specific hence the plurality, but in light of a reference to the universal, (…) which expresses the recognition that others have a dignity equal to mine.[80]

In short, the book makes a case for a concept of religious freedom amenable to pluralism and deepening of democracy and demonstrates that each selected country can find within itself its own idiosyncratic manifestation of it. Here is how the argument unfolds.

---

[72] *cf* B Markesinis and J Fedtke, *Engaging with Foreign Law* (Oxford, Hart Publishing, 2009).

[73] See P Fitzpatrick, *The Mythology of Modern Law* (Abingdon, Routledge, 1992) 65.

[74] Exploring legal concepts in their sociological and historical context ensures that one does not forget the bonds between law and culture, see R Unger, *Law in Modern Society* (London, Macmillan, 1976) esp 250; R Cotterrell, *Law Culture and Society* (Farnham, Ashgate, 2006).

[75] On the links between interdisciplinarity and comparative law methods, see P Legrand, *Le droit comparé*, 3rd edn (Paris, Press Universitaires de France, 2009).

[76] G Fletcher, 'Comparative Law as a Subversive Discipline' (1998) 46(4) *American Journal of Comparative Law* 683.

[77] On the normative force of the narratives surrounding laïcité (the French version of secularism), see A Ferrari, 'De la politique à la technique : laïcité narrative et laïcité du droit, Pour une comparaison France/Italie' in B Basdevant-Gaudemet and F Jankowiak (eds), *Le droit ecclésiastique de la fin du XVIIIème siècle en Europe* (Leuven, Peeters, 2009) 333; D Koussens, *L'épreuve de la neutralité. La laïcité française entre droits et discours* (Brussels, Bruylant, 2015). And more generally, E Balibar, *Des Universels* (Paris, Galilée, 2016) (from a philosophical perspective) and G Frankenberg, *Comparative Constitutional Studies: Between Magic and Deceit* (Cheltenham, Edward Elgar, 2018) (from a comparative law perspective).

[78] See J Habermas, *Between Naturalism and Religion. Philosophical Essays* (Ciara Cronin tr, Cambridge, Polity Press, 2016).

[79] See, by contrast, 'advocating a model of secularism suitable for Europe as a whole, L Zucca, *A Secular Europe: Law and Religion in the European Constitutional Landscape* (Oxford, Oxford University Press, 2012).

[80] D Schnapper, *De la démocratie en France : République, nation, laïcité* (Paris, Odile Jacob, 2017) 38: 'il faut refuser le général, l'unique ou le mondial, il faut choisir le particulier, donc la pluralité, mais en l'inscrivant dans une référence à l'universel qui est la condition même de son existence et de la possibilité de dialogue avec les autres, de la reconnaissance fondamentale que leur dignité est égale à la mienne'.

## III. STRUCTURE OF THE ARGUMENT

In the first part, 'The Broken *Vivre Ensemble* (Observations and Solutions)', I analyse the causes of current tensions and put forward solutions. Opening up with *Contextual Analyses*, I explore the sociological/cultural/historical context in which religious freedoms in Britain (with a focus on England) and France are anchored and make sense.

In Chapter 2, I submit that the French story of laïcité, the French version of secularism, has followed a schematic move from a militant form of secularism, rooted in Revolutionary ideals of democracy, to a separatist type, which contains inclusive elements more amenable to pluralism and minorities. However, in recent times, for fear of Islam, laïcité has reverted towards militant streaks, which I reveal and criticise. Through this analysis of the tortuous and at times violent history of laïcité, I make the too-often-neglected point that laïcité does not entail the relegation of religion to the private sphere.

A similar complexity and return towards illiberal trends characterise the hugely different story of church establishment in England, which I synthesise, praise and criticise in Chapter 3. This contextual analysis does not aim to provide a detailed definition of the 'best' secularism but to pick up, from 'within', features, which bring French laïcité and the English church establishment close to a type of secularism amenable to pluralism. Having argued that a type of secularism is *possible and suitable* in both national contexts (but via different manifestations specific to each selected country), I move on in Chapter 4 to arguing that a pluralism-friendly type of secularism is also the most *desirable*.

In Chapter 4, *Conceptual Analyses*, I explore the conceptual links between religious freedom, democracy and pluralism and develop the argument that the concept of religious freedom is vital to ensure a democratic-enriching pluralism. I first start by a dissection of and response to opposing views. I here bring in and discuss authors who identify secular values such as equality as the foundation of democracy as well as scholars who, more radically, doubt that religion and liberal democracy can be reconciled and consider that they should therefore each evolve in their own sphere. Having addressed these authors' objections, I then move on to make the case that religious freedoms have a positive value for democracy and put forward a framework of analysis based on the above-described method of avoidance, principle of inclusion and principle of revision.

In a second part, I confront my proposed pluralism-friendly democratic-deepening paradigm of religious freedom with concrete cases and thereby make theoretically-grounded normative proposals for change of some current legal outcomes in France and Britain.

In Chapter 5, *Lessons from Achbita*, I extract an important implication for law of the principles of inclusion and revision defended in earlier chapters, namely that law ought to refrain from assigning pre-political meanings to certain spheres of life or domains of activity. Based on a detailed analysis of the CJEU ruling in *Achbita*, I demonstrate how the ruling fails in that respect. I submit that the CJEU in *Achbita* confers upon neutrality policies decided by the employer a presumption of legitimacy and emphasises consistency over proportionality. These two features, I submit, muffle the consideration and expression of competing religious interests by employees and thereby risk undermining the democratic-deepening potential of religious freedom and of courts as democratic fora for debating conflicting interests in the workplace. Second, I refute the oft-made observation that the underlying deference to the laïque constitutional setting in that case (for good or bad reasons) allows for the continuation of dialogue at national level. I argue that the deference to laïcité was not only misplaced, as the principle of laïcité – as I explain – was actually not applicable, but also contradicts the principles of inclusion and revision. Indeed, far from allowing the national debate to endure, I will show that such undue deference acts as a conversation-stopper[81] both at local level, in the workplace, and in national courts.

In Chapter 6, *Ways Forward*, I analyse other concrete cases involving religious freedom claims in the workplace and make suggestions for reasoned and fair outcomes, in line with the democratic approach. Amongst the delicate issues I examine are: the rights of public agents in France to wear religious symbols in the workplace, in the *Ebrahimiam* case;[82] the rights of religious organisations to impose adherence to their religious ethos upon their employees, as in the CJEU rulings of *Ergenberger* and *IR*,[83] the ECtHR decisions of *Schüth Obst, Fernández Martínez* and *Travaš*,[84] and the US case of *Burwell v Hobby Lobby*.[85] Finally, I look at the rights of employees, as in the British *Ladele* case,[86] or of service providers, as the bakers, in the *Ashers Baker* case,[87] in Northern Ireland and the *Masterpiece Cakeshop* case,[88] in the US, or the hoteliers in *Bull v Hall*,[89] to refuse, on religious grounds, to serve same-sex couples. Many of these cases raise novel and delicate issues. The conflicting interests they reveal not only set public interests against individual rights but confront minority rights against each other, as when equality protection rights of same-sex couples clash with

---

[81] To use Richard Rorty's expression in relation to religion: R Rorty, 'Religion as Conversation-Stopper' (1994) 3 *Common Knowledge* 1, 2.

[82] *Ebrahimian v France* App no 64846/11 (ECtHR, 26 November 2015).

[83] Case C-414/16 *Vera Egenberger v Evangelisches Werk für Diakonie und Entwicklung*, Judgment of the Court (Grand Chamber) of 17 April 2018, ECLI:EU:C:2018:257; Case C-68/17 *IR v JQ*, Judgment of the Court (Grand Chamber) of 11 September 2018, ECLI:EU:C:2018:696.

[84] *Obst v Germany* App no 425/03; *Schüth v Germany* App no 1620/03, ECHR 2010 and ECtHR 3 February 2011; *Siebenhaar v Germany* App no 18136/02 (ECtHR Grand Chamber, 12 June 2014); *Fernández Martínez v Spain* App no 56030/07 (ECtHR 12 June 2014); *Travaš v Croatia* App no 75581/13 (ECtHR 4 October 2016).

[85] *Burwell v Hobby Lobby Stores, Inc*, 134 S Ct 2751 (2014).

[86] *Ladele v Islington London Borough Council* [2009] EWCA Civ 1357, [2010] IRLR 211, para [44] and before the ECtHR, *Eweida v UK* [2013] ECHR 285.

[87] *Lee v Ashers Baking Company Ltd & Others (Northern Ireland)* [2018] UKSC 49, [2018] 3 WLR 1294.

[88] *Craig v Masterpiece Cakeshop, Inc*, 370 P3d 272.

[89] *Bull v Hall* [2013] UKSC 73, [2013] 1 WLR 3741.

the religious freedom of citizens who hold minority religious views. Whilst the application of an avoidance method and inclusion and revision principles do not lead to one single outcome in each case, they allow the filtering of a few legitimate outcomes and the exclusion of others.

## IV. CONCLUSION

This book is therefore a reaction (and hopefully a response) to the current failed attempts at devising a harmonious *'vivre ensemble'*.[90] By offering a third way, which requires neither giving up on the notion of shared *vivre ensemble* nor abandoning the concept of religious freedom, the democratic approach fills a gap in the literature and helps us understand the vital connections between religious freedom, pluralism and democracy. The book thus seeks to unleash a more democratic reading of *vivre ensemble*, one that can be sufficiently inclusive to offer a legitimate and fair framework for citizens with different beliefs. To that end, I put forward a democratic paradigm, which offers a method for dealing with contemporary controversies involving religious freedom, under which religious freedom, pluralism and democracy reinvigorate one another.

[90] Amongst liberal Western democracies, the US and the UK, for example, are still struggling to deal with the generational, geographical and social divides, and resulting democratic crisis, which the 2016 election and referendum have respectively revealed and deepened. See MC Nussbaum, *The Monarchy of Fear: A Philosopher Looks at Our Political Crisis* (New York, Simon & Schuster, 2018); F Fukuyama, *Identity: Contemporary Identity Politics and the Struggle for Recognition* (London, Profile Books, 2019); A Weale, *The Will of the People: A Modern Myth* (Cambridge, Polity Press, 2018). These divides resonate well beyond and across the traditional political lines between the Left and the Right: see P Berman, 'The Philosophers and the American Left' *Tablet*, 25 November 2018; P Marlière, '«Lexit» ou la dangereuse illusion d'une sortie progressiste de l'Union européenne' (*Médiapart*, 30 May 2019) at blogs.mediapart.fr/philippe-marliere/blog/100519/lexit-ou-la-dangereuse-illusion-d-une-sortie-progressiste-de-l-union-europeenne.

# Part I

# The Broken *Vivre Ensemble* – Observations and Solutions

I N THIS FIRST part of the book, encompassing Chapters 2–4, I will analyse, out of the two national histories of France and Britain, why the *vivre ensemble* has broken down. Several features account for the current disharmony. In France, the principle of laïcité, whose roots and complex history I will retrace, is more and more frequently used as a tool to push for the assimilation of religious (and especially Muslim) minorities into a Republican mould. Whereas history shows that laïcité had gradually evolved towards a principle amenable to religious diversity and to an inclusive democratic paradigm of *vivre ensemble*,[1] the confrontation with Islam has prompted retrograde steps.

Laïcité has shifted away from the democratic approach I defend in this book in three ways: it is more inward-looking; it is at times used as a tool (in discourse at least)[2] to bolster majority ways of life; and it is a vehicle for Republican values. The move towards a closed version of laïcité,[3] under the 2004 Law banning the ostentatious display of religious symbols in state schools,[4] extends neutrality requirements from agents of public services to their users. Albeit confined to the highly symbolic remit of state schools, the 2004 law thus signals that religion and religious freedom potentially hinders learning, and especially the learning of Republican values. Laïcité, hereby used to channel anxieties over the preservation of existing majority values, appears to fall foul of the principle of revision, under which the terms of legitimacy should constantly be under review.[5] In the 2004 legislative framework, the terms of the *vivre ensemble* are no longer the object of an open debate but, as school pupils are encouraged to take a 'step back' from religion, are geared towards a horizon without religion, and especially one without a visible Islam.[6] More drastically, the 2010 legislative ban

---

[1] See Ch 2 below.

[2] But on the normative effect of discourse, see E Balibar, *Des Universels* (Paris, Galilée, 2016). It is nonetheless important to draw the distinction between laïcité as a legal concept and as a category in political/sociological/philosophical discourse, and the rest of the book will highlight the difference where appropriate.

[3] On the opposition between a closed and open version of laïcité, see the text at Ch 2, section II.A.

[4] Loi n. 2004-228 of 15 March 2004, JO 17 March 2004, 5190.

[5] See Introduction above, and more fully, Ch 3 below.

[6] For an analysis of the 2004 law, see the text at Ch 2, section II.A.ii.

on the full covering of the face[7] reverts to a pre-laïcité Revolutionary stance, in which Republican common values are invoked in order to create an imaginary consensus and justify on its elusive basis measures restrictive of religious freedom.[8] Contrary to the principle of inclusion,[9] the 2010 Law excludes marginal voices from the debate on the *vivre ensemble*. Third and finally, the argument whereby the dichotomous ideology spread by Islamist terrorists ought to be countered by a strengthening of Republican values and a restriction of visible religious signs in the public sphere feeds the narratives of an insurmountable opposition between a French *vivre ensemble* and religious freedom (especially when applied to Islamic visible signs).[10] Contrary to the dialogical discursive approach I promote,[11] it ossifies divisions and unduly simplifies the meanings of personal and collective stories behind the decision to wear a religious symbol.

As I will show, religious freedom in England is embedded in a hugely different political, historical and constitutional context of church establishment. Whilst church establishment might appear intrinsically exclusionary of those who do not belong to the established religion, I will argue that the English mild form of establishment is no more partial than other constitutional arrangements of church/state relationships. History shows that the establishment of Anglicanism has not precluded the English model from evolving gradually towards a non-coercive stance respectful of religious diversity and autonomy. Modern trends, however, stand in the way of a democratic *vivre ensemble* in line with the method of avoidance, principles of inclusion and revision, which I have advocated. Contrary to the method of avoidance, which postulates non-interference of the state with matters of religion, the new statutory duty, known as the 'Prevent' duty,[12] designed to prevent vulnerable people from falling prey to terrorism, throws suspicion on certain forms of religious views or practices. As construed under the Government guidance,[13] the Prevent duty targets 'extreme' religious views,[14] defined as such because of their rejection of elusive

---

[7] Loi n. 2010-1192 interdisant la dissimulation du visage dans l'espace public of 11 October 2010, JO 12 October 2010.

[8] On the 2010 law, see the text at Ch 2, section II.A.iii.

[9] See Ch 1 above, and Ch 4 below.

[10] On this argument, see section III.C below.

[11] See Ch 1 above, and Ch 4 below.

[12] Counter-Terrorism and Security Act 2015, s 26. The government announced on 12 August 2019 that Lord Carlile would lead an independent review on the Prevent duty: www.gov.uk/government/news/lord-carlile-to-lead-independent-review-of-prevent.

[13] Home Office, 'Prevent Duty Guidance', available at www.gov.uk/government/publications/prevent-duty-guidance.

[14] On the repeated failure to define extremism, see for example the lack of definition in the Counter-Extremism and Safeguarding Bill 2016 designed to 'prevent radicalisation, tackle extremism in all its forms, and promote community integration' by introducing a host of new powers to deal with extremism. The measures and powers announced under the Bill didn't materialise: www.theguardian.com/politics/2017/jan/29/theresa-may-counter-terrorism-bill-sinking-without-trace-extremism-british-values.

'fundamental British values'. As for the principles of revision and inclusion, they are in practice undermined (if not denied) by the social and economic divides which weigh more heavily on some cultures and religious groups and individuals than on others.

In response, I will propose a new democratic paradigm for religious freedom, which would be respectful both of context (as analysed in Chapters 2 and 3) and of a democratic-deepening effect of pluralism (as defended in Chapter 4).

# 2

# *Contextual Analyses: Laïcité and the Democratic* Vivre Ensemble

'La diversité des cultures doit s'inscrire dans une société qui accepte un certain nombre de valeurs et de principes communs'.

Dominique Schnapper[1]

'Il nous faut repenser cet espace intermédiaire, cet entre-deux nuancé qui permet au temps de faire son ouvrage'.

Jean Baubérot[2]

CONTEMPORARY STUDIES OF European societies have diagnosed a 'fracture',[3] a clash between religious absolutes and democratic pluralism,[4] itself possibly a sign of a broader 'clash of civilisations'.[5] In this chapter, I will explore these clashes and divisions and look to French policies for ways to handle today's religious (and social) diversity peacefully and fairly. The aim of this chapter is to provide the cultural/sociological/historical context against which legal conceptions and solutions pertaining to religious freedom are made and in which they are embedded and make sense. Undoubtedly, my own expertise (and its limits) motivates my choice of France, and, in the following chapter, Britain (with a focus on England), as selected national contexts of reference.[6] However, further justifications for the selection of these two

---

[1] 'Cultural diversity must inscribe itself in a society which respects a number of common values and principles': D Schnapper, *De la démocratie en France : République, nation, laïcité* (Paris, Odile Jacob, 2017) 325.

[2] 'We must rethink this intermediary space, this in-between nuanced sphere, which allows the passing of time to do its work': J Baubérot, *Vers un nouveau pacte laïque?* (Paris, Seuil, 1990).

[3] G Kepel, *La Fracture* (Paris, Gallimard, 2016).

[4] S Mancini and M Rosenfeld (eds), *The Conscience Wars: Rethinking the Balance between Religion, Identity, and Equality*, Reprint edn (Cambridge, Cambridge University Press, 2019).

[5] SP Huntington, *The Clash of Civilizations: And The Remaking of World Order*, Reissue edn (London, Simon & Schuster, 2002).

[6] I was brought up in a Franco-English family, have lived in both countries, graduated in both countries, worked as a teaching fellow or lecturer in both countries, have researched and written about each country and am a national of both countries.

countries lie in their differing and often contrasted policies of secularism versus multiculturalism;[7] in their rich philosophical and historical perspectives on religious freedom and in their common (but different) colonial pasts and resulting waves of immigration, notably immigration of Muslim families and more recently, sadly, in their confrontation with home-grown Islamist terrorism.[8] France and Britain therefore offer a rich soil out of which to think and rethink the connections between religious freedom, church/state national models, national identity, pluralism and democracy.

In this chapter, I will tell the French story of laïcité, the French version of secularism,[9] and explain its complex and at times contradictory trends of hostility and tolerance towards religious expressions. A brief historical perspective is indispensable to shed light on the roots and dynamics of laïcité. Using a typology suggested by constitutional law professor Dieter Grimm,[10] I will explore how laïcité evolved from a militant type of secularism, which left little space for religion in the public sphere, to a separatist type, which banned religion in institutional state spheres, but let freedom of religion prevail in private as well as public spheres independent of the state. At the end of the twentieth century, I will argue that laïcité, at least as an aspiration – albeit one which had never fully materialised and was stricken with inner contradictions – allowed a separatist/ inclusive type of secularism, which combined neutrality of the state and freedom of conscience.

Moving on to contemporary issues in section II, and in particular to the interaction between laïcité and Islam, I will examine how the inclusiveness potential reached by laïcité at the end of the last century has disintegrated. Prompted by the conviction that past moulds of integration had become dysfunctional, religious freedoms in France have been gradually more and more restricted. A dichotomous narrative, opposing French traditions to alien Islamist ways, supported the shift. Muslim voices would not be part of the national story but rather would offer a conflicting story, itself a consequence of growing conflicting values. The diagnosis of social fractures does not uniquely apply to Muslims.[11] However, in respect of Muslims, the impact is symbolically greater. Islam is not the cause of the failure of integration policies, but it has become a mirror, in which society looks at itself.[12] It is for this symbolic reason that the second section will focus

---

[7] B Bhandar, 'The Ties that Bind Multiculturalism and Secularism Reconsidered' (2009) 36(3) *Journal of Law and Society* 301.

[8] See RS Leiken, *Europe's Angry Muslims. The Revolt of the Second Generation* (Oxford, Oxford University Press, 2012).

[9] On the varied meanings of secularism, secular, secularisation, see for example, C Calhoun and others (eds), *Rethinking Secularism* (New York: Oxford University Press, 2011).

[10] See below (n 13).

[11] See Schnapper, *De la démocratie* (n 1) 272.

[12] O Roy, *La Laïcité face à l'islam* (Paris, Fayard, collection Pluriel, 2013) 34.

on Islam and Muslims. I will argue that faced with Islam, laïcité has retreated into a militant form of secularism. By contrast to the communitarian lines currently adopted in recent trends of laïcité, I will suggest that an inclusive type of laïcité should guide legal solutions.

According to Grimm, there are different secular constitutional states with quite different attitudes toward religion.

> There is a militant secularism that denies religious beliefs any public role and insists on their belonging strictly to the private sphere. There is also a secularism that separates church and state: the state accepts the role religion plays in society, but is prohibited from promoting religious activities or giving material or immaterial subsidies to religious communities. There is finally a type of secularism that recognizes religion as an elementary human urge that seeks public expression, an urge that the state not only has to respect, but also must protect and maybe even promote – altogether the opposite of a secular fundamentalism.[13]

The first type, militant secularism, imposes common values as the cement of the social and political bonds of the nation. Whilst the inspiration of a militant secularism can be egalitarian, it remains inherently assimilationist and is therefore unsuitable for our contemporary multi-religious and multicultural societies. The second type, separatist secularism, signals a position of compromise based on strict dividing lines between non-institutional spheres (where individual liberty reigns) and institutional spheres (where neutrality requirements prevail). This type two secularism embodies a negative constitutionalism based on a principle of non-interference of the state in non-institutional spheres. Reciprocally, however, citizens accept in return a restriction of their liberties in institutional spheres. Following a Holmesian model,[14] type two secularism thus relies on reciprocal consensual constraints of state power and individual liberties in order to protect religious liberties from state intrusions on the one hand and unencumber the political sphere from divisions and controversies on the other. Finally, under a type three model, secularism evolves into a positive constitutionalism under which religious freedoms are not only protected against state interference, but also valued as a positive good, capable of enriching political debate and contributing to society. That is why states that adopt a type three secularism will not only manage and contain religious diversity, so to speak, but will promote it, by embracing a generous and inclusive conception of religious freedom. However, inclusive secularism under this type three model is also conjectural and reciprocal,

---

[13] D Grimm, 'Conflicts Between General Laws and Religious Norms' in S Mancini and M Rosenfeld (eds), *Constitutional Secularism in an Age of Religious Revival* (Oxford, Oxford University Press, 2014).

[14] On Stephen Holmes, see Ch 4 below.

as the generous interpretation of religious freedom is subject to the condition that (religious) citizens accept in return the general framework of *'vivre ensemble'*. I will make the case in chapter 4 for an inclusive secularism along the lines of Grimm's type three secularism.

In the contextual chapters, I would like to draw from the political culture elements of this ideal inclusive secularism. Starting with France in this chapter, I will work from within the French culture to construe the interpretation of laïcité, which is closest to this inclusive type three model. Whilst the argument will rely on elements of inclusiveness that exist within French political culture and the complex history of laïcité itself, the goal here is neither to return to a pure, undistorted, original or perfect meaning of laïcité nor to identify a universal detailed concept of secularism. The ideal inclusive type of secularism is a paradigm, which lends itself to many varied manifestations, some more suited than others to a particular context and a particular period. The inclusive secularism I propose is thus inherently indeterminate in the sense that its precise substance depends on the contextual deliberations of stakeholders. In this first contextual chapter, my objective is not therefore to provide a detailed definition of the 'best' secularism but to pick up, from 'within', features that could bring French laïcité close to an ideal inclusive type of secularism.

## Table on laïcité

| Typology | Definition | Constitutional Moment | Motive | Current Contrary Trends |
|---|---|---|---|---|
| Type one: Militant pre-laïcité | • undermining of religion • assimilationist state ideology | The French Revolution | • political equality • anti-religious | • anti-religious policy • state ideology through common values |
| Type two: Separatist laïcité | • strict divide state and non-state spheres • religion tolerated in non-state spheres | 1905 Act | • negative constitutionalism • state non-interference • independence of each sphere | • expansionist interpretation of state spheres |
| Type three: Inclusive laïcité | • state support for religion • religion seen as public good | Aspiration | • positive constitutionalism inclusive of diversity • subject to acceptance by all of general framework | • communautarian |

## I. THE HISTORICAL LAYERS OF LAÏCITÉ: FROM HOSTILITY
TO TOLERANCE TOWARDS RELIGION

The French version of secularism – laïcité – is traditionally defined as an exemplar of the second separatist system,[15] in Grimm's typology, but is in effect often conceived as the epitome of the first militant type. In this section, I will explain why both these representations of laïcité are to an extent true but will argue that they hide the fact that laïcité – at least as an aspiration – also fit the third mode of secularism – one that is welcoming and inclusive towards religious freedoms. An incursion into the French Revolution, in section A, will account for the militant features of laïcité. Section B will show how the militant type of laïcité evolved towards a separatist type two laïcité, finally (partly) blossoming into an inclusive type three, thanks to the interpretation by the French Council of State (Conseil d'Etat) and the legacy of the 1789 French Declaration of the Rights of Man and the Citizen.

## A. Laïcité: A Militant Form of Secularism?

In this section, I will examine to what extent – if any – the Revolutionary period, from 1789 to 1799, can guide us in shaping the inclusive type of secularism I am aiming for. In our 'lieux de mémoire',[16] laïcité stems from the French Revolution. The same bust of Marianne symbolically represents the laïque Republic and the French Revolution: a young woman wearing the Revolutionary tricolour bonnet.[17] This section will explore the Revolutionary roots of French laïcité. It is customary to think of laïcité as a product of the French Revolution. On the one hand, the argument goes, the secularisation of French society, which the Revolution allegedly achieved, has supposedly paved the way to laïcité. On the other, the invention of a political sphere detached from religion would also have made a favourable terrain for laïcité. I will argue on the contrary that the Revolution only accelerated a process of secularisation that was already taking place and that secularisation does not necessarily lead to laïcité. Moreover, the Revolutionary conception of the political contradicted the public/private divide at the heart of the modern separatist concept of laïcité. However, I will go on to explain that the emergence of the political in Revolutionary France in reaction to the Catholic Church has left its marks on laïcité. It is because of the Revolutionaries' first experiments with democracy that laïcité in France is often still portrayed as a protection of the

---

[15] J Rivéro, *La notion juridique de laïcité* (Paris, Recueil Dalloz, 1949) 137.

[16] See, for an English version, the three volumes edited by P Nora: P Nora (ed), *Rethinking France: the State* (Chicago, University of Chicago Press, 2001); P Nora (ed), *Rethinking France: Space* (Chicago, University of Chicago Press, 2006); P Nora (ed), *Rethinking France: Legacies* (Chicago, University of Chicago Press, 2009).

[17] See M Aghulon and P Bonte, *Marianne : Les visages de la République* (Paris, Gallimard, 1992); F Furet and M Ozouf (eds), *Le Siècle de l'avènement républicain* (Paris, Gallimard, 1993).

political against the (non-democratic) influences of the Catholic Church (and, by extension, of religious communities). This first section will therefore make the argument that whilst the French Revolution does not explain the emergence of laïcité fully, it accounts for its militant tones,[18] and as such is unlikely to help in drawing the contours of an inclusive concept of secularism.

### i. Secularisation, Revolution and Laïcité: A False Connection

It is often believed that the French Revolution established an entirely new social order, which liberated 'the Third Estate'. According to this view, the Third Estate, namely those that were neither part of the aristocracy nor the clergy but belonged to the bourgeoisie and poorer classes, finally gained recognition.[19] In the Revolutionary struggles, the aristocracy and the clergy thus sided with the Ancien régime – which embraced a monarchist absolutist view of politics and a class-based unequal view of society – whilst the Third Estate brought in its stride an egalitarian perspective. In Revolutionary French society, the doctrines of the Church and the influence of the clergy would no longer dominate; secular ideals of the Enlightenment, giving credit to individual talent, independently of class, would instead reign. This presentation calls for nuances. In fact, as the French historian François Furet has shown,[20] building on Alexis de Tocqueville's analysis,[21] the secularisation of French society was already well under way under the Ancien régime.[22] The Church had already lost a lot of its influence. Since Louis XIV, the most decisive source of influence came from centralised state power, not the Church. 'This grip of the central power on French society is what links the new (Revolutionary) regime to the old; Bonaparte to Louis XIV'.[23]

Besides, class mobility existed prior to the French Revolution. Members of the bourgeoisie regularly acceded to aristocratic ranks through royal decree.[24] The Revolution only accelerated the process of secularisation by introducing key symbolic reforms in the heart of one of the areas traditionally controlled by the Church: civil status. A civil state system for births, marriages and deaths was established as soon as 1792, based on the Revolutionary ideals of freedom and consent.[25] The Revolutionaries introduced divorce, in blatant contradiction to the Catholic Church's doctrine of indissolubility of the sacrament of marriage. Upon mutual consent, faults or insanity on the part of the other

---

[18] See Table, above.

[19] A Soboul, *La Révolution française*, 4th edn (Paris, PUF Collection Quadrige, 2014).

[20] F Furet, *Penser la Révolution française* (Paris, Gallimard, 1985).

[21] A de Tocqueville, *L'Ancien Régime et la Révolution, re-edited version* (Paris, Gallimard, 1967) book 3.

[22] ibid, 33–66.

[23] ibid, 33.

[24] Furet, *Penser la Révolution* (n 20) 168 ff.

[25] Loi du 20 septembre 1792 sur l'état civil, on which see G Noiriel, 'L'identification des citoyens. Naissance de l'état civil républicain' (1993) 13 *Genèses* 3.

spouse, de facto separation or incompatible temperaments, spouses could easily divorce, without any judicial proceedings.[26] The new measures proved popular but this modern spirit of liberty did not pervade the whole of French society or the whole of French territory.[27] The Revolutionaries' nationalisation of the Church and consequent persecution of priests who refused to swear an oath of national allegiance moreover backfired. Overtly anti-religious measures ordered in the autumn of 1793, on the initiative of the Parisian Chaumette, such as the replacement of the Christian calendar by a Revolutionary one or the closure of all Parisian Churches, only increased divisions.[28] In many regions, especially in Vendée and Brittany, the tight control of Church affairs created intense resentment and undermined the Revolutionary cause and ideals, leading finally to bloodshed and the extermination of dissenters.

From what precedes, the notion of a rupture between an old religious-based French society and a new secular and egalitarian society born out of the French Revolution seems therefore an exaggeration. The Revolution did introduce emblematic secular institutions in areas up to then exclusively governed by the Church but secularisation of society and class mobility had already started prior to the Revolution. Moreover, it is difficult to see the secularisation achieved or, more accurately, continued in Revolutionary times as a precursor of modern separatist laïcité. Indeed, secularisation of society does not imply Church/state separation, as illustrated by the British experience[29] nor does Church/state separation imply the secularisation of society.[30] Whereas secularisation relates to the decreasing influence of religion in society, type two laïcité implies the separation of Church and state. The former relates to the descriptive, the latter to the normative. It is possible to argue that type two laïcité tends to encourage secularisation[31] but the two concepts remain distinct. In any case, in respect of Revolutionary France, as seen above, the secularisation of society did not produce laïcité in a type two sense. The competition for political influence between the Revolutionary state and the Church was too fierce. Revolutionaries did not seek separation from the church but control of it. In its relegation of

---

[26] J Tulard, J Fayard and A Fierro, *Histoire et dictionnaire de la Révolution française, 1789–1799* (Paris, Robert Laffont, 1998).

[27] See RG Phillips, 'Le divorce en France à la fin du XVIIIe siècle' (1979) 34 *Economies, sociétés, civilisations.* 385.

[28] See G Gengembre, 'Sur les origines révolutionnaires de la laïcité' (2013/14) 162 *Romantisme* 11.

[29] For a study of the secularisation of British society, see Grace Davie, *Religion in Britain since 1945: Believing without Belonging, 2nd edn (Oxford, Blackwell, 1995).*

[30] As in Turkey, where laïcité is in force but society remains religious. See JW Warhola and EB Bezci, 'Religion and State in Contemporary Turkey: Recent Developments in "Laiklik"' (2010) 52 *Journal of Church and State* 427.

[31] See R Adhar and I Leigh, *Religious Freedom in the Liberal State*, 2nd edn (Oxford, Oxford University Press, 2013). See also J Baubérot, *Histoire de la laïcité en France*, 7th edn (Paris, PUF, collection Que sais-je?, 2017) 109 ff, critically observing that the third stage of laïcité involves secularisation – laïcisation – of society. For a discussion of the terms secularisation, laïcité and laïcisation, see J Baubérot, 'Laïcité, laïcisation, secularisation' in A Dierkens (ed), *Pluralisme religieux et laïcités dans l'Union européenne* (Brussels, Editions de l'Université de Bruxelles, 1994) 9.

religion to the purely private sphere and its tight control of the Church, the conception of secularism embraced by the French Revolution was therefore of a militant type one 'that denies religious beliefs any public role'.[32] The Revolutionary vision of the political similarly leads us to a characterisation of the Revolutionary secularism as a militant type, unlikely to yield guidelines for managing religious diversity today.

### ii. The Political in the French Revolution: National Identity Through Universal Ideals

As identified by Furet,[33] building on Auguste Cochin,[34] what French Revolutionaries invented was a theory of political action based on a secularised national ideology. Politics in Revolutionary times was not procedural; it embodied a set of values and beliefs – for the sake of which all political actions were driven. This theory of the political was eminently democratic, in the sense that its legitimacy relied on popular sovereignty. The nation was the embodiment of all citizens, each equal to one another and the expression, through its laws, of the 'volonté générale', the general will of the people.[35] The nation was not a static entity but one open to anyone who had proven their commitment to the Revolutionary ideals.[36] The Revolutionary ideals in building the French nation had a universal inspiration. As French historian Bernard Cottret aptly puts it, 'the French people voted for the freedom of the world'.[37] Conversely, however, the Revolutionary nation felt it was legitimately entitled to crush its enemies from outside or within. Eminently democratic, the French Revolution was also illiberal and unstable. For lack of mediation between the executive power and the people, the legitimacy of the political was in a state of constant flux, dependent upon a permanent oratorical contest, in which members of the executive had to deliver persuasive speeches or face being ignored or even, in later times, guillotined.[38] To sharpen their arguments, political Revolutionary figures grew close to erudite salons.

As Tocqueville notes, the literary world (that is, literary and philosophical salons) took over the political.[39] This unusual position of erudite societies

---

[32] Grimm, 'Conflicts' (n 13).

[33] Furet, *Penser la Révolution* (n 20) 50–51.

[34] A Cochin, *La Révolution et la libre pensée* (Göttingen, Copernicus Diffusion. 1979) XVIII.

[35] This is reminiscent of course of Jean-Jacques Rousseau's writings, especially Le Contrat Social: J Rousseau, *Of The Social Contract and Other Political Writings* (Christopher Bertram ed, Quintin Hoare tr, London, Penguin Classics, 2012).

[36] S Wahnich, *L'impossible citoyen : L'étranger dans le discours de la Révolution française* (Paris, A Michel, 1997).

[37] B Cottret, 'Foreword' in B Cottret (ed), *Du patriotisme aux nationalismes (1700–1848), France, Grande-Bretagne, Amérique du Nord* (Paris, Créaphis, 2002); review by A Duprat in (2003) 333 *Annales historiques de la Révolution française* 7.

[38] Furet, *Penser la Révolution* (n 20) 94.

[39] ibid, book 3.

weighed against political pragmatism, not because philosophers or writers were less reasonable and realistic than others, but because they discussed ideas and principles without having to carry them out. Their exercise of political power remained abstract – akin to an opinion group – and did not have to operate within the confines of actual implementation. As Furet notes, 'Enlightened citizens of the time tended to favour rules over facts, principles over the balancing of interests, values and objectives over implementation'.[40]

The French Revolution lacked what Furet calls 'a political sociability', that is, a network linking citizens and the executive as well as political networks amongst citizens themselves.[41] The literary salons did not fill the gap. Instead, they embodied and spread the ideal of direct pure democracy[42] in which the sovereign power is indistinguishable from the people.[43] What lessons can we draw from Furet's perspective on the French Revolution?

### iii. A Type One Militant Form of Laïcité

Revolutionary France cannot be characterised as laïque in a type two separatist sense. It had become secular. Divine right no longer justified political sovereignty. The Revolutionaries shifted the notion of centralised state from a divine to a social entitlement: whereas the French monarchy had been of God's right, the new Revolutionary regime, even if it first invoked the 'Supreme Being', rested on 'the People'.[44] However, the Revolution did not amount to a separatist laïque regime, as the state sought to establish a form of state religion and control it tightly.[45] On 12 July 1790, the Civil Constitution of the Clergy placed the Church under the authority of the state and turned priests into civil servants. In 1791, these new civil servants were required to swear allegiance to the laws of the Revolution or face a clandestine life and persecution.[46] The laïque idea of a separation between religion and the political had not yet emerged.[47]

---

[40] ibid, 66.

[41] ibid, 67.

[42] It is tempting to link the notion of direct democracy to the work of Jean-Jacques Rousseau but Rousseau's social contract is far more complex than the imaginary consensus upon which Revolutionaries relied to establish political legitimacy. It would fall outside the scope of this chapter to discuss Rousseau's work. For a discussion, however, of political legitimacy, see Ch 4 of this book.

[43] Furet, *Penser la Révolution* (n 20) 272 ff.

[44] *cf* Baubérot, *Histoire de la laïcité* (n 31) 8 who highlights that, unlike the US 1776 Declaration of Independence, which refers to God as the source of the proclaimed rights, the 1789 French Declaration of the Rights of Man and the Citizen merely proclaims rights, in the presence and under the auspices of a Supreme Being.

[45] Nowadays non-laïque secular countries such as Britain adopt a position of neutrality towards religious beliefs.

[46] T Tackett, *Religion, Revolution, and Regional Culture in Eighteenth-Century France: The Ecclesiastical Oath of 1791* (Princeton, Princeton University Press, 2014).

[47] See A Mathiez, 'La Séparation des Eglises et de l'Etat a-t-elle existé réellement sous la Révolution française?' in JM Schiappa (ed), *1905 ! La Loi de séparation des Eglises et de l'Etat* (Paris, Syllepse, 2005) 15.

This lack of boundaries encouraged illiberal streaks. Interestingly, for Furet,[48] the period known as "The Terror", from 5 September 1793 until 28 July 1794, does not amount to a tragic accident in the history of the French Revolution. It is the logical climax of a political conception, which accepted no bounds other than oratory ineptitude, and relied upon a purely imaginary consensus. I acknowledge that this illiberal portrayal of the French Revolution, which I am putting forward, has attracted criticisms.[49]

What matters, for my purposes, is that these illiberal forces (whether they were inherent, as Furet argues, or accidental to the French Revolution)[50] derive from a certain conception of the political rather than from the concept of laïcité. The Revolutionary conception of the political was the exact opposite of a type two laïcité. Whereas type two laïcité, as I will explain below, rests on a distinction between the state and non-state spheres,[51] no such borders existed under the French Revolution. Citizens were to devote all aspects of their lives to the defence and promotion of the Revolutionary cause, with no distinction between their public and private lives.[52] The Revolution shared, in a secular version, the view of the Catholic Church that beliefs penetrate every aspect of believers' lives. According to American historian David Bell, the French Revolution conferred on the nation and the concept of law a sacredness, which has survived even our contemporary disenchanted secularised world.[53] As I will explain in the following section, modern laïcité, whilst departing from the Revolutionaries' encompassing illiberal ideologies, has however retained two elements from the Revolutionary period: its ideal of transcendence[54] and its hostility towards the Catholic Church.[55]

---

[48] ibid, 87 ff, 105.

[49] See C Mazauric, 'Réflexions sur une nouvelle conception de la Révolution française' (1967) 39 *Annales historiques de la Révolution française* 339. On the controversies between Furet and Marxist writers, see J Suratteau, *La Révolution française – Certitudes et controverses* (Paris, PUF, 1973) 95.

[50] For this thesis, see for example, T Tackett, The Coming of the Terror in the French Revolution (Cambridge MA, Harvard University Press, 2015).

[51] I will argue below that the distinction between State and non-State spheres is more accurate a description of the division in question than, and does not coincide with, the distinction between public and private spheres.

[52] Furet, *Penser la Révolution* (n 20) 49.

[53] D Bell, *The Cult of the Nation in France. Inventing Nationalism, 1680–1800* (Cambridge MA, Harvard University Press, 2001) 98.

[54] On these links between laïcité, the French Revolution and transcendence, see H Pena-Ruiz, *Dieu et Marianne: Philosophie de la laïcité* (Paris, PUF Collection Quadrige, 2015): 'the Revolutionary idea of the nation, devoid of all nationalistic ambiguities, ensures the mediation between the singular reality of a place, a story, a territory and the critical universality of principles which can be of value for the whole humanity. It is this mediation, which is remarkable as it denotes a universalisation process in which the laïque reasoning reconciles embeddedness and political will'. For a different conception, which presents laïcité from its socio-historical roots, rather than its philosophical ambitions of transcendence, see P Portier, *L'Etat et les religions en France: Une sociologie historique de la laïcité* (Rennes, Presses Universitaires de Rennes, 2016).

[55] M Vovelle, *La Révolution contre l'Eglise* (Brussels, Complexe, 1988).

## B. Laïcité: From Militant to Separatist and Liberal Secularism

The previous section has shown that, if the modern separatist form of laïcité is not the child of the French Revolution, the French Revolution still acted as a 'donor', transmitting fundamental genetic traits. Several questions emerge from this. If the French Revolution is merely a donor, when, then, was separatist laïcité born, and to whom? More importantly, what does laïcité look like? How have the two Revolutionary traits identified above (transcendence and suspicion towards the Church) manifested themselves in laïcité? What other (possibly more crucial) distinctive features characterise laïcité and how do all these features combine with one another? In this section, I will argue that whilst laïcité emerged out of a militant political fight of Republicans against the Catholic Church, its legal consecration, under the 1905 Law,[56] turned the concept into a separatist type two form of secularism. I will argue that this separatist type two laïcité[57] contains several useful elements for my purposes. Despite its deficiencies and ambiguities, I will show that the 1905 law shares many features with an ideal inclusive type of laïcité.

### i. The Revolutionary Heritage: 'Laïcité de Combat'

The Revolution had split France in two: Revolutionary and Catholic France; the state and the Church; the political and the religious. For a long time, from the end of the conciliatory politics of the Consulate[58] until the famous Law on Separation of Church and State of 9 December 1905,[59] laïcité reproduced these dichotomies and adopted a combative stance.[60] Laïcité was 'une laïcité de combat' carved from its opposition to the Catholic Church. During this period, the Catholic faith and laïcité offered two alternative and conflicting modes of belonging in France and two alternative and conflicting modes of living in France. They represented 'two partially idealist visions which linked patriotic feelings to a religious or ideological dimension that fought to win the hearts of the French people'.[61]

During the Second Empire, from 1852–1870, the tensions between the two faces of France reached their peak. Republicans and Catholics both vehemently professed their incompatibility with one another.[62] Intractable differences

---

[56] See below (n 59).

[57] See Table, above.

[58] See B Basdevant, *Le Jeu concordataire dans la France du XIXème siècle* (Paris, PUF, 1988).

[59] JO 11 December 1905; on the origins of the Act, see J Foyer, 'La Genèse de la loi de séparation' in La Laïcité (2005) 48 *Archives de Philosophie du droit* 75–83. Following French historian and sociologist Jean Baubérot (J Baubérot, *Laïcité 1905-2005, entre passion et raison* (Paris, Le Seuil, 2004)), I will argue that modern laïcité was born out of the 1905 Law.

[60] See Conseil d'Etat, *Rapport sur un siècle de laïcité* (Paris, La Documentation française, 2004) 279.

[61] R Rémond, *Religion et société en Europe* (Paris, Le Seuil, 1998) 157.

[62] On this, see Baubérot, *Histoire de la laïcité* (n 31) 36.

divided them. Culturally, Catholics discovered the 'miracle in Lourdes'[63] whilst Republicans read Darwin's evolutionary theories[64] and Auguste Comte's sociological positivism,[65] but the deeper divide was political. Republicans, who had lost to Napoleon III, feared a return of the monarchy, whereas many Catholics supported both Pope Pius IX and the Comte of Chambord, who was next in line to the French throne. When the Second Empire crumbled away in the Franco-Prussian War and the Third Republic was proclaimed in 1870, an active anti-Catholic state policy was put in force. In the 1870s, the Republic sought to control the hearts of the people and thereby avoid a return to the old regime. The Republic actively provoked the secularisation of French society[66] by introducing secular schools, abolishing Sunday as the day of rest, secularising hospitals,[67] health care[68] and cemeteries, banning public prayers and reinstating divorce.[69] At first, this forced secularisation left open the possibility of a parallel Catholic system, as illustrated by the 1886 Goblet Law.[70] However, with the election of the radical Emile Combes in 1902, Catholic France was hit hard: over 10,000 Catholic schools were closed, religious congregations were prohibited from delivering any teaching, assets belonging to religious congregations were confiscated by the state. Many Catholic priests and nuns chose exile.[71] A shift occurred in 1905. I will argue that the Act of 9 December 1905 amounts to a turning point: militant laïcité evolved into a separatist type.

## ii. The Turning Point of 1905: Separatist Laïcité

Without mentioning laïcité,[72] the 1905 Law defines new relationships between the state and the Church, based on two core principles: separation and freedom

---

[63] The first apparition of the Virgin Mary by Bernadette Soubirous dates from 1858. See M Blanton, *Margaret Grey, Bernadette of Lourdes* (London, Longmans, Green & Co, 1939).

[64] Darwin published his *Origin of the Species by means of natural selection by John Murray Publishers, London* in 1859 (but the French translation by Edmond Barnier, Alfred Costes Publishers, Paris, appeared in 1929).

[65] See, however, how Auguste Cochin reconciled his Catholic faith with a methodology inspired by Auguste Comte: Cochin, *La Révolution* (n 34).

[66] This active promotion of secularisation, by contrast to spontaneous secularisation, lies at the core of the difference sometimes drawn between the concept of laïcisation (active secularisation) and the concept of secularisation stricto sensu, when secularisation is spontaneous. See J Baubérot and S Mathieu, *Religion, modernité et culture au Royaume-Uni et en France* (Paris, Le Seuil, 2002). In my framework, borrowed from Dieter Grimm's typology, laïcisation corresponds to a militant form of laïcité.

[67] See J Baubérot and R Liogier, *Sacrée médecine. Histoire et devenir d'un sanctuaire de la Raison* (Paris, Entrelacs, 2010).

[68] See ibid.

[69] On these measures, see Conseil d'Etat, *Rapport* (n 60) 254.

[70] See Art 2 § 6 of the French Law of 30 October 1886 (Loi Goblet), JO 31 October 1886, according to which primary schools may be either state or privately run.

[71] C Sorrel, *La République contre les Congrégations* (Paris, Le Cerf, 2003).

[72] Laïcité was only explicitly proclaimed in law in 1946, under the Constitution of the Fourth Republic, *JORF*, 28 October 1946, vol 78ᵉ, n° 253, p 9166–9175 and can now be found in Art 1 of the

of conscience. Under Article 1 of the 1905 Law, 'The French Republic ensures freedom of conscience'.[73] Under Article 2, 'The French Republic neither recognises or subsidises any cult'. The 1905 framework recalls Grimm's above mentioned type two secularism, 'a secularism that separates church and state (in which) the state accepts the role religion plays in society, but is prohibited from promoting religious activities or giving material or immaterial subsidies to religious communities'.[74] In line with this separatist inspiration, the 1905 law sought to delineate separate spheres of competence for the state and the Church and no longer imposed anti-religious state policies on society. As Aristide Briand famously concluded at the end of his presentation of the law proposal before Parliament:[75]

> by voting in favour of this law, you will put the State back to its fair share of role and function; you will reconcile the Republic with its authentic revolutionary tradition and grant the Church what it is entitled to, namely the liberty to establish itself, grow and flourish, according to its own rules and own means, with no other restrictions but the respect owed to general laws and public order.

In this two-party compromise between the state and the Catholic Church, little regard, it seems, is shown to religious minorities.

### iii. 1905 Laïcité and Religious Minorities

The recognition of religious freedom under the principle of freedom of conscience in Article 1 of the 1905 Act served to appease conflicts with Catholics. In other words, freedom of conscience was thought of as an instrument to a social end, in the context of a culturally Catholic France. Jean Jaurès, one of the main supporters of laïcité, did not respect freedom of conscience because he considered religious voices important and valuable for the public good. On the contrary, in a Marxist inspiration, his objective was to put an end to religious tensions, to seal the issue of religion, in order to focus on the 'real' social questions.[76] Religious freedom was not valued in itself but only respected to the extent necessary to ensure social peace. As the social tensions of the time involved Catholics and non-Catholics, the drafters of the 1905 law consequently based their interpretation of religious freedom with the majority Catholic religion in mind. Religious minorities were not the main motivation behind the law.

---

present 1958 Constitution, available at www.legifrance.gouv.fr/affichTexteArticle.do;?idArticle=LE GIARTI000019240997&cidTexte=LEGITEXT000006071194&dateTexte=20140401.

[73] The votes in favour of the article were overwhelming: 412 in favour and 45 against in the lower Chamber of Parliament, and 214 versus 46 in the Senate.

[74] Grimm, 'Conflicts' (n 13).

[75] Quoted in Conseil d'Etat, *Rapport* (n 60) 399.

[76] E Balibar, *Des Universels* (Paris, Galilée, 2016) 126; R Castel, *Les Métamorphoses de la question sociale : Une chronique du salariat* (Paris, Fayard, 1995).

Up to the traumatic and tragic Dreyfus affair, in which the wrongful condemnation of a Jewish Army Officer, Alfred Dreyfus, for defence security breaches and collusion with Germany,[77] exposed the antisemitism rooted in the French army and civil society, the relationships between the Republic and its religious minorities had been more peaceful than with its religious Catholic majority. Historically, Protestants who had survived, had not converted to Catholicism and remained in France after Richelieu's policy of persecution, following the revocation of the Edit of Nantes,[78] had benefited from the French Revolution[79] and, in the war of the two Frances, had generally sided with the Republic and laïcité. The same is true for Jews, whose fate improved under the French Revolution[80] and for whom the Republic and laïcité opened more opportunities than royalist Catholic France. Both Protestants and Jews moreover gained in the nineteenth century national official representative bodies.[81] Protestants were heavily involved in the parliamentary report[82] that led to the 1905 Law.[83] Laïcité did not seek, unlike secularism in the United States, to manage religious diversity and ensure harmony amongst a plurality of religious faiths. The dividing line in France was not between diverse religious obedience but between traditionalist Catholics and others, known as 'free thinkers'.[84]

If religious minorities were not the focus of the 1905 framework, the trauma of the Dreyfus affair nonetheless contributed to the political resurgence of left-wing Republican values against right-wing nationalist voices and it is the former that were behind the 1905 compromise. Naturally, it would be too

---

[77] P Birnbaum, *L'Affaire Dreyfus, la République en péril* (Paris, Gallimard, 1994); V Duclert, *L'affaire Dreyfus. Quand la justice éclaire la République* (Toulouse, Privat, 2010).

[78] In 1685. See E Labrousse, *La Révocation de l'Edit de Nantes* (Paris, Payot, Paris, 1985) ch 'Une foi, une loi, un roi?'.

[79] Except for the period of Terror in which Protestants, Jews and Catholic priests who refused to swear a national oath were all affected, see Baubérot, *Histoire de la laïcité* (n 31) 14.

[80] In September 1791, Jews were granted full civic rights, under the status of citizens. See R Badinter, *Libres et égaux ..., L'émancipation des Juifs sous la Révolution française 1789–1791* (Paris, Fayard, 1989).

[81] Conseil d'Etat, *Rapport* (n 60) 396. Under the 17th March 1808 Decree for Judaism and the 18th Germinal an X or 8th April 1802 for those of the Protestant faith. Another Decree of 17th March 1808, known as the 'infamous decree', reinstated discrimination against Jews. This retrograde move is not however associated with laïcité but with Napoleon's policy of 'Concordat', in force between 1801 and 1905.

[82] Chambre des députés, *Rapport fait au nom de la commission relative à la séparation des Églises et de l'État et à la dénonciation du concordat, chargée d'examiner le projet de loi et les diverses propositions de loi concernant la séparation des Églises et de l'État par Aristide Briand, député.* Annexe au procès verbal de la séance du 4 mars 1905, n° 2302, chapter II, 103–112.

[83] Eugène Réveillaud, a radical MP of Protestant affiliation, submitted the proposal for the 1905 law. He was assisted by Dr Louis Méjean, a young doctor in law and militant Protestant, who later became Aristide Briand's main adviser. JP Scott, 'Protestants et juifs face à la séparation des Églises et de l'État' (2006) 1259 *Hommes et Migrations* 17, esp 23.

[84] The divide between (non-Republican) Catholics and (Republican) non-Catholics is naturally too crude. More accurately, the divide was between religious traditionalists and free thinkers. See J Lalouette, *La Libre pensée en France, 1848–1940* (Paris, Albin Michel, 1997); see also Baubérot, *Histoire de la laïcité* (n 31) 37.

crude to assign those who were pro-Dreyfus, known as *Dreyfusards*, to left-wing Republican and anti-Catholic forces, and those who were anti-Dreyfus, to conservative Catholic forces. Not all left-wing intellectuals sided with Dreyfus[85] nor all Catholics against. One of the staunch defenders of Alfred Dreyfus was the Catholic Colonel Picquart whose support against the military establishment led to him receiving a jail sentence.[86] However, the Dreyfus affair undoubtedly strengthened the resolve of left-wing progressive parties, some of which, such as the *Parti républicain radical-socialiste* (the Radical-Socialist Republican Party), were directly established as a result of the Dreyfus affair and with the support of Dreyfusard networks.[87] Following the victory of the left – *le bloc des gauches* – in the 1902 national elections, Jean Jaurès resumed the fight for Dreyfus,[88] whom public opinion had forgotten, leading finally to his acquittal.[89] Jaurès and later Georges Clémenceau[90] (also an active supporter of Alfred Dreyfus) then concentrated their energy on the 1905 legislative framework. Jaurès was involved in the drafting and promotion of the 1905 Law, whilst Clémenceau, head of the French government from 1906 until 1909 and then again from 1917 until 1920, later made the implementation of the law one of his government's priorities. Despite the deep subsequent divides within the left, and between Jaurès and Clémenceau themselves, on social issues[91] and on the war question,[92] Jaurès and Clémenceau thus embody an aspiration for religious tolerance and justice, which is reflected both in their support for the Dreyfus cause and in their commitment to the 1905 legislative framework. In that sociological sense, the 1905 Law was also a reaction against the religious intolerance, which, combined with antisemitism and nationalism, had reached its fever pitch in the Dreyfus Affair.

The 1905 Law did not, however, satisfy Catholics.[93] Even today, the 1905 Act is often accused of undermining religion: 'The collective memory of the French has made the 1905 law the glorious act of "Separation" that tore the

---

[85] M Dreyfus, *L'Antisémitisme à gauche. Histoire d'un paradoxe de 1830 à nos jours* (Paris, La Découverte, 2010).

[86] M Thomas, *L'Affaire sans Dreyfus* (Paris, Fayard, 1961). See also C Prochasson, '*Le Colonel Georges Picquart ou la vertu cachée*' (1993) 11 *Mil neuf cent: Revue d'histoire intellectuelle* 15 (part of issue: Comment sont-ils devenus dreyfusards ou anti-dreyfusards?).

[87] Duclert, *L'affaire Dreyfus* (n 77) 67.

[88] On Jean Jaurès' role in the Dreyfus affair, see G Candar and V Duclert, *Jean Jaurès* (Paris, Fayard, 2014); B Joly, *Histoire politique de l'affaire Dreyfus* (Paris, Fayard, 2014).

[89] Cour de cassation, Ch, réunies 12 July 1906, available at www.letempsarchives.ch/page/JDG_1906_07_13/1. Full text at fr.wikisource.org/wiki/Arr%C3%AAt_de_la_Cour_de_cassation_du_12_juillet_1906.

[90] On Clémenceau's involvement in the Dreyfus Affair, see M Winock, *Clémenceau* (Paris, Perrin, Collection Tempus, 2014) (1st edn, 2007).

[91] See for example the deep conflict between the two men regarding the 1907 demonstrations of wine producers: G Ferré, *1907, La guerre du vin. Chronique d'une désobéissance civique dans le midi* (Toulouse, Éditions Loubatières, 1997).

[92] G Doizy and J Jarnier, *Jaurès, apôtre de la paix* (Paris, Hugo-image, 2014).

[93] Gravissimo Officii Munere – Encyclical of Pope Pius X given in Rome, at St Peter's, on 10 August 1906 calling for disobedience towards the 1905 Law.

state from the Catholic Church and laid down a truth that each and everyone shares: religion is a private affair'.[94] Such is not the purpose or effect of the 1905 Law, however. The 1905 Law posits that the state accepts the role that religion plays in society and does not relegate religion to the private sphere. Here lies the crucial difference between a separatist and a militant form of laïcité. The 1905 Act acknowledged the Catholic influence on society: many Catholics feasts remained as national bank holidays; Sunday was the official national day of rest and Catholic religious signs were welcome in the public sphere. Jaurès explicitly asserted that the purpose of the law was the separation between Church and state and not the forced secularisation of society.

> Laïcité, he declared, is not the relegation of religion or its expression from the public to the private spheres. Laïcité is the protection of the State and society from religious domination and, reciprocally, the protection of religion and society from state domination.[95]

For the first time therefore, the issue was no longer about choosing religion over citizenship or vice versa. The issue was to allow coexistence of the two within an appeased Republic. Separation was the mode chosen to allow such coexistence. In all spheres related to the state, strict neutrality prevailed. The 1905 Law therefore logically prohibits religious symbols in state buildings.[96] By contrast, in all non-state spheres, be they private or public spheres, religious freedom reigns. The Conseil d'Etat thus struck down a decision by the mayor of Sens (in North Burgundy) to ban priests from wearing their cassocks during public funeral processions in the streets of his town. As long as these religious manifestations were compatible with public order, the Conseil d'Etat held, the mayor had no ground for prohibition.[97] However, the French have never strictly followed this separation between neutrality (in state spheres) and liberty (in non-state spheres).

### iv. Laïcité: A Separatist Secularism with Inclusive Elements

To the extent required by the principle of freedom of conscience, the principle of separation between religion and state has often been relaxed. The French state will, for example, fund private religious schools under contract with the state.[98] In return for a commitment to admit pupils non-discriminately and teach

---

[94] Blandine Chélini-Pont, 'Is Laicite the Civil Religion of France' (2010) 41 *Geo Wash Int'l L Rev* 765, 783.

[95] See Conseil d'Etat, *Rapport* (n 60) 263.

[96] Art 28 of the 1905 Law. TA de Besançon, 20 décembre 2001, *M. Guilleminot c/ville de Besançon*.

[97] CE 19 février 1909, Abbé Olivier, rec p 181.

[98] See B Poucet (ed), *La loi Debré, paradoxes de l'Etat éducateur?* (Amiens, CRDP, 2001); see further B Chélini-Pont, 'The French Model: Tensions between Laïc and Religious Allegiances in French State and Catholic Schools' in M Hunter-Henin (ed), *Law, Religious Freedoms and Education in Europe* (Farnham, Ashgate, 2012).

the state syllabus alongside other subjects more representative of the school's religious ethos, the state will take charge of the running costs of the school and staff salaries. Whilst such support for religion may seem at odds with the principle of separation between religion and state, it will actually be in perfect harmony with the 1905 legislative framework as long as freedom of conscience requires such intervention. Arguably, if the availability of religious schooling were only available to parents on the condition of paying high fees, freedom of conscience would in effect be restricted. Freedom of conscience here trumps separation.

Conversely, however, separation will trump freedom of conscience in cases involving requests by civil servants and public agents to wear religious symbols. Their status as representatives of the state will prohibit any manifestation of religious affiliation on their part.[99] Whilst strict separation reigns in the state spheres, in compliance with the second separatist type of secularism identified by Grimm, laïcité is therefore closer to the third liberal type in non-state spheres. According to Grimm, this third liberal type is one 'that recognizes religion as an elementary human urge that seeks public expression, an urge that the state not only has to respect, but also must protect and maybe even promote – altogether the opposite of a secular fundamentalism'. Indeed, laïcité will justify state support for religious options where freedom of conscience requires state intervention, but only in the non-state spheres.

Whilst the evolution of laïcité from a militant type to a separatist type takes place, as I have argued, under the 1905 Law, the introduction of inclusive elements is mainly owed to the interpretation of the Conseil d'Etat. In this interpretative work, the Conseil d'Etat relied, however, upon the 1905 Law itself (and notably Article 1, proclaiming freedom of conscience).[100] The Revolutionary ideals also played a role. Rather than the Jacobinist centralised and illiberal view of religion which the Revolutionaries implemented,[101] the Revolutionary principles invoked in twentieth century France in support of an inclusive laïcité were the individual rights contained in the 1789 Declaration of the Rights of Man and the Citizen. These individual rights, which included freedom of conscience and religion,[102] received constitutional standing by the French Constitutional Council's decision[103] of 16 July 1971 and encouraged a generous interpretation of religious freedom in non-state sectors.[104]

---

[99] CE Opinion 3 May 2000 *Demoiselle Marteaux*, RFDA 2001, 141, Conclusions R Swartz.

[100] J Rivero, *Les libertés publiques*, vol 2 (Paris, PUF, 2003) 156 ff.

[101] See section I.A above.

[102] Art 10 states that 'no one is to be aggrieved for reason of their opinions, including religious opinions, as long as their manifestation is compatible with public order, as determined by the law'.

[103] Décision n° 71-44 DC, *Liberté d'association*, 16th July 1971, available at www.conseil-constitutionnel.fr/en/decision/1971/7144DC.htm.

[104] Conseil d'Etat, *Rapport* (n 60) 276.

## C. Conclusion to Section I

Laïcité is therefore a complex concept with a rich multi-layered history. In this section, I have argued that laïcité does not entail the relegation of religion to the private sphere. Rightly understood, in light of the 1905 Law and subsequent Conseil d'Etat case law, laïcité is a separatist expression of Church/state arrangements which, in non-state spheres, is largely amenable to religious freedom. Going back to Grimm's abovementioned typology, laïcité, born out of a militant first type of secularism, has therefore evolved into a separatist form of secularism, with elements of a more inclusive approach, thus combining the second and third types referred to by Grimm.

However, this process, which led from a type one to an embryonic type three laïcité under the 1905 legislative framework, has been fraught with difficulties and ambiguities. Laïcité has always remained ambiguous in its reception of religious freedom and of religious minorities. Neither religious freedom nor religious minorities have indeed truly ever been recognised for themselves and for their own sake but merely as a broader component of justice and, more strategically, as a solution to a social conflict with Catholic (and, from a social perspective, bourgeois) France. In this latter more instrumental sense, laïcité represents less a liberating force and more 'the hearth of anxiety of an anxious France'.[105] Nowadays, the source of this anxiety resides in Islam. With the arrival of waves of Muslim immigration, following decolonisation, the focus of laïcité has consequently shifted from the Catholic Church to Islam.[106]

## II. LAÏCITÉ, COMMON VALUES AND ISLAM

As demonstrated in section I, laïcité has emerged from a political fight between the Republic and the Catholic Church. The confrontation with Islam could have been an opportunity to deepen the inclusive elements which laïcité had gradually come to incorporate.[107] However, fears of 'communautarism', of the dislocation of society into pockets of segregation on religious lines, prompted instead a return to archaic militant streaks, through an ever-extensive interpretation of neutrality requirements and invocation of national common values.

This section will critically examine these contemporary trends. The section will be divided into three sub-sections. Having set out recent distortive extensions of the concept of laïcité (section A), I will present the terms of the debate between what I would call promoters of a 'communautarian laïcité', as illustrated by Gilles Kepel's view (section B) and defenders of an inclusive laïcité, close to the type three model I am aiming for (section C).

---

[105] M Gauchet, *La religion dans la démocratie* (Paris, Gallimard, 1998) 474.
[106] J-P Costa, 'La conception française de la laïcité' (1994) 149(2) *Revue des sciences morales et politiques* 167.
[107] See section I.B above.

## A. Recent Extensions of Laïcité

In this section, I will examine two particular challenges posed – or allegedly posed – by Islam: the wearing of the Islamic headscarf in French state schools and the wearing of the full Islamic veil in the French public sphere. I will show how these two instances resulted in an extension of the concept of laïcité.

### i. The Headscarf Affairs

The 1980s and 1990s saw the first 'headscarf affairs', in which young Muslim girls claimed the right to attend French state schools wearing a headscarf. Immediately, these requests stumbled upon laïcité. A debate ensued as to the scope of religious freedom in state schools, and, concomitantly, as to the proper meaning of the principle of laïcité. The question raised was whether laïcité justified the prohibition of all religious signs in *places* (everyone and everything within state schools) closely associated with the state or whether it could only require such strict neutrality of *people* (civil servants and public agents)[108] and *buildings* (such as classroom walls)[109] representative of the state. Depending on the 'closed' or 'open' version adopted,[110] laïcité would consequently extend its neutrality requirements to pupils attending state schools or only restrict state school teachers' and other public staff members' rights to religious freedom.[111] By stretching the institutional sphere from state buildings and state agents to users of emblematic Republican sites, such as state school pupils,[112] neutrality requirements, under a closed version of laïcité, would considerably increase in scope.

### ii. From the Separatist/Inclusive Interpretation of the Conseil d'Etat to the Separatist/Militant Conception of Laïcité Endorsed by the 2004 Law

Asked to deliver an opinion on the matter, the Conseil d'Etat[113] considered, in 1989, that the wearing of the headscarf by pupils was not contrary to the principle of laïcité. Prohibitions were only possible *in concreto* if the wearing of

---

[108] See, subjecting public agents to such neutrality requirements, CE Ass *Delle Lamotte* 17 février 1950, *Rec Lebon* n° 86949.

[109] See prohibiting religious symbols on state buildings: Besançon (n 96).

[110] See the contrasting views of D Schnapper, *La Démocratie providentielle. Essai sur l'égalité contemporaine* (Paris, Gallimard, 2000) and JP Willaime, *Le Retour du religieux dans la sphère publique. Vers une laïcité de reconnaissance et de dialogue* (Lyon, Editions Olivétan, 2008).

[111] On this distinction, see Commissaire du gouvernement D. Kessler in CE *Kherouaa* 2 novembre 1992, *Rec Lebon* n° 130394.

[112] See Baubérot, *Histoire de la laïcité* (n 31); G Haarscher, *La Laïcité*, 6th edn (Paris, PUF (Que sais-je ?), 2017). And, more generally, F Mayeur, *Histoire générale de l'enseignement et de l'éducation en France (vol 3), 1789–1930* (Paris, Tempus Perrin, 2004).

[113] CE 27 November 1989 Opinion, RFDA 1990, 1, J Rivero; AJDA 1990, 39–42; J Bell, 'Religious Observance in Secular schools: A French Solution' (1990) 2 *Education and the Law* 121.

the headscarf proved incompatible with safe participation in classes[114] or was accompanied by demonstrations which hindered the peaceful running of the school day.[115] Ultimately, the French Parliament banned the headscarf as well as all other ostentatious religious signs in all French state schools, under the 2004 Act.[116]

To avoid the charge that the law was protecting state ideology and that laïcité was giving up on its inclusiveness, the promoters of the law sought to argue that the restriction protected Muslim girls' freedom of conscience.[117] Allegedly, the ban did not protect French values (or not only), but the young girls themselves. There was indeed a fear that should schools allow a few pupils to wear the headscarf, other Muslim girls who did not wear it would feel under pressure to. Following that reasoning, which the European Court of Human Rights (ECtHR) had already adopted in *Dahlab v Switzerland*,[118] and which the House of Lords (now Supreme Court) subsequently followed in the leading English case of *Begum*,[119] the headscarf itself would have a proselytising effect. To be fair, elements of coercion into wearing the headscarf had indeed been observed from boys of the 'cités', the deprived suburbs of major French towns.[120] However, the causal link between these instances of coercion and the French legal ban on the headscarf was open to question.

Methodologically, the two reports that had led to the 2004 Law – the Stasi Report[121] and the Obin Report[122] – raised doubts as to the connection. Was the evidence of coercion contained in these reports enough to justify a ban in *all* cases, even when the decision to wear the headscarf was voluntary?[123] Was the evidence of coercion the genuine justification for the recommendation, when the recommendation seemed to have preceded the evidence? Was the evidence

---

[114] CE 10 mars 1995 *Epoux Aoukili* (PE classes); CE 20 October 1999, *Ministre de l'Education nationale, de la recherche et de la technologie c./ Epoux Ait Ahmed* (DT classes).

[115] CE 27 October 1996 *Ligue islamique du Nord et Epoux Chabou*.

[116] Loi n. 2004-228 of 15 March 2004, JO 17 March 2004, 5190.

[117] P Weil, 'Why the French Laïcité is Liberal' (2009) 30 *Cardozo Law Review* 2699.

[118] *cf* underlying the risks of indoctrination, *Dahlab v Switzerland* (2001) V ECHR 449, App no 42393/98.

[119] *R (Begum) v Governors of Denbigh High School* [2006] UKHL 15, [2006] WLR 719. In *Begum*, Miss Begum requested the right to wear a *jilhab* – a long and loose-fit coat garment, which covers the entire body but leaves the hands and face visible – in derogation from the school uniform policy which, in consultation with local religious communities, only allowed the *shalwar kameeze*, consisting of wide trousers underneath a tunic. The House of Lords ruled in favour of the school. The Court expressed concern that allowing her to wear the *jilhab* might trigger pressure on her peers also to adopt a stricter form of dress. For more detail on the case, see M Hunter-Henin, 'Children's religious expression in state schools: Exemptions, Participation and Education' in J Dwyer (ed), *Oxford Handbook of Children and the Law* (Oxford, Oxford University Press, 2019).

[120] Stasi Report, *Rapport de la Commission présidée par M. Bernard Stasi de réflexion sur l'application du principe de laïcité dans la République* submitted on 11 December 2003 (La Documentation française, 2004), section 3.3.1, 57; section 4.2.2.1, 99 ff.

[121] Lamotte (n 108).

[122] Les Signes d'appartenance et manifestation religieuse dans les établissements scolaires, juin 2004, n° 2004-115.

[123] See R Liogier, *Une Laïcité légitime : La France et ses religions d'Etat* (Paris, Entrelacs, 2006).

reliable, given the few interviews carried out?[124] In a more abstract way, the ban arguably sought to preserve the emerging conscience of students, by encouraging them to take a step back from their families and communities outside of school.[125] This approach is in line with the abstract trends identified in French laïcité above, as well as with the French ideal of education as an intellectual endeavour detached from the world,[126] but in practice, it leads to a rather paternalistic view of children.[127] Besides, far from merely allowing pupils to take a step back, it actively encourages them to think of themselves outside of religion.[128]

Through its confrontation with the headscarf, laïcité was thus reverting to a type one/type two mode of secularism.[129] Whilst not relegating religion to the strict private sphere, as a pure type one form of militant secularism would do, the wide construction of the institutional state sphere and of the neutrality requirements it triggered under the 2004 Law introduced militant streaks of secularism within a separatist type two model. As to the inclusive elements – amenable to a generous approach to religious freedoms – under a type three form of secularism, they were gone. The concern over the integration of Islam into the French Republic had chased them away. At least the 2004 solution seemed to be restricted to state schools and to children.[130] At universities and other higher education institutions, freedom of conscience prevailed.[131] Freedom also won over restriction in the private sector. Many private Catholic schools (heavily subsided by the state) thus welcomed French Muslim girls (and their headscarves). In the historical divide between Republican and Catholic France, religious minorities now felt more at ease on the Catholic side. Once the 2004 Law had been passed, controversies around Islam and laïcité soon subsided in French schools[132] but

[124] For a summary of the methodological concerns raised by the Reports which led to the 2004 ban, see Leiken, *Europe's Angry Muslims* (n 8) 26–30.

[125] See C Kintzler, 'Laïcité et Philosophie' (2005) 48 *Archives de Philosophie du Droit, La laïcité* 43.

[126] See K Williams, 'Religious Worldviews and the Common School. The French Dilemma' (2007) 41 *Journal of Philosophy of Education* 675: 'The French view school as the perfect institution to teach future citizens to exploit their faculties of reason and to help them exercise freedom of thought. (…) Freedom of thought ensures that pupils enjoy the right to independently re-examine beliefs received from family, social group and society as a whole. This way a person can freely adhere to these beliefs, adapt them or turn from them to something else'.

[127] On children's rights in that context, see Hunter-Henin, 'Children's religious expression' (n 119). See further M Freeman, 'The Human Rights of Children' (2010) 63 *Current Legal Problems* 1.

[128] R Adhar, 'The Child's Right to a Godly Future' (2002) 10 *International Journal of Children's Rights* 89.

[129] See Dieter Grimm's typology in 'Conflicts' (n 13).

[130] See, however, extending obligations of religious neutrality to a mother taking part in a school visit: TA Montreuil 22 November 2011, Droit Administratif (2012) 163. The 2004 Law will also apply to pupils over the age of 18 if they are still attending secondary state schools.

[131] See, however, for one of the latest proposals to extend laïcité to universities and institutions of higher education, E Ciotti et al, 'Proposition de loi visant à étendre le principe de laïcité aux établissements publics d'enseignement supérieur', submitted to the French National Assembly on 30 May 2018, www.assemblee-nationale.fr/15/propositions/pion1009.asp.

[132] Report of July 2005 by H Chérifi, quoted in the Report on the full Islamic veil, *Mission d'information sur la pratique du port du voile intégral sur le territoire national*, Report submitted to the President of the National Assembly on 26 January 2010, at 91, JCP 2010, act 142, comments

the confrontation of laïcité and Islam then bounced back with a new vigour. Six years after the ban on the headscarf (and other ostentatious religious signs) in French state schools, another Islamic religious sign seemed to threaten the French model: the full-face Islamic veil, known as the *burqa* or *niqab*.[133]

### iii. The Republic and the Burqa

Six years after the 2004 Law banning ostentatious symbols in state schools, the French Parliament passed the 2010 Law to prohibit the full covering of the face in the public sphere, namely, in more explicit terms, the wearing of the full Islamic veil.[134] While the 2004 Law, as demonstrated above, reverted to a sepa-ratist stance on laïcité, mixed with militant streaks, the 2010 Law, I will submit, reverted to a pre-laïcité Revolutionary mode of reasoning, which sets common values ahead of freedom of conscience. Unlike the ban on the headscarf, the ban on the *burqa* did not originate from actual tensions between *burqa* wearers and representatives of state institutions but from a presidential comment expressing distaste for such clothing.[135] On 22 June 2009, before both Houses of Parliament in Versailles, President Nicolas Sarkozy declared that 'the *burqa* wasn't welcome in France'.[136] Apart from the unease it provokes, it is difficult to see what ground could justify banning the *burqa* in the whole of the public sphere. The Conseil d'Etat, when asked to review the question, found no possible legal basis for a general prohibition.[137]

Unless we are to legislate to prohibit all practices that appear socially shock-ing,[138] or consider that a right not to be offended might rival a right to express one's religion, no legal ground can be put forward to justify a general ban on the *burqa*. Laïcité does not offer such a legal ground. If, under a closed accepta-tion of the concept, laïcité could still be relied upon to ground the prior 2004 Law,[139] it could not secure a ban on the *burqa*. The special committee set up to

by A Levade. R Leiken, *Europe's Angry Muslims* (n 8) 31, reports that by January 2005, 44 students had been excluded from school for not observing the ban and 639 students were officially censured for violation of the rule. Of those 639 disputes, 550 were solved through dialogue.

[133] The *niqab* is a veil for the face that leaves the area around the eyes clear. The *burqa* covers the body and face completely, often leaving a mesh screen to see through.

[134] Loi n. 2010-1192 interdisant la dissimulation du visage dans l'espace public of 11 October 2010, JO 12 October 2010.

[135] On the origins and the reasons of the French ban on the *burqa*, see M Hunter-Henin, 'Why the French Don't Like the Burqa: Laïcité, National Identity and Religious Freedom' (2012) 61 *International Comparative and Law Quarterly* 1.

[136] *cf* A Chrisafis, 'Nicolas Sarkozy says Islamic veils are not welcome in France' (*The Guardian*, 23 June 2009) www.guardian.co.uk/world/2009/jun/22/islamic-veils-sarkozy-speech-france.

[137] Conseil d'Etat, *Rapport sur les solutions juridiques d'interdiction du port du voile intégral*, 25 March 2010, 35.

[138] D Koussens, 'Sous l'affaire de la burqa ... quel visage de la laïcité française?' (2009) 41 *Sociologie et Sociétés* 327, 328.

[139] However, as I have argued, see section II.A above, the deeper motivation for the 2004 Law probably did not lie in concerns around laïcité but already in anxieties linked to the integration of Muslims.

consider the issue of the wearing of the full veil had to admit that the concept of laïcité was not relevant to the discussion[140] and the government's text which led to the 2010 law did not rely on the notion. Indeed, purely ordinary places such as public streets and purely ordinary citizens, such as passers-by in their daily lives,[141] have never been subjected to religious neutrality requirements under the principle of laïcité. It is not therefore to laïcité but to a pre-laïcité Revolutionary style invocation of common Republican values to which the legislative drafters, followed by the French Constitutional Council[142] and, to an extent, by the ECtHR,[143] reverted in order to justify the banning of the *burqa*.

From the headscarf to the *burqa* bans, religious freedoms have thus become more and more restricted in France. In practice, reports indicate that few women were wearing a *burqa* in France before the ban entered into force.[144] The increased restrictions to religious freedom have therefore had little impact in quantitative terms. It is in qualitative terms, in the way that French law now understands religious freedom, that the restrictions have considerably increased. Whereas freedom of religion had always been the starting point in non-institutional state spheres, since the 2010 *burqa* ban, compliance to social consensus (the minimum requirements of living together, as construed by social consensus) now comes first.[145] This appeal to common national values is not an isolated phenomenon, focused on an extreme and uncommon religious symbol; rather, it is part of a current trend to adopt dichotomous narratives, which place national values in opposition to Muslim extremism, in the hope of cutting terrorism at its root.[146]

## B.  Gilles Kepel's Laïcité

French political scientist Gilles Kepel is one of the prominent voices who argue that there is a continuity between religious radicalisation and terrorism and that the fight against the latter would therefore justify curbing extreme manifestations of religious freedom. In this section, I will critically present Kepel's view.

---

[140] See Report, Mission d'information (n 132). See further Conseil d'Etat, *Rapport* (n 137) 17.

[141] These considerations prompted the ECtHR to hold that the prohibition of a peaceful religious procession in the streets was a disproportionate interference with rights under the ECHR, Art 9: *Ahmet Arslan v Turkey* App no 41135/98 (ECtHR 23 February 2010).

[142] Conseil Constitutionnel 7 October 2010, JO 12 October 2010, 18345.

[143] *SAS v France* [2014] ECHR 695.

[144] Allegedly, fewer than 400 women used to wear the veil in France before the 2010 ban: 'Moins de 400 Femmes Porteraient Le Voile Intégral En France' (*Libération*, 29 July 2009) www.liberation.fr/societe/2009/07/29/moins-de-400-femmes-porteraient-le-voile-integral-en-france_573216.

[145] For a detailed and critical analysis of this shift in reasoning, see M Hunter-Henin, 'Living Together in an Age of Religious Diversity: Lessons from Baby Loup and SAS' (2015) 4 *Oxford Journal of Law and Religion* 94.

[146] On the crude connections made between Islam and terrorism, see section II.C below.

*i. The Argument for a Link between Religious Radicalisation and Terrorism*

According to Kepel, between 2005, which he calls a pivotal year,[147] and 2015–2016, the 'awful year',[148] a sequence of related events unfolded. In 2005, riots erupted in poor and heavily Muslim suburbs in France (the banlieues) and its enclave (the cités), bringing the problem of Muslim integration to the forefront.[149] Following weeks of social unrest and an astonishing amount of property damage, in excess of €200 million, France declared a state of emergency, just as the violence was starting to die down. Ten years later, in 2015, France suffered a wave of terrorist attacks. From the attacks against *Charlie Hebdo* on 7 January 2015, the murder of two police officers, and the killings of Jewish customers of a Kosher supermarket in Porte de Vincennes, to the bloodied celebrations of Bastille Day in Nice on 14 July 2016, followed by the murder of an eighty-year-old priest during mass, only 12 days later, France was hit hard.

Kepel notes that when the French 'banlieues' erupted in rioting in 2005, and again when jihadist terror struck France in January 2015, many Britons attributed France's troubles to its unwise policy of forcing North African immigrants to adopt all aspects of French culture, including a reverence for the French language and a secular and republican ideology.[150] The title of the last chapter of Kepel's book *La Fracture* captures what the scholar thinks of these attacks on the French model: 'Djihadism and "Islamophobia": double deception'.[151] Kepel[152] thus depicts and deplores how the beaches of the South of France, in Nice, which had seen so many victims of the terrorist attacks on 14 July 2016, soon became symbols of French Islamophobia when Muslim women wearing burkinis[153] were refused access to these same beaches, and subsequent town regulations banned the burkini.[154] For Kepel, we should stay away from these 'polemics'; the fight against terrorism would, on the contrary, involve the protection and promotion of the French model of assimilation. From the 2005 riots,

---

[147] See G Kepel with A Jardin, *Terreur dans l'Hexagone: Genèse du djihad français* (Paris Gallimard, 2015) and the review by M Lilla, 'How the French Face Terror' (24 March 2016) *New York Review of Books*.

[148] Kepel, *La Fracture* (n 3) 17.

[149] For an analysis in English of the 2005 riots and of the recommendations that followed, see D McGoldrick, *Human Rights and Religion: The Islamic Headscarf Debate in Europe* (Oxford, Hart Publishing, 2006).

[150] C de Bellaigue, 'The New Europeans' (7 June 2018) *New York Review of Books*.

[151] My translation – the French title is 'Djihadisme et "islamophobie": la double imposture': Kepel, *La Fracture* (n 3) 199.

[152] ibid, 260–61.

[153] A type of swimsuit that covers the whole body except the face, the hands and the feet.

[154] These municipal regulations were subsequently struck down by the Conseil d'Etat CE Ordonnance du 26 août 2016 *Ligue des droits de l'homme et autres – association de défense des droits de l'homme collectif contre l'islamophobie en France*, Nos 402742, 402777, www.conseil-etat.fr/ressources/decisions-contentieuses/dernieres-decisions-importantes/ce-ordonnance-du-26-aout-2016-ligue-des-droits-de-l-homme-et-autres-association-de-defense-des-droits-de-l-homme-collectif-contre-l-islamophobie.

the burkini affairs of 2016 to the wave of terrorism, Kepel suggests a common thread – an attack on common French national values – and a common remedy: a stronger assertion of these values.

### ii. The 2005 Riots: Social Rather than Religious Divides

Let us look more closely at the alleged connections between the three highlighted events: the 2005 riots, the 2016 burkini affairs and the wave of terrorist attacks. The 2005 riots stand out, as their relation to religion is tenuous – if not non-existent. The areas, known as 'cités', at the centre of the riots were (and still are) heavily populated by Muslims, but not exclusively so. In any case, the revolts did not aim to advance a Muslim identity or challenge the French Republican model of assimilation. The 2005 revolt was a cry for social and economic inclusion, not separation. As Ian Buruma[155] underlines in his review of Kepel's 2010 book, Kepel[156] shows that the riots of the French banlieues – joined by Africans, Arabs, Berbers, Muslims, and non-Muslims – were not so much a declaration of independence from French society, as a protest against being excluded from it, by discrimination in jobs or education: 'In a message burned onto television and computer screens throughout France, the rioters seemed to be saying, "We're here! Notice us! Let us in!"'.

The rioters were not asking for separation but denouncing the forced segregation in which they lived. The geographical configuration of the 'cités' in the 'banlieues', these massive architectural ensembles built in the 1960s on the outskirts of town centres to house people of moderate means, inscribed this exclusion in the scenery. Geographically, the cité stands apart from the town-centre, often separated by a network of high-speed roads.[157] Economically and sociologically, it stands apart from professional success, as unemployment rates will score much more highly in the cité; legally, it stands apart from law-abiding society, as criminality is more common in the cité, hence the frequent reference in the media to the cité as a zone of 'non-droit', of non-legality. The anger generated from these fractures had sparked the 2005 revolts.[158]

Religious identity was not at stake in the 2005 riots. On the contrary, the young Muslims (just like others) who took part in these weeks of violence did not claim the right to be different (religiously or otherwise), but the right to be treated as the same as other citizens. They embraced the Republican ideal of

---

[155] I Buruma, 'Living with Islam. Review of Gilles Kepel, Beyond Terror and Martyrdom: The Future of the Middle East and Tzvetan Todorov, La Peur des barbares: Au-delà du choc des civilisations' (14 May 2009) *New York Review of Books*.

[156] G Kepel, *Beyond Terror and Martyrdom: The Future of the Middle East* (P Ghazaleh tr, Cambridge MA, Harvard University Press, 2010).

[157] As in Clichy-sous-Bois, see G Kepel, with L Arslan and S Zouheir, *Banlieue de la République, Institut Montaigne 2011* (Paris, Gallimard, 2012).

[158] See McGoldrick, *Human Rights and Religion* (n 149).

equality but denounced its hypocrisy. Compared to second-generation migrants in Britain, they enjoyed longer schooling and higher educational achievements. Yet access to the workplace proved far more problematic for them than for British migrants' children.[159] The riots were the expression of a bitter rupture between the cité youth's aspirations (inherited from French Republican values) and the reality of their limited prospects.[160] Why then does Kepel mention 2005 as one of the key steps towards radicalisation? Kepel argues that since 9/11, in 2001, two dominant worldviews have clashed in the global arena: a neoconservative nightmare of an insidious Islamic terrorist threat to civilized life, and a jihadist myth of martyrdom through the slaughter of infidels.[161] Marginalised Muslims, he says, have begun to credit this idea of an eternal dichotomy between Islam and the infidels. Social fractures would push towards an ideological rift. In that sense, social fractures, Kepel claims, are the first step towards religious radicalisation. If social fractures themselves naturally need to be addressed, the urgently needed solution, Kepel goes on to suggest, would therefore be to ban signs of religious radicalisation.

### iii. Conflicting Ideological Dichotomous Discourses

In this context of ideological tensions, Kepel claims that religious radicalisation and visible signs of a Muslim religious identity contribute to setting Islamic values against the essential values of what it is to be French. Kepel is not conflating young girls wearing headscarves or swimmers in burkinis with potential terrorists. He accepts that the road leading to terrorism is complex. However, if terrorism and jihadism are complex, the reaction their attacks provoke is often binary: jihadism engenders a reaction 'against all Muslims', subsequently exploited by populist politicians, which is exactly the dichotomous narrative that terrorists are trying to spread in Europe. It is at this ideological level of meta-narratives that Kepel sees dangerous analogies between religious radicalisation and home-grown terrorism. Advocating for a visible Muslim identity in the public sphere would give wings to anti-Islamophobia lobbies and feed the narrative that French values are necessarily oppressive of and incompatible with Islamic identity. Kepel is very critical of those he sees as opportunists, who use religious identity cases such as the headscarf affairs to demonise the French model of integration and denounce its rampant Islamophobia.[162] Whilst it is important to draw distinctions and be aware of inner divisions, it is therefore crucial, according to Kepel, to fight the ideological discourse he sees at work in

---

[159] Schnapper, *De la démocratie* (n 1) 268.

[160] See D Schnapper, 'Intégration et exclusion', *De la démocratie* (n 1) 69.

[161] Kepel, *Beyond Terror* (n 156).

[162] Kepel, *La Fracture* (n 3) 19, where Kepel urges us to raise above polemics and adopt a lucid attitude.

both terrorism and religious radicalisation by an ideological counter-narrative: an assertion of French traditions of Republicanism and secularism (the principle of laïcité). Confronted with these fractures, France should not, Kepel recommends, undermine its Republican traditions and principle of laïcité (here construed as an invocation of national common values) but strengthen them, in a 'vital burst'.[163]

Whilst Kepel's concerns about terrorism are legitimate, his views remain controversial. Other prominent authors argue, by contrast, that – faced with the threat of terrorism – laïcité need not renew itself along communautarian lines, but can on the contrary retain its bridge-building potential and inclusive nature.

## C. Communautarian versus Inclusive Laïcité

### i. Laïcité as an Instrument for Assimilation of Islam

In his exhortation to strengthen laïcité, Kepel in fact defends a post-colonialist model of assimilation of minorities against hegemonic communautarism.[164] As Buruma underlines:

> Kepel makes a strong argument in favour of the French model of imposing a common secularist culture (…): almost 40 percent of Britons, according to a 2007 *Financial Times* poll, felt that Muslims posed a threat to national security, versus only 20 percent of the French who felt that way. According to the same poll, 80 percent of French respondents believed that being a Muslim and a French citizen were quite compatible, whereas less than 60 percent of the British took a similar view.[165]

Kepel thus sees the headscarf affairs as the tip of the iceberg, with the iceberg being a push for communautarism.[166] As anthropologist John Bowen notes,[167] the headscarf affairs concealed underlying concerns about the integration of Islam, along with fears of communautarism and of gender discrimination. Rather than laïcité, it was the French model of assimilation, inherited from France's colonial policies and often opposed to the British model of local administration, which was in tension with the headscarf.[168]

---

[163] 'un sursaut vital' – ibid, 14.

[164] This invocation of laïcité in support of a post-colonialist model of assimilation is paradoxical given that laïcité was never applied in French colonies. See P Vermeren, *La France en terre d'Islam. Empire colonial et religions, XIXème–XXème siècles* (Paris, Belin, 2006). See notably Ch 8, in which the author analyses the active support of the French state for Catholic missionaries in Muslim colonies and the tight control of religion by the state.

[165] Buruma, *Living with Islam* (n 155).

[166] Kepel, *La Fracture* (n 3) 221.

[167] JR Bowen, *Why the French Don't Like Headscarves: Islam, the State and Public Space* (Princeton, Princeton University Press, 2006).

[168] On the alleged continuity of representation and instrumentalisation of women's bodies and of sexuality between colonialists' narratives and contemporary laïque discourse, see JW Scott, *The Politics of the Veil* (Princeton, Princeton University Press, 2010).

Independent, for now, of the value of Kepel's assimilationist ambition, the question remains as to whether there is truly a contradiction between the head-scarf and French values. French anthropologist Edwige Rude-Antoine[169] suggests not. Young girls wearing the headscarf are not, Rude-Antoine says,[170] trying to radicalise French Muslims or subvert French values. They are only seeking to define a 'space of specificity'. Their decision is personal and their reasons for wearing the headscarf as varied as their own experience. This complexity and individuality of meanings behind the headscarf contrast with the dichoto-mous and 'pre-made' meaning[171] which Kepel and others have assigned to the headscarf. Ultimately, however, the pre-made meaning prevailed and French Parliament banned the headscarf as well as all other ostentatious religious signs in all French state schools, under the 2004 Act.[172] Laïcité in this construction is thus a remedy to fears of communautarism and a tool for enforcing a dubious model of assimilation.

## ii. Critique of Kepel's Reasoning

For the sake of avoiding dichotomies between jihadists and infidels, Kepel himself thus adopts a dichotomous discourse in which questions as varied as social problems and religious freedom of expression requests all merge into a potentially terrorist issue as soon as they vaguely relate to Islam. The conflation of Muslims and Islamic terrorism is the work of anti-Islamophobia lobby-ing groups, Kepel would answer, not his. It is because of a lucid awareness of how these Muslim issues will be used to fuel terrorist propaganda that French law must be vigilant towards seemingly innocuous requests of Muslim female swimmers to wear a burkini. However, the risk is that the counter-dichotomous narrative, which Kepel invites us to adopt, only reinforces the perception of Islam and Muslims as a whole as a problem, and further feeds terrorist propa-ganda's own dichotomies. Olivier Roy, a French political scientist specialist on Islam and secularism, says it eloquently: 'Why should we fight an ideological discourse by another ideological discourse when our aim is to find ways to avoid adopting an ideological discourse?'[173]

The challenge, therefore, is to find ways of thinking about laïcité outside of this dichotomous opposition between Islam and common French values.

---

[169] E Rude-Antoine, *Des Vies et des familles, Les immigrés, la loi et la coutume* (Paris, Odile Jacob, 1997).
[170] ibid, 185.
[171] See F Gaspard and F Khosrokhavard, *Le Foulard et la République* (Paris, La Découverte, 1995) 34: 'Les Français voient le foulard et, à partir d'une représentation liée à l'histoire ancienne (le danger du communautarisme) ou récente (la menace de l'islamisme), ils donnent un sens préfabriqué au voile'.
[172] See section II.A above.
[173] O Roy, *La Laïcité* (n 12) 37.

*iii. Beyond Dichotomies*

Is it possible to think of laïcité and Islam in non-dichotomous terms? French philosopher Etienne Balibar offers a counterpoint to Kepel in that respect. In his recent book, *Secularism and Cosmopolitanism: Critical Hypothesis on Religion and Politics*,[174] Balibar seeks solutions based on a dialogical approach. Balibar rejects the stark opposition between the core of laïcité and the core of religious claims, which stems from what he calls a 'conflict of religious universalisms'.[175] Balibar also rejects the temptation to fetishise the veil into either a symbol of oppression or liberation.[176] Instead of thinking in terms of transcendence and exclusivity (within one model of thought elevated into abstraction), Balibar reasons with a multiplicity of cosmopolitanisms in mind and conceives secularism, not as an abstract model of representation, but as an historically institutionalised instrument through which subjects represent themselves for one another.[177] Thanks to this focus on multiplicity, context and inter-subjectivity, Balibar finds, in Baubérot's words, '*cet espace intermédiaire*', 'this intermediate space'. It is in this supplementary place carved out by the opposition of concepts that Balibar encourages us to look for the absent cause of religious tensions.[178] Should we adopt a dichotomous rather than a dialogical approach to religion and culture, Balibar warns, we will expose ourselves to a skewed debate in which communautarian identity will vex discussions.[179] Balibar thus usefully reminds us of the complexity of the debate. The ban on the *burqa* is often justified in terms of an opposition between the requirements of a 'vivre ensemble' and (extreme) Islamic symbols. This concept of 'vivre ensemble' was the main justification in the French Constitutional Council's decision and later, in the ECtHR's *SAS v France* decision,[180] for upholding the 2010 legislative ban.[181] However, as Balibar thus usefully underlines, neither the decision to wear a full veil nor the notion of *vivre ensemble* can be reduced to one identifiable and unique meaning, and the full complexity of the problem cannot be captured by examining issues in isolation.

The notion of *vivre ensemble* is an interpretative one, which lends itself to a diversity of definitions. The decision by a few French Muslim women to

---

[174] E Balibar, *Secularism and Cosmopolitanism: Critical Hypothesis on Religion and Politics* (New York, Columbia University Press, 2018).

[175] ibid, xxxii.

[176] ibid, 16.

[177] ibid, 32.

[178] ibid, 37.

[179] Balibar, *Des Universels* (n 76) 40.

[180] *SAS v France* (n 143) paras 121 and 122.

[181] See, however, how the ECtHR, whilst endorsing the notion of living together, immediately seeks to set limits to it. The Court shows concerns about using such a malleable notion as a justification for restricting Convention rights: ibid, para 122.

wear a *burqa* is also (perhaps paradoxically) a way of interpreting the concept of *vivre ensemble*. Putting forward the notion as a legal justification for the *burqa* ban, as if leaving one's face uncovered was the *only* possible interpretation for living together, therefore betrays the dialogical approach, which Balibar has recommended. It dismissed the voice of the *burqa* wearers.[182] In fact, the suggested interpretation of *vivre ensemble* that underlies the 2010 French ban is not the only one possible but merely the one favoured by social consensus. The *empirical* observation – that the majority construes the full veil as infringing the minimum requirements of living together – fails to offer a justification for the *normative* conclusion that the full veil *should* be banned.[183] Precisely though, as authors like the French sociologist Dominique Schnapper have argued,[184] the social expectations to leave one's face visible are legitimate because they express the requirements of a truly democratic society. The view of *vivre ensemble* endorsed by the 2010 ban would express the reciprocity necessary in democratic societies. Healthy democracies would require a vibrant agora in which exchange and opening to the other can occur, unfettered. Naturally, there can be no duty, as the dissenting opinion notes, in the ECtHR *SAS* case,[185] to engage with one's fellow citizens at all times but there would be a duty not to close down *the possibility* of such exchange – by keeping one's face uncovered. However, as I will demonstrate in Chapter 4, democracy not only entails the possibility of dialogue, exchange and reciprocity; it also implies that such dialogues and exchanges are inclusive and open to the voices of the marginal fractions of society. One should therefore probably pause before rushing to exclude Muslim *burqa*-wearers from this democratic process for the sake of democracy.

## D. Conclusion to Section II

In this section, I have argued that, under the (perceived) threat of Islam, there has been a regressive move in French thinking, which has gradually put common values ahead of commitments to religious freedom rights. In Grimm's typology, it may be said that contemporary French trends have therefore provoked a move

---

[182] For an empirical study based on interviews with women who wear/wore a face veil in Belgium and France, see E Brems, 'SAS v. France: A Reality Check' (2016) 25 *Nottingham Law Journal* 58. See also M Khan (ed), *It's Not About the Burqa. Muslim Women on Faith, Feminism, Sexuality and Race* (London, Pan Macmillan, 2019).

[183] See Hunter-Henin, *Living Together* (n 145) 11.

[184] Schnapper, *De la démocratie* (n 1) 305. Note, however, that Schnapper leaves open the question as to whether this democratic consideration is strong enough to justify a *legal* prohibition of the *burqa*. Compare with Guy Haarscher, who clearly supports a legal ban for the sake of democracy: G Haarscher and G Gonzales, 'Consécration jésuitique d'une exigence fondamentale de la civilité démocratique. Le voile intégral sous le regard des juges de la Cour européenne (Cour eur. dr. h., Gde Ch., 1er juillet, 2014, S.A.S. c. France)' (2015) 19 *Revue trimestrielle des droits de l'homme* 219.

[185] *SAS v France* (n 143), dissenting opinion of Judges Nussberger and Jäderblom, para 8.

away from a type three inclusive concept of laïcité and a return to militant type one forms of secularism along communautarian lines. Following Balibar, I have suggested, however, that it would be possible to retain a bridge-building dialogical approach to Islam and laïcité, in which laïcité would remain close to an ideal inclusive type three secularism.

### III. CONCLUSION TO CHAPTER 2

In this chapter, I have shown that the French concept of laïcité, in its synthesis achieved under the 1905 legislative compromise, contains features of an inclusive ideal type of secularism:

> a type of secularism that recognizes religion as an elementary human urge that seeks public expression, an urge that the state not only has to respect, but also must protect and maybe even promote.[186]

The 1905 laïcité offers many positive traits. The improvement of the fate of religious minorities; the delineation of a political sphere free (at least in principle) from national or religious ideology; a divide between state and non-state spheres, which allows free expression of religion in both private and public non-state spheres and fosters neutrality of the state in state spheres; and, finally, a principle of self-restraint from the state over religious matters and issues of freedom of conscience, are all useful guidelines for shaping an inclusive ideal type of secularism.

Yet, as section II has shown, French secularism has in more recent times often (wrongly in my view, as I have argued) reacted to fears of Islamic radicalisation by a relegation of religion to the private sphere and an assertion of national common values in the public sphere, itself broadly construed. In the chapter that follows, I want to bring in the English experience and highlight similar trends. I will show that, if, similarly to laïcité, English establishment had evolved historically into a mode of church/state relationships (potentially) amenable to a type three secularism, it is often now also adopting an exclusionary stance.

---

[186] Grimm, 'Conflicts' (n 13).

# 3

# Contextual Analyses: The English Experience of Vivre Ensemble

I N THIS CHAPTER, I would like to analyse the English story. The English narrative seems an inverse reflection of the French landscape examined in the previous chapter: in the role of religion in national identity formation; in the legal relationships between Church and state, in the historical and philosophical conception of law, the English story seems to offer a counterpoint to the French. Whereas in France, the national myth depicts the birth of the nation out of a rupture from Church authority,[1] the Church in/of England has contributed to the formation of national identity.[2] The emergence of the political in England reinforced the symbolic links between the majority Church and the political sphere. Since Henry VIII, albeit for reasons of political dynasty rather than ideology, England has had its own established Church: the Church of England.[3] Even the episode of the Revolution in Cromwell's times did not separate religion from the state in England.[4] On the contrary, Cromwell's staunch Protestantism was at the heart of the Revolution and its politics.[5] This alliance of religion and the state in England coincided with a distance between law and the executive. Unlike in France, the political in England was born through an idea of representative democracy, which placed limits on royal power and gradually (with some upheaval) increased parliamentary rights.[6] Finally, England, unlike France, does

---

[1] TJ Gunn, 'French Secularism as Utopia and Myth' (2005) 42 *Houston Law Review* 81.

[2] GM Trevelyan, *History of England* (London, Longmans, Green & Co, 1926); see further I Bradley, *God Save the Queen: The Spiritual Dimension of Monarchy* (London, Darton, Longman & Todd, 2002).

[3] See DG Newcombe, *Henry VIII and the English Reformation*, e-edition (Milton, Park, Taylor & Francis, 2001).

[4] This book focuses on England. For a presentation of Church/state arrangements in Scotland, under the Church of Scotland Act 1921, see JHS Burleigh, *Church History of Scotland* (Oxford, Oxford University Press, 1960); Wales, under the Welsh Church Act 1914, see R Adhar and I Leigh, *Religious Freedom in the Liberal State*, 2nd edn (Oxford, Oxford University Press, 2013); see further, J Lucas and RM Morris, 'Ireland and Wales' in RM Morris (ed), *Church and State in 21st Century Britain: The Future of Church Establishment* (London, Palgrave Macmillan, 2009).

[5] See C Davis, 'Cromwell's religion' in J Morrill (ed), *Oliver Cromwell and the English Revolution* (London, Longman, 1990); see further DL Smith, 'Oliver Cromwell, the first Protectorate Parliament and Religious Reform', from (2000) 19 *Parliamentary History*, in DL Smith (ed), *Cromwell and the Interregnum, The Essential Readings* (Oxford, Blackwell Publishing, 2003) 139 and 167.

[6] The King's Answer to the Nineteen Propositions, 18 June 1642 in JP Kenyon (ed), *The Stuart Constitution: Documents and Commentary* (Cambridge, Cambridge University Press, 1966).

not traditionally see an inherent risk of social dislocation in communautarism. On the contrary, religious communities have historically proven to be worthy interlocutors and useful mediators and promoters for civil peace.[7] The traditional conception (or mythology) of law itself reflects this model: the doctrine of parliamentary sovereignty,[8] despite its numerous encroachments, has for many retained its position at the constitutional apex,[9] whilst the Common Law embodies the incremental bottom-based approach more in line with a restricted executive.[10]

In this chapter, I seek to analyse the implications of the English approach for religious freedom. I will show that the English establishment has traditionally (at least in principle) been compatible with a type three form of secularism 'that recognizes religion (including minority religions) as an elementary human urge that seeks public expression, an urge that the state not only has to respect, but also must protect and maybe even promote'.[11] Just as the preceding chapter has shown that the separatist model of laïcité could contain (and has in the past contained) elements favourable to an inclusive approach to religious freedom, I wish to make the claim here that English church establishment can also be interpreted in ways compatible with an inclusive approach towards religious minorities (Section I). More recent trends, however, reveal a tendency to curb religious freedom or free speech rights for the sake of avoiding risks of unfathomable consequences, triggering unprecedented and unpredictable encroachments of the state into traditional spheres of autonomy (Section II). I will criticise these new trends, not because traditional domains of non-interference must remain autonomous, but because of the ways in which these new encroachments betray a type three form of secularism. I will argue that these new tendencies should be resisted and that renewed models of law and religion relationships in England, if needed, should retain an inclusive approach to religious freedom.

---

[7] See J Rivers, *The Law of Organized Religion: Between Establishment and Secularism* (Oxford, Oxford University Press, 2010).

[8] AV Dicey, *Introduction to the Study of the Law of the Constitution*, 8th edn (London, Macmillan, 1915).

[9] See for example, M Gordon, *Parliamentary Sovereignty in the UK Constitution: Process, Politics and Democracy* (Oxford, Hart Publishing, 2015), and the (critical) review by S Larkin, 'The Manner and Form Theory of Parliamentary Sovereignty: A Nelson's Eye View of the UK Constitution' (2018) 38 *Oxford Journal of Legal Studies* 168. On a recent debate over how the decision by the Prime Minister to prorogue Parliament may be exercised, see *R (on the application of Miller) (Appellant) v The Prime Minister (Respondent)* [2019] UKSC 41.

[10] For details on how the Common Law is thought to be outside of royal authority, see FW Maitland, 'Rede Lecture, English Law and the Renaissance' (Cambridge University, 5 June 1901), on which see D Jenkins, 'English law and the renaissance eighty years on: In defence of Maitland' (1981) 2 *The Journal of Legal History* 107. I am not hereby making the claim that executive powers can still be characterised as constrained in current UK constitutional times, although see *Miller* (n 9).

[11] D Grimm, 'Conflicts Between General Laws and Religious Norms' in S Mancini and M Rosenfeld (eds), *Constitutional Secularism in an Age of Religious Revival* (Oxford, Oxford University Press, 2014) Ch 2.

From a comparative perspective, the approach adopted in this chapter will lead to observing points of divergence and convergence in each of the two selected countries. However, the selection of the two countries in question does not purport to draw an exhaustive list of differences and similarities in the way that each country deals with religious freedom. The aim is to demonstrate how both, within their own different historical and sociological contexts, can offer elements of a type three secularism. In other words, I do not therefore seek to examine which of the French or English model is better, but to identify which features of French and English arrangements allow for a democratic approach to religious freedom, which is the conception I will defend in Chapter 4 and adopt to guide my normative legal proposals in Part II.

**Table on English Church Establishment (CE)**

| Typology | Definition | Constitutional Moment | Motive | Current Contrary Trends |
|---|---|---|---|---|
| Type 1: Militant CE | National religious ideology<br><br>Church monopolies in several civil areas<br><br>Restrictions on civic participation of minorities | Henry VIII: break from Rome | Fusion of state and religion<br><br>Support for Anglican faith | Instances of state meddling into the definition of 'proper' religion |
| Type 2: Neutral CE | Respect for all faiths<br><br>Only few remaining privileges for CE | Successive nineteenth century Acts | State neutrality | Stigmatising effects on Muslims |
| Type 3: Inclusive CE | • state support for religion without discrimination<br>• religion seen as public good | Aspiration | • positive constitutionalism inclusive of diversity<br>• subject to acceptance by all of general framework | Communautarian |

## I. CHURCH ESTABLISHMENT: AN INCLUSIVE TYPE OF SECULARISM?

In this section, I argue that the English church establishment is compatible with a type three inclusive form of secularism. My argument of compatibility, developed in section B, will rest on two points. First, English establishment is a tolerant model: there is no (longer) coercion to adhere to the tenets of the official Church. Second, English establishment is a democratic model: there is no (longer) fusion between the religious and the political spheres. It is because of these two features – tolerance and democracy – that church establishment in

England has proven conducive to religious freedom, not because of any inherent superiority of establishment versus separation. Before I prove my point, I need, however, to address the objections of those who think that establishment can *never* be compatible with religious freedom and democracy (section A).

## A. The Possibility of Church Establishment

It could be argued that a system in which one religion is accorded special privileges (be they merely symbolic) can never qualify as a type three inclusive form of secularism, because promotion of religion would by definition be greater for the established church and its members than for others. In this section, I intend to challenge this view. There are many forms of church establishment.[12] Establishment will here be taken in its loose sense of state/church arrangement whereby 'the State has for some purpose of its own distinguished a particular Church from other Churches, and has conceded to it in a greater or less degree a privileged position'.[13]

Some have argued that church establishment is inherently more protective of religious freedom than constitutional arrangements based on separation,[14] while others have on the contrary made the case for a mild separation system.[15] The former group contend that a separatist model will always be, to more or less severe degrees, dismissive of the importance of religious commitments. Religious freedoms could only genuinely strive, in this perspective, under a system of (mild) church establishment. By contrast, the second group of authors claim that mild separation is preferable because church establishment, however mild, will always undermine to an extent the value of minority religious voices[16] and will struggle to capture the importance of secular commitments.[17]

---

[12] See R Adhar and I Leigh, 'Is Establishment Consistent with Religious Freedom?' (2004) 49 *McGill Law Journal* 635, 642 ff.

[13] Lord Cecil of Chelwood, *Church and State – Report of the Archbishops' Commission on the Relations between Church and State*, Vol 2 (London, Church Assembly, 1935) 171. Establishment will therefore here be taken in a far narrower sense than the US term. On the meanings of 'Establishment', see, for example, ER Norman, *Church and State: Some Reflections on Church Establishment in England* (London, Constitution Unit of UCL Department of Political Science, 2008) 9, who considers that establishment exists whenever the state – and its subordinate institutions – sustains a relationship between law and religious opinion.

[14] See N Doe, *Law and Religion in Europe: A Comparative Overview* (Oxford, Oxford University Press, 2011); Adhar and Leigh, *Religious Freedom* (n 4) 87 ff; J Garciá Oliva and H Hall, *Religion, Law and the Constitution: Balancing Beliefs in Britain* (Abingdon, Routledge, 2017).

[15] See discussion and references in C Laborde, 'Political Liberalism and Religion: On Separation and Establishment' (2013) 21 *Journal of Political Philosophy* 67 and in K Greenawalt, *Religion and the Constitution vol 2, Establishment and Fairness* (Princeton, Princeton University Press, 2009) 182–91.

[16] M Nussbaum, *Liberty of Conscience: In Defence of America's Tradition of Religious Equality* (New York, Basic Books, 2008).

[17] R Dworkin, *Is Democracy Possible Here?* (Princeton, Princeton University Press, 2006), even though Dworkin is willing to concede that vestiges of establishment may not be harmful: R Dworkin, *Religion without God* (Cambridge MA, Harvard University Press, 2013) 134 fn 16. For

*i. The Equality Objection to Establishment*

According to American philosopher Martha Nussbaum,[18] establishment is in principle contrary to religious freedom. Those who do not belong to the established faith will feel marginalised, perhaps even demeaned. Even symbolic endorsement of the majority religion will send the signal that members of minority religions are merely second-class citizens. The alignment of state institutions with symbols of the majority religion will diminish the sense of self-respect of minority religion members, as their minority religion membership will stand in the way of their full identification with state institutions. Respect for equality between citizens therefore demands, the argument goes, that the state abstain from siding with a religion. However, the prohibition of all religious signs in state institutions may also be alienating for religious citizens. Law Professors Rex Adhar and Ian Leigh have convincingly argued in their book, *Religious Freedom in the Liberal State,*[19] that separatist systems are no more neutral towards religion than establishment models: 'Even if a state does not have an established church it will have an established position on religion'.[20]

The state will always take a certain position towards religion. Separation is not per se the neutral ideal model for respecting religious freedom. Nor is it the model in which minority religion members necessarily feel the most at ease. In England, some[21] prominent members of minority religions have expressed support for establishment.[22] Tariq Modood,[23] a British Muslim sociology professor, far from calling for the abolition of establishment, has thus defended an extension of the establishment model, in the form of a multi-establishment.[24] Despite the numerous practical difficulties of its implementation,[25] Modood's

---

a robust position against establishment, see R Audi, 'The Separation of Church and State and the Obligations of Citizenship' (1989) 18 *Philosophy and Public Affairs* 259, 264: 'The state should give no preference to religion (or the religious) as such, that is, to institutions or persons simply because they are religious'.

[18] M Nussbaum, *Liberty of Conscience* (n 16), 225–27.

[19] Adhar and Leigh, *Religious Freedom* (n 4) (1st edn, 2005) ch 5.

[20] ibid, 128.

[21] Support for establishment is not, however, unanimous. Amongst Christians, many Non-Conformists, whilst acknowledging that practical difficulties have been removed, retain the view that the principle of establishment is wrong: Norman, *Church and State* (n 13), which contains the views of members of the Free Churches, the Quakers and the United Reformed Church, at 14, 33 and 23 respectively.

[22] See the Chief Rabbi of the United Hebrew Congregation, J Sacks, *The Persistence of Faith: Religion, Morality and Society in a Secular Age* (London, Continuum, 1991) 97.

[23] See, advocating such a model, T Modood, 'Establishment, Multiculturalism and British Citizenship' (1994) 65 *Political Quarterly* 53; T Modood, *Multiculturalism: A Civic Idea* (Cambridge, Polity Press, 2007).

[24] Statements by minority religion leaders suggest, however, that minority religions in England would prefer to retain the model of a single established Church rather than move towards a multi-establishment model: Morris, *Church and State* (n 4) Ch 11.

[25] On these, see S Laegaard, 'Moderate Secularism and Multicultural Equality' (2008) 29 *Politics* 160.

proposal usefully reminds us that separation is not therefore the only way to protect religious freedom in diverse societies. Separation is not inherently more neutral than – and hence superior to – establishment models.

## ii. Establishment Beyond the Majority/Minority Divide

Even if separation were more neutral,[26] there may be good reasons for the state to depart from neutrality. As political theory professor Cécile Laborde writes:

> A state can support religious activities and practices, not because it endorses and affirms the good that they pursue, but in the name of the public values of religious freedom or equality between citizens.[27]

Consequently, as Laborde elaborates in her book, *Liberalism's Religion*,[28] there is a diversity of permissible state-religion arrangements in liberal democracies. 'Secularia', a fictional state, which endorses strict separation between state and religion would not be the unique or even ideal type of state-religion arrangement. 'Divinitia', another fictional model, based on symbolic church establishment, would qualify as a reasonably liberal state too.[29] Laborde's approach on this issue has been criticised by two opposite sides of the spectrum. On the one hand, some liberal authors have accused her of partiality towards Secularia. On the other hand, others would object to her inclusion of Divinitia within the permissible models. Let me present briefly each position in turn.

## iii. The Stronger Case for Establishment

In a recent article,[30] professor of political theory David Miller suggests that Laborde's endorsement of establishment is but lukewarm. According to Miller, Laborde shares with anti-establishment authors the premise that 'establishment conveys a message of disparagement to those outside the favoured church', but unlike them, Laborde would be willing to make concessions towards mild forms of establishments such as the English type. Against Laborde's mild acceptance of mild church establishment, Miller offers positive reasons to embrace soft forms of church establishment, notably the fact that an established church may act for religious minorities as 'a shield against the pervasive secularism of most modern liberal societies'.[31]

---

[26] On neutrality, see, for example, R Dworkin, *A Matter of Principle* (Oxford, Clarendon Press, 1985). And for counter-arguments, see A Koppelman, *Defending American Religious Neutrality* (Cambridge MA, Harvard University Press, 2013).

[27] Laborde, 'Political Liberalism' (n 15) 72.

[28] C Laborde, *Liberalism's Religion* (Cambridge MA, Harvard University Press, 2017) 150–59.

[29] On the 'Secularia' and 'Divinitia' models, see Laborde's tables in ibid, 152.

[30] D Miller, 'What's Wrong with Religious Establishment?' (2019) *Criminal Law and Philosophy*, at doi.org/10.1007/s11572-019-09496-7, esp 2.

[31] ibid.

Miller has a point. If Laborde's classification seems at first sight to put establishment and separatist systems on an equal footing, I argue that her conceptual framework in fact privileges her model of Secularia. Laborde herself concedes that her 'preferred conception of justice is closer to the progressive arrangements of Secularia'.[32] I would maintain that Laborde's inclination towards Secularia is not only one of personal taste, but also the logical conclusion of her particular conceptual framework. Critics of church establishment might underline the view that state support for religion is particularly problematic because unlike other views, religious views often entail truth claims, which necessarily exclude non-religious members, hence causing an 'expressive harm' to non-religious members.[33] Miller is right to point out that Laborde endorses this familiar objection,[34] even if she then argues that mild church establishment may nonetheless be compatible with liberal requirements. Laborde's position postulates that the exclusion of minority religious identity (of the non-established Church) is necessarily heightened by church establishment, at least when that religious identity coincides with a social 'marker of vulnerability'.[35] However, evidence of such effect remains to be put forward.[36] As Miller submits,[37] Laborde's claim therefore suffers from abstraction. More profoundly, I suggest that Laborde's greater caution towards establishment stems from her 'disaggregative' approach to religious freedom, under which the liberal state, although it may accept religious expression, ought never to *value* religious expression as such as a positive democratic good.[38] In that sense, the fact that religious minority members might welcome church establishment as an opportunity for *religious* views to be heard in the public sphere would simply have no place in Laborde's liberalism, for only secular values warrant protection in her system.[39]

Despite her intrinsic (unacknowledged) reservations towards church establishment, then, Laborde does support the possibility of church establishment in principle. Despite her remaining abstract approach, Laborde also introduces contextual elements into the analysis and is thus willing to defend models of

---

[32] Laborde, *Liberalism's Religion* (n 28) 152.

[33] ES Anderson and RH Pildes, 'Expressive Theories of Law: A General Restatement' (2000) 148 *University of Pennsylvania Law Review* 1509, esp 1520.

[34] Laborde, *Liberalism's Religion* (n 28) 136.

[35] ibid, 137: 'When a social identity is a marker of vulnerability and domination, it should not be symbolically endorsed and promoted by the state'. See further C Eisgruber and L Sager, *Religious Freedom and the Constitution* (Cambridge MA, Harvard University Press, 2007).

[36] See, pointing to the contrary, N Perez, J Fox, and J McLure, 'Unequal State Support of Religion: On Resentment, Equality, and the Separation of Religion and State' (2017) 18 *Politics, Religion and Ideology* 431.

[37] Miller (n 30), 14.

[38] For a full analysis and critique of that approach, see Ch 4.

[39] For an argument that symbolic religious establishment has an exclusionary effect because of the difference between religious and political reasons, see J Cohen, 'Establishment, Exclusion and Democracy's Public Reason' in R Jay Wallace, R Kumar and S Freeman (eds), *Reasons and Recognition: Essays on the Philosophy of TM Scanlon* (Oxford, Oxford University Press, 2011).

church establishment in circumstances where social markers of vulnerability do not put minority religion members at a greater risk of stigmatisation. The equality between citizens referred to in Laborde's scheme does not equate therefore to the more abstract concept of equality used by Nussbaum to argue against establishment in principle.

### iv. Responding to the Equality Objection

Nussbaum rejects establishment because it undermines religious minority members' sense of self-worth. The equality Nussbaum has in mind is one that would require the state to take into account citizens' religious identities equally, in the abstract. However, even supposing that this could be achievable,[40] it is not clear why the state should treat religious identities even-handedly. Is there not a risk that such abstract quest for neutrality strips societies of their cultural historical references?[41] The suggestion here is not that the majority would have a right to the 'culture it prefers',[42] but that we may all benefit from a culturally vibrant society, which builds on its history and develops organically. Minority rights, however, must keep us alert to the risks of cultural oppression.[43] When does religious majority culture stop being a richness to all and become an instrument of coercion upon minority religion members? This is a crucial question but one, I submit, of degree, rather than principle. If one is, for example, a devout Protestant in France, a Jew in the US or a Muslim in the UK, one will be – and feel – part of the minority. The divide between majority/minorities is not, however, in itself problematic. It only becomes a problem if membership of minorities means that one's view or contribution will be less valued. Precisely, Nussbaum would argue that any state-endorsed majority religion will automatically mean that minorities are less valued. The ECtHR considered a similar argument in the *Lautsi* case, where it held, in a Grand Chamber decision,[44] that the obligatory presence of crucifixes on Italian state school classroom walls did not infringe the Convention rights of (in that case, atheist) dissenters. However, a state Church system must, in order to satisfy religious freedom rights under Article 9 of the European Convention on Human Rights, include specific safeguards for the individual's freedom of religion.[45] The purpose of the next section is to show that the English form of church establishment does include sufficient safeguards in principle.

---

[40] A claim that I have refuted above, given that a strict separation model faces a similar hurdle as it runs the risk of undermining religious citizens' sense of self-worth.

[41] RC Sinopoli, 'Liberalism and Contested Conceptions: The Limits of Neutrality' (1993) 55 *Journal of Politics* 644, making the argument that state funding of religion increases general knowledge of religion and our understanding of art and history.

[42] Dworkin, *Is Democracy Possible* (n 17) 75.

[43] See, for example, alerting us to this risk, V Bader, 'Religious Diversity and Democratic Institutional Pluralism' (2003) 31 *Political Theory* 265.

[44] *Lautsi and Others v Italy* (2012) 54 EHRR 3.

[45] *Darby v Sweden* (1991) 13 EHRR 774 (ECtHR), para 45.

## B.  English Establishment: An Inclusive Form of Secularism

In this section, I will examine English establishment more specifically and draw from within it features which make it compatible with a type three secularism, as described in Grimm's typology. The demonstration of compatibility will rely on two features of English establishment: its tolerance towards dissenters and its democratic boundaries between the political and the religious spheres. The Church of England does enjoy a few special privileges qua its established position[46] but I will argue that these privileges do not exert coercion upon religious minorities or non-believers. Legal discriminations against dissenters, as I will show, have now been abolished. It is, however, in the socially embedded advantages of the Christian majority, when (and only when) religious privilege matches a socially and economically favoured standing, that the English tolerance towards dissenters takes in practice a darker tone: one of indifference towards and marginalisation of (religious) minorities.

### i.  The Abolition of Discrimination against Dissenters

Legal provisions for discrimination against dissenters have been removed through a gradual process. First, since 1727, the state has in practice allowed dissenters full civic participation by means of annual Indemnity Acts.[47] Discrimination was then legally removed in successive waves: dissenting Protestants, under the 1828 Act,[48] Roman Catholics, under the 1829 Act,[49] Jews, under the 1846[50] and 1858 Acts[51] and finally, non-believers, under the 1888 Act[52] were legally granted the right to full civic participation on a par with Anglicans. Freedom of conscience also came to be protected amongst Anglicans: the civil penalties of excommunication were abolished in 1813[53] and state sanctions for non-attendance at Anglican services were suppressed in 1846.[54] The Church of England has moreover lost most of its legal monopolies. In 1836 and 1880 respectively, marriage[55] and burial[56] thus became mostly[57] civic secular institutions, and

---

[46] See summary in Adhar and Leigh (n 4) 101 ff.

[47] See F Cranmer, J Lucas and B Morris, *Church and State, A Mapping Exercise* (London, Constitution Unit of UCL Department of Political Science, 2006) 40; see further Morris, *Church and State* (n 4) Ch 1.

[48] Repeal of Test and Corporation Acts 1828 (9 Geo IV c 17).

[49] Roman Catholic Relief Act 1829 (10 Geo IV c 7).

[50] Religious Disabilities Act 1846 (9 & 10 Vict c 59).

[51] Jewish Relief Act 1858 (21 & 22 Vict c 49).

[52] Oaths Act 1888 (51 & 52 Vict c 45).

[53] Excommunication Act 1813 (53 Geo III c 127).

[54] Religious Disabilities Act 1846.

[55] Marriage and Registration Acts 1836 (6 & 7 Wm IV cc 85 and 86).

[56] Burial Act 1880 (43 & 44 Vict c 41).

[57] The Church of England retains minor privileges in the formation of marriage. Currently, the Anglican route is thus the only purely religious route to marriage, one in which both preliminaries to marriage and the ceremony are governed by Church of England rules (Marriage Act 1949).

in 1857 the ecclesiastical courts lost their jurisdiction over civil family law matters.[58] I argue that this non-coercive feature of English establishment is an element characteristic of an inclusive type three secularism.

### ii. The Compatibility of Non-coercive Establishment with an Inclusive Type Three Secularism

Non-coercive establishment is, I submit, compatible in principle with a type three secularism as it respects citizens' freedom of conscience equally.[59] Non-coercive establishment is consistent with a 'principle of personal responsibility', which the late American philosopher Ronald Dworkin places at the core of liberalism.[60] According to the principle of personal responsibility, everyone has a responsibility for realising the success of his/her own life.[61] Under that principle, any constitutional arrangement which defers to the state or a religious authority the power to decide on behalf of their citizens/followers how to lead their lives, would fall foul of liberalism. By contrast, a non-coercive establishment such as the English establishment leaves room for personal responsibility – at least in principle. Moreover, this leeway not only applies to how people decide to live their own personal lives; it also preserves their decisions as citizens by making sure that democratic decision making is not dependent upon the doctrines of the official religion.

### iii. Independence between the Church of England and Politics

The institutional privileges granted to the Church of England do not generally[62] lead to a confusion between religion and political matters. The state will not encroach on matters pertaining to Anglican tenets nor will Anglican tenets have a higher claim to truth in political debates. Originally, Church, state and

---

Other religious marriages will necessarily have to abide by civil preliminary rules, although Quakers and Jews, since an exemption granted in 1753, are able to follow their own usages for the conduct of the ceremony, unlike other religions, which will need to comply with the requirements set out under the Matrimonial Causes Act 1973. For a summary of the current rules, see the Law's Commission, 'Getting Married – A Scoping Paper' (17 December 2015) www.lawcom. gov.uk/app/uploads/2015/12/Getting_Married_scoping_paper.pdf. See, however, the announcement on 1 November 2018 that the Law Commission will be looking at reform proposals in the area: F Cranmer, 'Law Commission to Conduct a Full Review of Wedding Law in England & Wales' (*Law & Religion UK*, 1 November 2018) at www.lawandreligionuk.com/2018/11/01/law-commission-to-conduct-a-full-review-of-wedding-law/.

[58] Under the Divorce and Matrimonial Causes Act 1857 (20 & 21 Vict c 85), the jurisdiction of the ecclesiastical courts over marriage and probate was transferred to civil courts.

[59] See D Brudney, 'On noncoercive establishment' (2005) 33 *Political Theory* 812. See also Adhar and Leigh, 'Is Establishment Consistent' (n 12).

[60] Dworkin, *Is Democracy Possible* (n 17).

[61] ibid, 10.

[62] With the qualification mentioned below (n 72).

society were conceived as one. As Bob Morris, a specialist on Church establishment writes:

> In 1800, however, state and church were, formally, a single enterprise. A largely Anglican Parliament legislated for secular and ecclesiastical affairs in a structure which in theory treated the entire population outside Scotland as a uniform entity.[63]

Since 1800, however, the picture has changed.[64] The state will no longer interfere with Anglican internal matters. The Crown still has powers of appointment[65] and Church legislation still needs the approval of Parliament.[66] However, as demonstrated by the opening of priesthood to women in 1993,[67] the norm is now to leave the initiative of structural changes within the Church of England to the Church itself. Both houses of Parliament may have formally scrutinised the change in favour of female priests, but to all protagonists it was an internal move. As such, the decision to allow the ordaining of female priests attracted the attention of psychologists specialised in internal group behaviour,[68] more than that of constitutional lawyers. Reciprocally, the Church of England will not interfere with political affairs. It receives a high symbolic constitutional standing through its role in the coronation of the Monarch[69] and has a say in parliamentary debates, through the voices of 26 of its senior Bishops sitting in the House of Lords. However, the coronation of the Monarch is more ceremonial than political and the involvement of the senior Bishops in the House of Lords has been described more as a conduit for religion in general into the legislative affairs of the nation than an exclusive Church of England entitlement.[70]

---

[63] Morris, *Church and State* (n 4).

[64] ER Norman, 'Church and State since 1800' in S Gilley and WJ Sheils (eds), *A History of Religion in Britain* (Oxford, Blackwell, 1994) 277.

[65] Bishops are appointed by the Queen, on the recommendation of the Prime Minister. The Prime Minister chooses from two names proposed in a ranked order by the Crown Appointments Commission, a church body. Prime Ministers are not obliged to follow the order in which the Commission ranks candidates and may ask for alternative names. On the remaining role of the state in the appointment of Church of England Bishops and other eminent dignitaries, see Cranmer, Lucas and Morris, *A Mapping Exercise* (n 47) 29 ff. See further B Palmer, *High and Mitred: A Study of Prime Ministers as Bishop-Makers, 1837–1977* (London, Cromwell, 1992). See also the reports and recommendations made by Lord Howick of Glendale, *Crown Appointments and the Church* (London, Church Information Office, 1964) and W van Straubenzee, *Senior Church Appointments* (London, Church House, 1992).

[66] Parliament will need to approve Church legislation under the Church of England Assembly (Powers) Act 1919 (as amended by the Synodical Government Measure 1969). On the procedure, see N Doe, *The Legal Framework of the Church of England*, 2nd edn (Clarendon Press, Oxford, 2000).

[67] Priests (Ordination of Women) Measure 1993 (1993 No 2).

[68] See for example, F Sani and S Reicher, 'Identity, Argument and Schism: Two Longitudinal Studies of the Split in the Church of England over the Ordination of Women to the Priesthood' (1999) 2 *Group Processes & Intergroup Relations* 279.

[69] Bradley, *God Save the Queen* (n 2).

[70] Archbishop Carey, quoted in Cranmer, Lucas and Morris, *A Mapping Exercise* (n 47) 11.

One may be more or less convinced about the significance and fairness of the Church of England's parliamentary representation.[71] Moreover, there may be examples where the presence of Church of England Bishops in the House of Lords has been used to further the Church of England's own interests,[72] but it is undeniable that religion and the political largely remain in separate spheres in England. Certainly, 'it would be politically fatal for a British Prime Minister to claim religious authority for state policy'.[73] The existence of an established Anglican Church does not, therefore, preclude the existence of an autonomous political sphere whose legitimacy and functioning is external to religious authority or divine entitlement.[74] Whilst a socio-legal analysis will lead to a far more measured assessment in the next section, I would therefore conclude that, as a matter of principle, the English church establishment is in line with the ideal inclusive type of secularism I am striving for.[75]

## C. Conclusion to Section I

In this section, I have argued that the established position of the Church of England is compatible in principle with a type three form of secularism because the promotion of the public expression of religion is not confined to Anglican beliefs and because political decisions are not bound by Church doctrines. Since the end of the nineteenth century, the Church establishment in England has even arguably generated a welcoming climate, which acknowledges the positive value of religion for society and democracy. However, this positive assessment is, as I will show in section II, tainted by underlying social divisions, which weigh

---

[71] PW Edge, 'Religious Remnants in the Composition of the United Kingdom Parliament' in R O'Dair and A Lewis (eds), *Law and Religion: Current Legal Issues*, vol 4 (Oxford, Oxford University Press, 2001). More generally, see PW Edge, 'Secularism and Establishment in the United Kingdom' in P Cumper and T Lewis (eds), *Religion, Rights and Secular Society* (Cheltenham, Edward Elgar, 2012) Ch 3.

[72] M Warnock, *Dishonest to God: On Keeping Religion out of Politics* (London, Continuum, 2010) 163–65, describing the episcopal ambush on an Equality Act government amendment when an unusually large number of bishops – eight – attended and voted to achieve a majority of five defeating the amendment which would have confined religious employment exemptions from equality provisions to strictly religious officials rather than all employees of religious organisations. I am grateful to Bob Morris for drawing my attention to this episode. See HL Deb 25 January 2010, vol 716, cols 1211–48.

[73] Dworkin, *Is Democracy Possible* (n 17) 57.

[74] See Morris, *Church and State* (n 4). See further Phillimore J in *Marshall v Graham* [1907] 2 KB 112, [1907] 4 WLUK 3, [126].

[75] My argument is one of compatibility between English church establishment and inclusive secularism. It does not carry the stronger claim that English church establishment is the best model, even in an English context, for promoting inclusive secularism. For insightful arguments in favour of reform, see B Morris, 'The future of high establishment' (2011) 13 *Ecclesiastical Law Journal* 260. See also C Smith, 'A very English affair: establishment and human rights in an organic constitution' in P Cane et al (eds), *Law and Religion in Theoretical and Historical Context* (Cambridge, Cambridge University Press, 2008) 162.

particularly heavily on ethnic (and religious) minorities.[76] Moreover, in recent times, under the fear of religious extremism and terrorism, the value of (some forms of) religion has been called into question. It is to these trends, and to the challenges they raise for reconciling British values, religious autonomy and liberalism, that I will now turn.

## II. BRITISH VALUES, RELIGIOUS AUTONOMY AND LIBERALISM

As demonstrated in the preceding section, English establishment at the eve of the twentieth century had blossomed, on paper at least, into an inclusive type three secularism, which protected and even promoted religious expression for all and carved out a political sphere independent of church influence. Naturally, the Christian influence on English (political) history and within it, the competing influence of the Church of England and of Roman Catholics, has left its marks on English society. In education, for example, Church of England and Catholic schools significantly outnumber schools with a different denomination[77] and in state schools devoid of a religious ethos, the daily act of worship must be of a mainly Christian character.[78] Non-Catholic minorities have struggled to obtain the recognition granted to the minority of Roman Catholics. It was not until 1998 that the Secretary of State granted permission to open a school with a religious Islamic ethos and nowadays, there are still few Islamic and Jewish state schools in proportion to the numbers of Muslims and Jews resident in England.[79] As I will show in section A below, this imbalance is largely attributable to the historical context of education provisions in England. Despite being compatible in principle with a type three secularism, the inclusiveness of the English model towards religious minorities calls for nuances. The answer does not lie, however, in a crude curtailment of religious autonomy. On the contrary, I will argue that the decline of religious autonomy in contemporary times in England has moved the English approach further away from a type three secularism (section B).

---

[76] See T Modood et al, *Ethnic Minorities In Britain: Diversity And Disadvantage* (London, Policy Studies Institute, 1998).

[77] See R Long and P Bolton, *Faith Schools: FAQs*, House of Commons Briefing Paper no 06972, 13 March 2017.

[78] Education Reform Act 1988, s 7(1); Education Act 1993, s 138(2).

[79] Approximately 37% of state-funded primary schools and 19% of state-funded secondary schools were faith schools as of January 2017. The great majority of these are associated with Christian traditions (primarily Church of England and Catholicism) but there are also a modest number of state-funded schools of other faiths: 48 Jewish, 27 Muslim, 11 Sikh and 5 Hindu schools at the start of January 2017. A substantial proportion of independent schools also have a religious designation. In the case of Muslim schools, there are more in the independent sector than state-funded ones. See Long and Bolton, *Faith Schools* (n 77). Data from the 2011 census shows 1 in 12 schoolchildren were Muslim. There are more than 26,000 Jewish pupils attending Jewish schools today.

## A. Religious Minorities in England

The greater presence of Church of England schools is a relic of the early prominence of church schools, which compensated for the lack of any compulsory state-funded elementary education until 1880.[80] Until then, the need for education fell mainly upon the Church of England, and to a lesser extent upon the Roman Catholic Church. In 1870, state-funded elementary schools started to be introduced but their limited number could only cater for the educational needs of less than half of all children.[81] At the same time, Church schools were increasingly struggling financially.[82] In 1902, the Balfour's Education Act therefore controversially[83] sought to address both problems of funding of Church schools and the paucity of state schools by allowing state-funding of church schools, through decisions made by local education authorities (LEAs).[84] State-funded Church schools remain a characteristic feature of today's English school framework, as do the controversies that they attract. Despite the controversies raised by this entanglement of state and Church in the provision of education, subsequent Acts of Parliament followed in the same direction. In a pushback against anti-religious fascist ideology, the Butler Act 1944 reinforced the connections between state and Church in the educational sector. Under the Butler Act, Church schools could opt for a voluntary controlled status and sacrifice some independence in return for increased state funding or retain greater independence, under the status of voluntary aided schools.[85] As a historic residue of the past influence of the Church on education, schools with a religious denomination, commonly known as 'faith schools', have thus always been part of the English school framework, alongside non-faith state schools. For structural reasons (until the School Standards and Framework Act 1998, the creation of a new faith school entailed a lengthy and difficult process),[86] these faith schools have moreover been predominantly of a Christian (and mainly Church of England and Catholic) denomination. However, this lesser representation of (non-Catholic) minorities in the state sector has been no obstacle to individual and collective religious autonomy in non-state spheres.

---

[80] Mundella Education Act 1880.

[81] By 1900, two-thirds of schools, educating a little over half of all children, were still voluntary Church schools. See Rivers, *Organized Religions* (n 7) 238.

[82] See, for example, the plea of the Bishop of Rochester, quoted in M Cruickshank, *Church and State in English Education* (London, McMillan, 1963) 70.

[83] On these controversies, see NR Gullifer, 'Opposition to the 1902 Education Act' (1982) 8 *Oxford Review of Education* 83.

[84] These new LEAs were entrusted with the maintenance of voluntary (church) schools and the control of the schools' secular curriculum. Maintenance of the school's buildings remained the responsibility of the church for those schools that opted to provide denominational teaching.

[85] Education Act 1944, s 25.

[86] See Rivers, *Organized Religions* (n 7) 241.

*i. Religious Autonomy*

Religious autonomy has thrived in England for several reasons. First, *religious* autonomy is in line with the traditional view, embodied by English-style church establishment, whereby religion is intrinsically of positive value for society. Unlike in France, the recognition of a universal secular option is not always seen as necessary (as in marriage laws)[87] and when it is (as in education),[88] it is not exclusive of religion, as evidenced by the existence of state schools with a religious character. Religion is not a concession of the state to other ways but a valued and intrinsic part of institutions. Second, religious *autonomy* concords with a general principle of non-interference of the state. Outside of state institutions, individuals and communities will thus traditionally enjoy a high degree of leeway to live according to their own customs. As Woold J stated in *R v Secretary of State for Education and Science, ex p Talmud Torah Machzikhei Haddass School Trust*, 'there is no requirement to educate the child in the way of life of the country as a whole'.[89] Finally, autonomy also matches the administrative model used by the British Empire in its colonies. As the late Robert S Leiken aptly put it:

> Britain and France each viewed their Muslim immigrants in the light of their considerable colonial experiences, and these experiences themselves reflected divergent nation-building histories. Immigrants arriving in the United Kingdom from the Imperial subcontinent were encouraged to look to their communal leaders to resolve their grievances in a polity where Muslims enjoyed autonomy but little chance of entry into British social circles. (…) In France, such communal mediation was unknown. As in the French empire, immigrants were to adhere directly to France.[90]

However, empirical studies revealing the connection between the role of religious affiliation and racial designation of ethnic minorities and the lack of achievement in the educational and labour market in England and Wales prompt us to temper any enthusiastic conclusions.[91]

*ii. Limits: Entrenched Social Divides*

In England, controversies over religious freedom and autonomy often hide social questions. Those who argue for the abolition of faith schools (or at least of faith state schools) often suggest that segregated-religious schooling increases social division.[92] Despite the socially more advantaged intake of

---

[87] See Law Commission, *Getting Married* (n 57).

[88] See Rivers, *Organized Religions* (n 7).

[89] *R v Secretary of State for Education and Science, ex p Talmud Torah Machzikhei Haddass School Trust* [1985] 1 WLUK 778, (1985) Times, 12 April.

[90] RS Leiken, *Europe's Angry Muslims. The Revolt of the Second Generation* (Oxford, Oxford University Press, 2012) 108–109.

[91] See, for example, N Khattab, 'Ethno-religious Background as a Determinant of Educational and Occupational Attainment in Britain' (2009) 43 *Sociology* 304.

[92] British Humanist Association, *Religious Schools: the Case Against* (London, British Humanist Association, 2001).

faith state schools,[93] it is probably unfair to blame faith schools for the social divides of English society and unrealistic to expect religious policy to solve social problems. Non-faith state schools are no less socially divisive.[94] It may be less the religious ethos of faith schools than the deep divides of the English social fabric, that encourage in some areas a recrudescence (and possibly for the better) in religiosity in education. The Birmingham schools involved in the so-called 'Trojan Plot' scandal,[95] an alleged plot to Islamise and take over state schools,[96] did not have a religious ethos but catered for a geographically, socially and economically heavily marginalised community: 'of the fourteen state schools assessed (...), not one had an ethnic minority intake of less than 96 per cent'.[97] It would fall outside of the present chapter to suggest solutions to these tensions between social and religious divisions. For now, awareness of these deeper social issues usefully reminds us, however, that an inclusive type three secularism can only flourish in a social environment that offers genuine equal opportunities.[98] In their 2007 study, Clark and Drinkwater on the contrary observe that: 'being Muslim was associated with poorer employment outcomes for many ethnic groups and that this penalty was greater for women'.[99]

According to a 2009 study by Nabil Khattab,[100] recently confirmed by a 2018 report drafted by Modood,[101] compared to Christian White-British, we

---

[93] R Allen and A West, 'Why Do Faith Secondary Schools Have Advantaged Intakes? The Relative Importance of Neighbourhood Characteristics, Social Background and Religious Identification amongst Parents' (2011) 37 *British Educational Research Journal* 691.

[94] See S Hollingworth and K Williams, 'Multicultural mixing or middle-class reproduction? The white middle-classes in London's comprehensive schools' (2010) 14 *Space and Polity* 47, revealing that white middle-class pupils were, through various practices and processes, set apart, which resulted in a reification of social and racial divides.

[95] See J Fergusson, *Al Britannia, My Country. A Journey through Muslim Britain* (London, Bantam Press, 2017) 101 ff.

[96] See www.theguardian.com/world/2017/sep/01/trojan-horse-the-real-story-behind-the-fake-islamic-plot-to-take-over-schools.

[97] ibid.

[98] On the contrary, British policies have been described as creating 'an underclass': L Morris, *Dangerous Classes. The Underclass and Social Citizenship* (Abingdon, Routledge, 1994); see also L Morris, *Social Divisions. Economic Decline and Social Structural Change*, 2nd edn (Cambridge, Cambridge University Press, 2014).

[99] K Clark and S Drinkwater, *Dynamics and Diversity: Ethnic Minorities in the Labour Market* (Bristol/York, The Policy Press/Joseph Rowntree Foundation, 2007) 45. See, however, M Mirza, A Senthilkumaran and Z Ja'far, *Living Apart Together: British Muslims and the Paradox of Multiculturalism* (London, Policy Exchange, 2007) 68, who have argued that: '... there is little evidence to suggest a significant *direct* causal link between religion and employment discrimination. Looking at the employment statistics for all groups, it seems that socio-economic background and educational achievement exert a primary effect'. However, given the lower opportunities of educational achievement of (at least some) ethnic minorities, Mirza's observation does not refute the disadvantage suffered by ethnic minorities, it only encourages a displacement of the focus from the workplace to schools.

[100] Khattab, 'Ethno-religious Background' (n 91) 317.

[101] Modood, *Ethnic Minorities* (n 76).

can classify ethno-religious groups into three main categories in terms of their educational and occupational attainment:

(1)    the first category includes the advantaged groups (in terms of their educational and occupational attainment) such as Jewish White-British, No-religion White-British, and, to some extent, Christian White-Others (in the case of men);

(2)    the second category includes groups that are advantaged in their educational attainment but disadvantaged in terms of occupational attainment such as Christian Black-African and Christian Black-Caribbean;

(3)    the third category consists of groups that were disadvantaged in both their educational and occupational attainment such as three out of the four Muslim groups (Pakistanis, Bangladeshis and Whites) and Sikh-Indians.

As the study concludes:

> whiteness seems to operate in a direction that facilitates educational and occupational success among groups that belong or are close to the dominant culture, while religion functions to reinforce disadvantage among groups that are culturally 'alien', regardless, or in spite, of whether their skin colour is white or not.[102]

For my purposes, these empirical enquiries therefore reveal that, whatever the generous interpretation of religious freedom and autonomy in black-letter law, the reality of living in England may be more inclusive for some than for others. In any case, for better or for worse, religious autonomy seems to have weakened in recent times in English law.

## B. The Decline of Religious Autonomy in English Law

As noted regretfully by British law professor Julian Rivers, the importance of religion seems to have recently declined in English law:

> Ensuring the weight of religious claims not only requires an appreciation of their social and moral value; it requires institutional anchoring in the recognition of a quintessentially religious domain – a core field – which is important enough to be immune from state interference.[103]

The purpose of this section is not to analyse whether such restrictions on religious autonomy are justified in principle or not. I will explore the question of the importance of and legitimate limits to religious autonomy in the following chapter. The aim of this section is to demonstrate that recent judicial, legislative and governmental interventions into the affairs of religious communities have strayed away

---

[102] ibid, 319.

[103] J Rivers, 'The Secularisation of the British Constitution' (2012) 14 *Ecclesiastical Law Journal* 371, esp 399.

from the principle at the heart of an inclusive type three form of secularism: the principle that the state is to protect freedom of conscience, whatever the doctrines of the Church, and whatever the state's own view about religion.

### *i. Protection of Freedom of Conscience Independently of Doctrinal Views on Religion*

As shown in Section I, the state no longer lends its coercive power to enforce the Church of England's doctrines and rituals. Civil penalties of excommunication and state sanctions for non-attendance at Anglican services have long been abolished.[104] Moreover and more generally, since the decision of the ECtHR in *Eweida v UK*,[105] English courts will no longer distinguish between practices which are mandatory or 'core' to the religion in question and others.[106] Whatever the importance of the practice in light of the pertinent religious dogma, it will be protected as long as there is a sufficiently close and direct nexus between the act and the underlying belief.[107] In other words, religious freedom is to be protected independently of religious authorities. Religious practices, which are required by religious authorities, will not be backed by civil state sanctions in case of non-compliance; reciprocally, religious practices, which are not specifically required by religious authorities, may still receive protection from the state.

I argue that such dissociation of religious freedom and religious authorities is beneficial both for religious freedom (which can thrive more fully outside of majority expressions of religious faith) and for the state (which thus avoids discussions of scholastics for which it is ill-equipped).[108] Yet, there has recently been a move back to a deference towards religious authorities, in respect of admission to state schools with a religious ethos. Since 2008, the Government has required that faith state schools have their admission criteria approved by their own religious authorities.[109] Following a challenge by parents whose children had been refused entry, the High Court Judge, in the *London Oratory Catholic School* case,[110] was consequently asked to ascertain whether the board of governors had failed to have due regard to the Archdiocese Guidance and in doing so was requested to assess the importance of baptism in the definition of Catholic membership. I would argue that discussion of the opportunity of

---

[104] See Section I above.

[105] *Eweida v UK* [2013] ECHR 285.

[106] See Ch 5, section II below.

[107] *Eweida v UK* (n 105), [82].

[108] For that argument, see M Hunter-Henin, 'L'Impact de l'arrêt Eweida de la Cour européenne des droits de l'homme sur le droit anglais' in B Callebat, H de Courreges and V Parisot (eds), *Les Religions et le droit du travail. Regards croisés, d'ici et d'ailleurs* (Brussels, Bruylant, 2018).

[109] Under the code issued by the Department for Education Schools' Admission under the Education and Inspections Act 2006.

[110] *R (on the application of London Oratory School Governing Body) v Schools Adjudicator* [2015] EWHC 1012 (Admin), [2015] 4 WLUK 285.

particular religious criteria would best be left to the relevant religious schools.[111] There may be good reasons for wanting to curtail the autonomy of religious schools but non-compliance with religious dogma set by diocesan authorities should not be one of them. The adjudication of such doctrinal matters, even if purely for secular purposes, clouds the abovementioned distinction between freedom of conscience and church authorities and may suggest that the state is indirectly protecting religious dogma over religious autonomy. Similarly, protection of freedom of conscience should not depend on its conformity with the state's view on 'proper' religion.

### ii. Protection of Freedom of Conscience Independent of State Views on Religion

In the UK, schools have, since September 2014, been under a duty to promote fundamental British values (FBV), which the advice by the Department of Education defines, as including notably: 'democracy, the rule of law, individual liberty and mutual respect and tolerance of different faiths and beliefs'.[112] In the state-maintained sector, FBV feature in the context of social, moral, spiritual and cultural development[113] and appear in the Teachers' Standards, which apply to the training, appraisal and discipline of teachers.[114] The duty to respect FBV extends to the independent sector with equal weight.[115] Naturally, there is nothing objectionable about schools teaching fundamental values. Nor are there any serious points of contention with the list of values contained in the Government's advice. Research has shown that support for liberal values was strong amongst young people, including those from ethnic minorities.[116] If the new duty to promote FBV has raised eyebrows in England,[117] it is because of fears of stigmatisation of Muslims in its implementation. Indeed, the new duty emerged out of concerns about Muslim integration and Islamic threats

---

[111] See M Hunter-Henin, 'Believing in Negotiation: Reflection on Law's Regulation of Religious Symbols in State Schools' in F Guesnet, C Laborde and L Lee (eds), *Negotiating Religion: Cross-disciplinary Perspectives* (Abingdon: Routledge, 2017) and M Hunter-Henin, 'English Schools with a Religious Ethos: For a Re-Interpretation of Religious Autonomy' (2018) 13 *Religion and Human Rights* 3, 16 ff.

[112] Department for Education, *Promoting fundamental British values as part of SMSC in schools* (November 2014).

[113] ibid.

[114] Teachers' Standards, Department for Education, July 2011, which have had statutory force since 2012: SI 2012/115, reg 6; SI 2012/560, reg 4; Education Act 2002, s 78.

[115] Education (Independent School Standards) (England) (Amendment) Regulations 2014, SI 2014/2374.

[116] Centre for Research on Learning and Life Chances, 'Citizenship Education Longitudinal Survey' www.llakes.ac.uk/research-project/166/citizenship-education-longitudinal-survey-cels.

[117] AEC Struthers, 'Teaching British Values in Our Schools: But why not Human Rights Values?' (2017) 26 Social & Legal Studies 89; see further, M Hunter-Henin and C Vincent, 'The problem with teaching "British values" in School' (*The Conversation*, February 2018) at theconversation. com/the-problem-with-teaching-british-values-in-school-83688.

of terrorism, and now evolves in parallel with a new Prevent duty,[118] which closely associates religious radicalisation with terrorism. The 2014 FBV curriculum Guidance for English schools was drafted as a direct consequence of the so-called 'Trojan plot' scandal, after a number of English state schools in the Birmingham area were reported to allegedly have been overtaken by Islamist groups.[119] Moreover, schools, universities and nurseries have since September 2015 been subject to a duty to have due regard to the need to prevent people from being drawn into terrorism (the Prevent duty).[120] The accompanying statutory guidance suggests a direct discrepancy between FBV and religious extremism, defined as the vocal or active rejection of FBV and as the first step towards terrorism.[121] It is not surprising,[122] in this context, that inspectors in charge of controlling compliance with the FBV duty have focused on Islam. The decision, for example, of Ofsted inspectors to interview pupils wearing the hijab at school in the course of testing the school's score on FBV[123] is likely to feed suspicions that the FBV discourse hides suspicions of Islam and to antagonise Muslims. Likewise, the slippery slope contained in the guidance and advice on FBV from 'non-violent extremism' to 'terrorism', despite the wealth of scholarship refuting the connection,[124] contributes to casting suspicions on Muslims as a whole. In light of these criticisms, the government announced an independent review on the Prevent duty.[125]

As exceptions increase to the principle that the state is to protect freedom of conscience, whatever the doctrines of the Church, and whatever the state's own view about religion, the ideal of a *vivre ensemble* open to religious autonomy and diversity crumbles. The school system in England and Wales is thus frequently the site of heated conflicts, in which moral views as to the place

---

[118] Counter-Terrorism and Security Act 2015, s 26.

[119] See above. See further, J Arthur, 'Extremism and Neo-Liberal Education Policy: A Contextual Critique of the Trojan Horse Affair in Birmingham Schools' (2015) 63 *British Journal of Educational Studies* 311.

[120] Counter-Terrorism and Security Act 2015, s 26.

[121] Section 26 is to be read in conjunction with the statutory guidance issued by the Home Secretary under section 29 of the Act, namely: HM Government, *Revised Prevent Duty Guidance for England and Wales: Guidance for specified authorities in England and Wales on the duty in the Counter-Terrorism and Security Act 2015 to have due regard to the need to prevent people from being drawn into terrorism*, 12 March 2015, revised 16 July 2015 (Crown Copyright, 2015); and the specific Guidance for Higher and Further Education Institutions 16 July 2015, available at www.gov.uk/government/publications/prevent-duty-guidance/prevent-duty-guidance-for-further-education-institutions-in-england-and-wales.

[122] B Spalek, *Terror Crime Prevention with Communities* (London, Bloomsbury, 2013) Ch 4: the insistence on FBV stems not 'from the foundation of equality, non-discrimination and respect for human dignity, but rather from fear, suspicion and prejudice'.

[123] 'Inspectors to Quiz Schoolgirls in Hijabs' (*BBC News*, 19 November 2017) at www.bbc.co.uk/news/education-42046371.

[124] See references in J Bartlett, J Birdwell and M King, *The Edge of Violence* (London, Demos, 2010).

[125] The government announced on 12 August 2019 that Lord Carlile would lead an independent review on the Prevent duty, see www.gov.uk/government/news/lord-carlile-to-lead-independent-review-of-prevent.

of LGBT issues[126] or worship at school[127] clash in irreconcilable difference. The erosion of pluralism, through an intransigent official narrative in the style of the FBV rhetoric, is not, as I have suggested, the way forward. Far from protecting a sphere of (religious) autonomy, it leads to erratic encroachments of the state into matters of religion. Far from fostering an inclusive dialogue, it imposes an official discourse and stigmatises those who hold minority views. Far from encouraging protagonists to review and revise their positions, it ossifies antagonisms.

## C. Conclusion to Section II

In this section, I have examined the challenges and hurdles which stand in the way of a fully inclusive secularism in England. Social divisions, more pronounced in respect of certain religious minority groups, have undermined rights to and aspirations for equality. Under the threat of terrorism, there has moreover been a regressive move in English thinking, most notably in the area of education, where the narrative of Fundamental British Values, itself tainted by fears of the 'other' in the context of the Prevent duty, has curbed religious autonomy of schools in unprecedented, unpredictable and chaotic ways.

### III. CONCLUSION TO CHAPTER 3

In this chapter, I have shown that, similarly to the French concept of laïcité, but through different routes, the English form of mild establishment contains features of an inclusive ideal type of secularism – one which, according to Grimm's typology, 'recognizes religion as an elementary human urge that seeks public expression, an urge that the state not only has to respect, but also must protect and maybe even promote'. I have argued that English establishment has evolved from a fusional model of religion and politics into an inclusive secularism, respectful of religious diversity and of political autonomy. However, I have shown that, just like in France, the inclusive aspirations of the English model of secularism have never fully materialised. In light of socially entrenched divisions, which weigh more heavily on (certain) religious minorities, the equality aspiration inherent in an inclusive model of secularism has never been able to express itself fully in England. Besides, in England too, just like in France, the

---

[126] See, for example, D Aaronovitch, 'Mutual tolerance means we don't ban lessons' (*The Times*, 17 July 2019) www.thetimes.co.uk/article/we-can-t-bow-to-faith-protesters-who-want-lessons-banned-00dv8h6t0.

[127] See the successful complaint lodged by Lee and Lizanne Harris against Burford primary school in Oxfordshire for offering no alternative to their children when opted out of worship activities: www.theguardian.com/education/2019/nov/20/oxfordshire-parents-win-right-to-prayer-free-school-assembly.

fear of religious (Islamic) radicalisation and terrorism has prompted certain illiberal and exclusionary trends.

This comparative incursion does not, therefore, lead to the conclusion that one national model is better than the other. The conclusion reached is that there are different ways of achieving an inclusive equilibrium in which democracy and religious freedoms both foster one another. Laïcité can be inclusive and so can Church Establishment. Vice versa, however, as contemporary trends have shown, neither model is immune from illiberal streaks. Calls for common national ways of living together now often pervade laïcité and turn it into an instrument of forced assimilation. On this side of the Channel, calls for national values have cast a doubt on the legitimacy of certain religious ways, which, previously, had been acknowledged, if not encouraged. It is in these potentially stigmatising implementation problems that the Fundamental British Values discourse echoes the dichotomous narrative, which now dominates in France, between Republican values and Islam.

This chapter therefore leads us to the conclusion that if neither laïcité nor church establishment are inherently flawed or ideal, they can both potentially collapse into illiberal streaks when they close themselves along communautarian lines, built upon a dichotomous thinking between 'us' and 'the other'. Following Balibar, I conclude that a secularism 'guided essentially by imperatives of national unity, national identity or national security will soon find itself entangled in contradictions and eventually become self-destructive'.[128] My goal, again borrowing Balibar's words, is to propose, by contrast, a 'secularism that is a critical and self-critical form of what has been historically thought and institutionalised under that rubric'.[129] In the chapter that follows, I will therefore seek ways forward, ones that are true to a liberal paradigm, in which freedom of religion, democracy and pluralism reinforce one another.

---

[128] E Balibar, *Secularism and Cosmopolitanism: Critical Hypothesis on Religion and Politics* (New York, Columbia University Press, 2018) 7.
[129] ibid, 50.

# 4

# Conceptual Framework: The Liberal Democratic Vivre Ensemble

Liberalism should provide the devout with a reason for tolerance.[1]

> Freedom of thought, conscience and religion is one of the foundations of a 'democratic society' within the meaning of the Convention. It is, in its religious dimension, one of the most vital elements that go to make up the identity of believers and their conception of life, but it is also a precious asset for atheists, agnostics, sceptics and the unconcerned. The pluralism indissociable from a democratic society, which has been dearly won over the centuries, depends on it.[2]

As the previous chapters have revealed, recent trends have strengthened and spread the idea that liberalism and religion are in competition over the control of the political sphere. Tensions between religious and secular views, values and ways of life have emerged and the narrative of a fracture between religion and democracy, as well as between secular and religious values, has gained traction. In the preceding chapters, I have denounced this dichotomous presentation of religion versus democracy and the underlying suggestion that democracy would be stronger if citizens reunified around a core of immutable secular(ised) values. Chapters 2 and 3 have developed a critique of this militant form of secularism from a sociological and historical perspective. Recent developments in France and Britain reveal signs of heightened social divisions, greater risks of terrorism and a regained attraction for extremist thoughts, leaving the promise of tighter national bonds and the calls for respect and tolerance a dead letter. Instead of redefining a *vivre ensemble* along inward-looking values, I would like to explore in this chapter whether the statement of the European Court of Human Rights (ECtHR) in *Kokkinakis v Greece*[3] can guide us towards a more inclusive, fairer, peaceful and stable approach to current problems. The aim is to move closer to the ideal type three secularism outlined in the preceding chapters: 'a type of secularism that recognizes religion as an elementary human urge that seeks

---

[1] T Nagel, 'Moral Conflict and Political Legitimacy' (1987) 16 *Philosophy & Public Affairs* 215, 229.
[2] *Kokkinakis v Greece* Series A No 260-A (1993) 17 EHRR 397, para 31.
[3] ibid.

public expression, an urge that the state not only has to respect, but also must protect and maybe even promote'.[4]

To that end, I will suggest that the two connections hinted at by the ECtHR in *Kokkinakis* should be explored further, namely, the connection between freedom of religion and democracy on the one hand and the connection between pluralism and religious freedom on the other. In this chapter, I would like to explore these links from a conceptual perspective. Why does religious freedom matter for liberalism and democracy? What are the relationships between pluralism and democracy? What does pluralism entail for religious freedom? If we adopt a demanding, radical[5] conception of democracy, institutional rules relating to elections, parliamentary representation etc, albeit essential, are but manifestations of democracy, and do not contain it all. Its fundamental traits lie not in its institutional manifestations but in its discursive qualities,[6] as an inclusive and open-ended reason-giving process.[7] In this chapter, I will demonstrate that a generous and inclusive reading of religious freedom would enrich democracy thus conceived. It would help, in the words of Stanford University political philosophy professor Joshua Cohen,[8] 'to constitute a political community of equals' and 'enable co-deliberation among political equals on a terrain of public reason'. It would ensure that the terms of the liberal *vivre ensemble* are constantly subject to review and that religious marginal voices have their say in this ongoing democratic debate.

In section I, I will examine and respond to claims that deny or undermine the first part of the ECtHR's statement whereby 'freedom of thought, conscience and religion is one of the foundations of a "democratic society" within the meaning of the Convention'. Authors who have doubted the foundational connection between democracy and religious freedom come from opposite sides of the spectrum. Some liberals deny that religion should receive any special privilege or status. They claim that religion, for the liberal state, is, in effect, diluted into secular interests and that these secular interests, rather than the *religious* request, are in truth the values protected when courts accommodate a religious claim. Consequently, the foundation of democracy would not be religious freedom, but equality. On the other side of the spectrum, liberal sceptics resist the connection between democracy and religion because they see it as a pernicious

---

[4] D Grimm, 'Conflicts Between General Laws and Religious Norms' in S Mancini and M Rosenfeld (eds), *Constitutional Secularism in an Age of Religious Revival* (Oxford, Oxford University Press, 2014) Ch 2.

[5] J Cohen, *Philosophy, Politics, Democracy: Selected Essays* (Cambridge MA, Harvard University Press, 2009). Under a radical conception, democracy goes beyond majority rules and aggregation of interests, to include broader conditions of participation and deliberation.

[6] J Habermas, *Between Facts and Norms: Contributions to a Discourse Theory of Law and Democracy* (W Rehg tr, Cambridge, Polity Press, 1998).

[7] J Rawls, *Political Liberalism*, 2nd edn (New York, Columbia University Press, 1996).

[8] J Cohen, 'Establishment, Exclusion and Democracy's Public Reason' in R Jay Wallace et al (eds), *Reasons and Recognition: Essays on the Philosophy of TM Scanlon* (Oxford, Oxford University Press, 2011) 256.

way for the liberal state to tame and interfere with religious beliefs. The only way for religious beliefs and liberal ideals to remain true to themselves, they contend, is if they remain apart. Each of these claims, from opposite starting points, see religion and liberalism as competing for control of the public sphere.

Having examined these claims of competition between religion and liberalism in section I, I will then explain in a second section that religious freedom, on the contrary, has a positive value for democracy and hence, in the ECtHR's words, 'is also a precious asset for atheists, agnostics, sceptics and the unconcerned'. Drawing on the work of NYU political theorist professor Stephen Holmes, I will argue that if these connections impose constraints both on democracy and on religious freedom, these restraints can be enabling, both for democracy and for religious freedom. Going further, with late American philosopher John Rawls, I will argue that religious freedoms ensure a healthy pluralism, which invigorates democracy. In that sense, as the ECtHR has said, 'the pluralism indissociable from a democratic society, which has been dearly won over the centuries, depends on (religious freedom)'.

This chapter will consequently argue that religious freedoms are inherently political rights, rights to participation, to opt in, rather than (purely) negative rights to be left alone. Under the democratic paradigm I have set out, liberalism should not feel threatened by religious freedom and nor should religious citizens fear the liberal state.

## I. WHY RELIGIOUS FREEDOM MATTERS FOR DEMOCRACY

The first question is one of definition. What do we mean by 'religion' in law and religion debates? Is the concept of religious freedom useful and important in understanding and deciding, for example, whether a school should grant a child's request to opt out from religious education courses? How should the liberal state through its courts and legislators approach religion in these legal matters? At stake behind these epistemological problems is the question of what interactions, if any, should exist between religious freedom and democracy. On one reading, which I call the 'analogous-to-secular view', the liberal state should only protect religious freedom when and to the extent that the secular values underpinning the religious claim deserve protection (section A). On another, opposite, view, which I call the 'accommodationist view', the liberal state should abstain from assessing religious claims or, when it – inevitably – does so, should recognise that this intervention is a betrayal both of religious freedom and of liberal ideals of neutrality and hence defer to the religious citizen's assessment. This would mean that the religious citizen's claim is likely to be accommodated (section B). Rather than being recognised as 'one of the foundations of a "democratic society"' the concept of religious freedom in these perspectives either dissolves into the values it encompasses or threatens to stand outside of democracy and liberalism altogether.

## A.  The Dilution of Religious Freedom

In this section, I will examine and refute the 'analogous-to-secular' position according to which the liberal state does/should not confer any special value on religious commitments for reasons of their being religious and should not consequently protect religious freedom intrinsically but only when courts can identify underlying legitimate secular interests. I will argue, by contrast, that there is something special in *religious* freedom for democracy and that the concept of religious freedom is important in law.

Let us first examine the reasons why some have suggested that the liberal state should steer away from the *religious* in the concept of religious freedom. There is a perception that religious freedom cases are more problematic than other cases. From an epistemological point of view, that is, from an intellectual perspective of seeking understanding of the facts, courts seem less equipped to assess the situation at hand when it involves a religious claim because they face another, alien, normative system. However, this epistemological problem, 'the problem of how courts are to understand normative systems other than those to which they are themselves committed'[9] should not be exaggerated. First, courts need not understand the entirety and full complexity of the religious system in question to assess the legitimacy of the religious claim put forward. Thus, courts need not be persuaded that a requirement to wear a full-face covering garment flows from the Quran[10] to conclude that the request to wear a *burqa* in the public sphere potentially expresses a deep religious commitment constitutive of the claimant's sense of identity.[11] Second, religious arguments presented to judges can be translated into secular reasons and thus incorporated into and assessed in light of law's own system of meaning: its sets of concepts, prior case law and precedents.[12] Note that this process of adjudication of religion – through public reason (see section B) – is not the same as the dilution of religious freedom into secular values (see below).

### i. *Practical Importance of the Concept of Religious Freedom*

Public reasons serve to explain and support the importance of the particular religious freedom claim and of religious freedom more generally. By contrast,

---

[9] C McCrudden, *Litigating Religions. An Essay on Human Rights, Courts and Beliefs* (Oxford, Oxford University Press, 2018) 87.

[10] On these Quranic origins, see A Barlas, *Believing Women is Islam: Unreading Patriarchal Interpretations of the Qur'an* (Austin, University of Texas Press, 2002) 53.

[11] I am here reasoning in the context of the European Convention on Human Rights, under which the test of what constitutes religious protected beliefs is subjective and does not rely on the official or mainstream religious position. I am grateful to George Letsas for prompting me to add this clarification.

[12] R Audi and N Wolterstorff, *Religion in the Public Square: The Place of Religious Convictions in Political Debate* (Lanham, Rowman and Littlefield, 1997) 180. On the concept of public reason more generally, see below, section II.

when religion dissolves into secular interests, the importance of the concept of religious freedom is *ab initio* undermined. The distinction may appear thin but will have a practical impact in contentious cases. A baker's refusal, for religious reasons, to write a message on his cake supporting gay marriage[13] is thus bound to be weighted more heavily in the former approach. The latter approach will also lend itself more easily to allowing neutrality clauses, which ban all expressions of personal beliefs and commitments in the workplace, as long as the prohibition applies even-handedly.[14] The process of adjudicating religious claims undoubtedly presents challenges, however, and can sometimes go wrong.

## ii. The Epistemological Problem

In the *Jewish Free School (JFS)* case[15] for example, the Supreme Court seemed to have stumbled upon this epistemological hurdle, the difficulty in understanding the religious claim presented. In that case, the disputed school policy gave priority to children recognised as Jewish by the Office of the Chief Rabbi of the United Hebrew Congregation of the Commonwealth, namely children who are Jewish by matrilineal descent or through a conversion recognised by Orthodox authorities. The applicant, who was born to a Catholic Italian mother who had converted to Judaism under the auspices of the Masorti, did not meet the school's definition of 'Jewish pupils' and was consequently refused admission. The Supreme Court ruled that the school's decision amounted to direct discrimination on the ground of race because the test applied by the school hinged on the ethnicity of the applicant's mother.[16] The decision showed a misunderstanding of Jewish affiliation. In drawing sharp lines between 'religion' and 'ethnicity', the Court framed religion in Protestant terms and projected the individual conscience of the believer as being of paramount importance in the definition of religious Jewish affiliation. The Court's reasoning thus distorted the meaning of religion.

Can one conclude, however, from this case that courts should steer away from considerations of the religious? On the contrary, it seems that, had the Supreme Court focused more on the religious dimension of the case instead of setting it aside to reason on racial discrimination grounds, the meaning of the 'religious' in that case would have been more appropriately defined by the court. Ignorance is hardly to blame for the distortive approach that the Supreme Court chose to adopt. The Chief Rabbi had provided evidence that one could be Jewish under Jewish law whilst rejecting any conscious affiliation with the Jewish faith. The Supreme Court did not struggle to *understand* the religious aspects of

---

[13] See *Lee v Ashers Baking Co Ltd* [2018] UKSC 49, [2018] 3 WLR 1294. For a discussion, see Ch 6, section III.B.

[14] For a discussion of these neutrality clauses, see Ch 5.

[15] *R (E) v Governing Body of JFS* [2009] UKSC 15, [2010] 2 WLR 153.

[16] ibid, para 41, per Lord Phillips.

the case but felt compelled to *undermine* this religious dimension because of the large scope given in earlier cases to racial discrimination,[17] under the then applicable section 1 of the Race Relations Act 1976.[18] It thus rejected the argument put forward for the school that the matrilineal test is not a test of ethnic origin or ethnic status but a test of religious origin and religious status.[19] As long as there was an ethnic basis to the test, it had to be characterised as racial discrimination, according to the Court, regardless of the religious dimension, because direct discrimination is unlawful, even in the absence of any intention to discriminate.[20] It is doubtful, however, that religion was here merely a motive for discrimination on another ground. Where religious believers invoke their faith in order to justify treating men and women differently for example, the law will disregard these religious reasons if the differences of treatment amount to direct discrimination. In *JFS*, however, the difference of treatment (itself allowed under a statutory exemption from religious discrimination),[21] coincided with the definition of religion itself. It may be that the Supreme Court in *JFS* felt tied by the practical difficulty of overturning its own precedent in *Mandla v Lee*.[22] In that previous case, a similar overlapping of religious and ethnic membership was at play. At a time when the law did not protect against discrimination on ground of religion, the extensive definition of 'racial group' for the purposes of the 1976 Act then allowed the courts to hold that the school's decision to refuse admission to a Sikh wearing a turban amounted to racial discrimination under the Act and was unlawful. Arguably, the Supreme Court could have distinguished *JFS* from *Mandla*. Whereas the effect of racial anti-discrimination inhibited the school's religious freedom and autonomy in *JFS*, the two grounds of protection on the basis of race and religion (had they both been available) would have reinforced one another in *Mandla*. However, the Supreme Court considered that legislative intervention would need to entitle such judicial balancing between grounds of discrimination.[23] By contrast, considerations of separation of powers and practical difficulties are not the drivers of the 'analogous-to-secular' view. The motivation behind the analogous-to-secular view, as I will now explain, is that equality rather than religious freedom should be the basis of legal reasoning and the foundation of democracy.

---

[17] See *Mandla v Dowell Lee* [1983] 2 AC 548, [1983] 2 WLR 620.

[18] For a detailed and insightful analysis of these new tensions, C McCrudden, 'Multiculturalism, Freedom of Religion, Equality, and the British Constitution: the *JFS* case considered' (2011) 9 *International Journal of Constitutional Law* I•CON 200.

[19] *R (E) v Governing Body of JFS* (n 15) para 34.

[20] ibid, para 35.

[21] Under Department for Children, Schools and Families, *School Admissions Code* (Norwich, TSO, 2009) para 2.47.

[22] *Mandla* (n 17).

[23] *R (E) v Governing Body of JFS* (n 15) para 70, per Lady Hale, calling for legislation to allow such departure.

### iii. Equality as the Foundation of Democracy

In their important book, *Religious Freedom and the Constitution*,[24] US law professors and constitutional theorists Christopher Eisgruber and Lawrence Sager start with the observation of the impasse to which the metaphor of the wall of separation has led US courts.[25] Their goal is to revive 'the project of finding fair terms of cooperation for ourselves as a religiously diverse people'.[26] To that end, they suggest that 'Equal Liberty' would be a more workable and consensual basis for legal reasoning: 'Our hope is that Equal Liberty, by focusing attention on equality and removing it from imponderable questions about the goodness of religion, can reduce the partisanship and confusion that now plague America's public argument about religious freedom'.[27]

However, their project goes far beyond the search for practical remedies. It makes an important theoretical claim (to which I will return) that the concept of religious freedom can (and should) be streamed into underlying equality/liberty concerns and that fair terms of cooperation should rest on Equal Liberty, rather than religious freedom. In the same vein, Oxford political theorist professor Cécile Laborde, in her recent book *Liberalism's Religion*,[28] proposes to disaggregate religion under the law and political philosophy into the various legitimate secular interests underlying a particular religious claim. For example, Laborde supports the accommodation of religious minority members who request exemptions from Sunday laws or wish to wear religious garments in the workplace. In both cases, the law should grant their request, she argues, not because of the force of their religious beliefs, but because their claim involve an 'integrity-related liberty', 'a liberty that is essential to the exercise of their core moral powers: notably, their capacity to formulate and live by their own ethical commitments and projects'.[29] Whilst pointing to the practical advantages of her proposal, Laborde acknowledges that her argument is not practical, but conceptual. Indeed, Laborde dedicates the first chapter of her book to proving that the epistemological hurdles that the liberal state faces when it tackles religious considerations are surmountable. The law may distort the meaning of religion as believers see it but the objection is not fatal because legal and semantic meanings need not overlap. 'What matters is that the law, or the theory, expresses and protects the correct underlying values'.[30] For Laborde, these correct underlying values must be secular.

---

[24] CL Eisgruber and LG Sager, *Religious Freedom and the Constitution* (Cambridge MA, Harvard University Press, 2007).
[25] ibid, 7.
[26] ibid.
[27] ibid, 20.
[28] C Laborde, *Liberalism's Religion* (Cambridge MA, Harvard University Press, 2017).
[29] ibid, 147.
[30] ibid, 31.

### iv. Religious Freedom Through Secular Analogies or Equivalents

The conceptual paradigm for these authors is that religious freedom can fuse into secular equivalents, hence my characterisation of their position as the analogous-to-secular view. Laborde, Eisgruber and Sager share the conviction that religion is not special. According to Laborde, whatever treatment religion receives from the law, it receives because of features that it shares with non-religious beliefs, conceptions and identities.[31] She thus elaborates on Eisgruber's and Sager's position, which:

> denies that religion is a constitutional anomaly, a category of human experience that demands special benefits and/or necessitates special restrictions. It insists that, aside from our deep concern with equality, we have no reason to confer special constitutional privilege or to impose special constitutional disabilities upon religion.[32]

The analogous view is rooted in a (refined and extended) principle of liberal neutrality whereby the liberal state must refrain from deciding what counts as a good life. Accommodating religious requests because of their religious dimension would be granting greater weight to religious commitments and practices as opposed to secular ones. Citizens deserve, in the terms of the renowned late American philosopher Ronald Dworkin,[33] a right to ethical independence and this ethical independence – the argument goes – would require that law treat religion no more or no less favourably than any other ways of life. One may draw from Dworkin's theory the conclusion that the liberal state *may* still accommodate religious practices as long as its reason for doing so does not solely lie in the assumption that the corresponding religious way of life is ethically better than other ways of life.[34] This conclusion then prompts liberal egalitarians, in Dworkin's footsteps, to look for secular reasons for accommodation.[35] Whilst departing from Dworkin's stance on neutrality and arguing, contrary to Dworkin, that the liberal state must define at a meta-level what pertains to the religious and what does not,[36] Laborde belongs to this line of thought, which considers religious interests only to the extent that there is a secular equivalent.

### v. The Search for a Secular Comparator

Unlike for Eisgruber and Sager, there is no need, in Laborde's framework, for a religious claimant to point to an existing corresponding secular hypothesis before

---

[31] ibid, 32.

[32] Eisgruber and Sager, *Religious Freedom* (n 24) 6.

[33] R Dworkin, *Justice for Hedgehogs* (London, Harvard University Press, 2011).

[34] See G Letsas, 'Accommodating What Needn't Be Special' (2016) 10 *Law & Ethics of Human Rights* 319, esp 328.

[35] Another approach of course would be to argue against accommodations altogether, see B Barry, *Culture and Equality: An Egalitarian Critique of Multiculturalism* (Cambridge, Polity Press, 2001).

[36] Laborde, *Liberalism's Religion* (n 28) 48.

the judge is entitled to grant the request. As long as the underlying value that is to be protected can conceivably and legitimately apply to a secular scenario, this is enough to justify consideration of the exemption/accommodation request. For example, the integrity-liberty claim, which the religious citizen makes when she asks to wear a religious symbol at work, could equally support the claim of a vegan[37] who asks for dietary accommodations. In Eisgruber's and Sager's framework on the other hand, the search of a comparator is more demanding, as it applies to the situation at hand and not only to the underlying protected value. Eisgruber's and Sager's emblematic example[38] is the US *Newark* case[39] in which two officers challenged their employer's policy requiring all police officers in the Newark police force to be clean-shaven. As Sunni Muslims, the applicants argued that the policy breached their religious duty to wear a beard and requested an exemption. Newark regulations already provided exemptions for officers who suffered from folliculitis, a skin condition that makes shaving painful. If some officers could benefit from an exemption on secular medical grounds, Eisgruber and Sager argue (endorsing the opinion written by Judge Samuel Alito, then at the US Court of Appeals for the Third Circuit), equal regard demands that the applicants also benefit from an exemption on religious grounds. This comparative approach also usefully illuminates the solution in *Sherbert v Verner*,[40] where South Carolina prohibited employers from firing workers who refused to work on Sundays, on account of conscientious objections, but provided no such protection for employees who consciously objected to working on other days. The comparators, according to Eisgruber and Sager, help to ensure that 'no members of our political community be disadvantaged in the pursuit of their important commitments and projects on account of the spiritual foundations of those projects and projects'.[41]

Following this rationale, however, equality does not appear to be the exclusive foundation of the liberal state. Rather, it may be characterised as a second-order commitment, one that serves a primary fundamental value. Equality would be designed to guarantee that citizens benefit fairly from the opportunities to pursue their personal commitments. The freedom to pursue these commitments would be the foundational value amongst which freedom of religion cases are paradigmatic.

---

[37] For a recent case about whether veganism amounts to a 'philosophical belief', protected under the Equality Act 2010, see *Mr Casamitjana v League Against Cruel Sports ('LACS')*. cf, holding that vegetarianism was a life-style choice and lacked the 'clear cogency and cohesion' that vegan beliefs had, *Conisbee v Crossley Farms Ltd & Others* [2019] ET 3335357/2018. For a critique of the sharp distinction between veganism and vegetarianism, see P Edge, 'Vegetarianism as a protected characteristic: another view on *Conisbee*' in *Law & Religion UK*, 23 September 2019, www.lawandreligionuk.com/2019/09/23/vegetarianism-as-a-protected-characteristic-another-view-on-conisbee/.

[38] Eisgruber and Sager, *Religious Freedom* (n 24) 90–91.

[39] *Fraternal Order of Police Newark Lodge No 12 v City of Newark*, 170 F3d 359 (3d Circ 1999).

[40] *Sherbert v Verner*, 374 US 398 (1963).

[41] Eisgruber and Sager, *Religious Freedom* (n 24) 15.

*vi. Critique of the Search for Comparators*

It is not clear why a comparator test is most suited to protect religious freedom claims. Religious requests will sometimes rely mainly on an equality argument but there can be an infringement of religious freedoms regardless of how the law treats others in an equivalent situation. Where the equality argument exists, it is important to put it forward. In the *Sherbert* case, for example, equality considerations were indeed, I would argue, at the heart of the case. The selection of Sunday as the only day on which South Carolina allowed exemptions from work on conscientious grounds unduly advantaged members of the majority Christian religion. Framing the argument in equality terms importantly underlines the greater burden members of minority religion face as they alone have the dilemma of choosing between their work and religious commitments. Such disparity of treatment amounts, in Eisgruber's and Sager's terms, to 'a failure of *equal regard* – a failure by the state to show the same concern for the fundamental needs of all its citizens'.[42] In the European legal framework, anti-discrimination provisions would capture such failure.

Not all freedom of religion protection, however, is essentially egalitarian and comparative.[43] Take the *Newark* case. The fact that exemptions from clean-shaven requirements had been granted on medical grounds only marginally strengthens the applicants' claim. It certainly provides evidence that accommodating the request is feasible and makes any objections to the applicants' claims on practical grounds unconvincing. However, it does not prove anything as to the legitimacy of the applicants' request. The medical-based exemptions from the clean-shaven requirements do not render all other requests for exemptions from the same requirement legitimate, nor would the lack of comparable exemptions on medical grounds have made the applicants' request on religious grounds illegitimate. There may be good reasons for judging that medical grounds are legitimate reasons whereas the aesthetic motivation to hide a chin scar, for example, is not. It may be expedient to refrain from examining the employee's motivations in each case and allow accommodations as long as the cost/benefit equation lies in favour of employees but, in my view, these pragmatic considerations cannot amount to a legitimacy test.[44]

The focus on the respective burdens which would follow on the employer and employee respectively should the accommodation be granted or, on the contrary, denied, necessarily pre-supposes that all requests have a prima facie legitimate

---

[42] ibid, 89.

[43] See McCrudden, *Litigating Religions* (n 9) 75, analysing the relationships between freedom of religion and freedom from discrimination.

[44] Contra, Letsas, 'Accommodating' (n 34) 322: 'What is distinctive about the argument from fairness is that it is irrelevant why the employee breaches his contractual obligation. What makes accommodation reasonable does not depend on the reasons for the breach and their strength. Rather, it turns on the nature of the threatened harm (dismissal) and the extent to which the employer can easily accommodate the alternative that the employee is proposing'.

expectation of being accommodated. However, it is not clear why aesthetic, religious, medical and family commitments, for example, should all benefit from that presumption alike. If courts draw analogies too broadly, religious requests will be trivialised, in the vein of late philosopher Brian Barry's analogy between refusing to wear a motorcycle helmet as a Sikh man with enjoying the thrill of the wind whipping through your hair.[45] If courts draw analogies more restrictively, limiting secular analogies to requests that reach a certain level of depth, as illustrated by Laborde's integrity-liberty value criterium for example, the test should then focus on identifying the level of coherence and depth required under the concept of integrity-liberty. The existence of a similar request on other grounds is irrelevant. Even if no officers in the Newark police force had suffered from folliculitis, denying the applicants' requests would still have been unfair. The applicants would still face the difficult dilemma of choosing between their work and religious duties. If we were to choose a comparator, a better one would be with Christian officers, who can comply with the police force clean-shaven requirements without compromising their religious commitments. We would then be back to the *Sherbert* case hypothesis.

### vii. Eisgruber's and Sager's Response to the Critique

Eisgruber and Sager largely accept the objection. They recognise that the existence of an exemption for folliculitis is morally an arbitrary accident[46] and acknowledge that the Sunni officers' entitlement to an exemption should not depend *in principle* upon the existence of a skin condition like folliculitis.[47] However, they maintain that an inherently comparative approach is appropriate. Only then can the liberal state treat comparably serious religious and non-religious needs equally. To avoid the arbitrariness of the existence of a comparator whilst maintaining their comparative approach, Eisgruber and Sager accept counter-factual comparisons. If the Forest Service, they state as an illustration,[48] decided to run a service road across sites sacred to Native Americans,[49] the relevant comparator could be purely hypothetical. One might ask whether the Forest Service would run a similar road if it threatened a conservationist area well-known for its rare redwood trees or a well-established community of Catholics or Orthodox Jews. The answer to that question, in both cases,

---

[45] Barry, *Culture and Equality* (n 35).

[46] Eisgruber and Sager, *Religious Freedom* (n 24) 105. And for the objection of the accidental arbitrary nature of the equivalent exemption, see CG Lund, 'A Matter of Constitutional Luck: the General Applicability Requirement in Free Exercise Jurisprudence' (2003) 26 *Harvard Journal of Law and Public Policy* 627, 648–49.

[47] Eisgruber and Sager, *Religious Freedom* (n 24) 106.

[48] ibid, 91.

[49] The issue was raised in *Lyng v Northwest Indian Cemetery Protective Ass'n*, 485 US 439, 441–42 (1988). The Court held that the government could build the road as 'government simply could not operate if it were required to satisfy every citizen's religious needs and desires', at 452.

is almost certainly no, Eisgruber and Sager write,[50] but is it? How does one know the answer, if the comparison is purely hypothetical? Is the approach still comparative? Is the counter-factual comparator not a convenient way to hide an ethical assessment of what the answer should be? In fact then, Eisgruber and Sager do adopt a generous approach to religious freedom. The requirement of a comparator would rarely – if ever – restrain considerations of religious requests. Nonetheless, conceptually, religious freedoms in their scheme remain subordinate to secular equivalents and to equality concerns. Laborde removes the requirement of a comparator but adopts the same conceptual premise: the protection of religious freedom relies on secular features, which non-religious beliefs and ways of life share.

## viii. Consequences for Religious Freedom

What are the consequences of such frameworks for religious freedom? Interestingly, the protection of religious freedom may still be extensive in the analogous conceptions discussed above. Religious believers may still enjoy a sphere of autonomy and privacy in which to express their faith; they may also ask for exemptions from contractual or public duties, when these unduly burden them for reason of their membership of a vulnerable religious minority group. According to Eisgruber and Sager, the state should moreover avoid siding with symbols of the majority religion lest disparaging messages be sent to minority religion citizens as a result. Would any of the 'correct underlying values' of religious freedom be missing? Does it matter that the concept of religious freedom lose its salience? In his recent book, *Litigating Religions*,[51] human rights professor Christopher McCrudden identifies three main rationales for protecting religious freedom: avoiding civil strife; protecting a private sphere of autonomy and privacy; and protecting the pluralism of the public space. At first sight, the analogous stance meets these objectives. However, unlike the ECtHR, it does not see religious freedom as '(also) a precious asset for atheists, agnostics, sceptics and the unconcerned'. The picture is reversed. According to the analogous-to-secular view, it is the secular value of equal-liberty that is an asset, not only for atheists, agnostics, sceptics and the unconcerned but also for religious believers. I submit that this secular premise is exclusionary of religious believers. It certainly does not, in the words of NYU philosophy and law professor Thomas Nagel, provide the devout with a reason for tolerance[52] or the non-religious person with a reason for tolerance of the religious devout person. Before I suggest ways for a more inclusive liberalism, one that might provide such reasons for tolerance, I need to consider arguments that have denied any possibility of such rapprochement between liberalism and religion and have consequently promoted the isolation of religious freedom from the liberal democratic project.

---

[50] Eisgruber and Sager, *Religious Freedom* (n 24) 92.
[51] McCrudden, *Litigating* (n 9) 66 ff.
[52] Nagel, 'Moral Conflict' (n 1) 229.

## B. The Isolation of Religious Freedom

Humanities and law professor Stanley Fish famously declared that the regulation of religion by the liberal secular state was 'mission impossible'.[53] Fish means that the liberal state cannot govern religion without losing its claim to neutrality, that is, its commitment to respect citizens' own conceptions of the good. Running deeper is the charge that liberalism is but another ideology and that the liberal state would have no legitimacy in privileging its own ideological secular values. In that presentation, religious freedom is crucial, to quote the ECtHR again, 'in its religious dimension, (as) one of the most vital elements that go to make up the identity of believers and their conception of life'[54] but its importance for non-believers and the unconcerned and its value for democracy are denied. Indeed, as liberalism is, according to Fish, a rival doctrine, liberalism and religion necessarily lie in tension/competition and often contradiction with each other.

### i. Religious Freedom and Liberalism: Inevitable Enemies?

According to Fish:

> Politics, interest, partisan conviction and beliefs are the locations of morality. It is in and through them that our sense of justice and of the good lives is put into action. Immorality resides in the mantras of liberal theory – fairness, impartiality and mutual respect – all devices for painting the world various shades of grey.[55]

This statement contains several claims. Fish contends: that the divide between the private and public spheres, on which the liberal state traditionally rests, is inherently biased in favour of state interests; that the divide necessarily trivialises religious commitments and beliefs; that the liberal state's self-declared tolerance cannot – logically – explain liberalism's intolerance towards illiberal views. No rational or reasonable justification, Fish concludes, can logically explain why the devout religious person should accept the liberal framework. Liberalism and religion, in this view, are inherently and irreducibly conflicting. Let us unpack the position.

### ii. The Accusation of Liberalism' Partiality

Fish first notes that regulation of religion by the liberal state is inherently biased. The liberal state has an interest in taming religious views into a certain direction –

---

[53] S Fish, 'Mission Impossible: Settling the Just Bounds between Church and State' (1997) 97 *Columbia Law Review* 2255.

[54] *Kokkinakis* (n 2) para 31.

[55] Fish, 'Mission Impossible' (n 53) 2333.

towards moderate, inner, private beliefs accommodating of conflicting perspectives and of a shared public realm. Presenting the resulting public/private divide at the heart of liberalism's treatment of religion as the paradigm of neutrality is therefore, according to Fish, pure pretence. As liberalism has a stake in the problem, it cannot claim to adjudicate the conflict between religious and secular views with impartiality. The observation builds on American professor Steven D Smith's anti-theory stance. For Smith, the liberal formulation is already inflected in a particular direction; the definitions selected by the liberal state will have been borrowed from one or another of the competing interests, which means that, rather than mediating conflicts, the liberal theory will be entering them on a particular side. A liberal theory of religious freedom would therefore be a 'foreordained failure'.[56] It would inevitably fail for lack of any higher moral standpoint. Embedded in the conflicts it strives to solve, liberalism would have no claim to impartiality. The other objections follow from this starting point of impossibility.

### iii. Liberalism's Contradictions: Its Intolerance for the Intolerant

In the absence of a higher moral liberal order, liberalism cannot – the argument goes – give any reasons that might persuade the religious devout person to adhere to liberal values of tolerance.[57] Faced with this failure, the accommodationist position, which defers to religious citizens' points of view, would be the only possible logical outcome for liberalism. To make his point, Fish refers to the famous case of *Mozert v Hawkins County Board of Education*,[58] in which a fundamentalist Christian mother objected to her daughter's participation in the school's critical reading programme. Interestingly, the mother's objections did not target any particular aspect of the programme's syllabus. What the mother criticised was her daughter's exposure to a diversity of views and the underlying liberal assumption that consideration of a problem from a multiplicity of perspectives is enriching. From her point of view, exposure to diversity was not enriching but threatening, as it risked undermining her daughter's faith. To Fish, liberalism's attempts to justify why the mother should not have a right to opt her daughter out of the critical reading programme cannot be persuasive. How can the fundamentalist accept a requirement to tolerate different points of view when her profound conviction is that her outlook is the one and the only one to embody truth and morality? How can the liberal state invoke tolerance to

---

[56] SD Smith, *Foreordained Failure: The Quest for a Constitutional Principle Religious Freedom* (Oxford, Oxford University Press, 1995) 30.

[57] See for example, Smith's criticisms of the liberal value of equality, which he traces back to religion and whose modern secular manifestations he describes as akin to religious dogma: SD Smith, 'Equality, Religion, and Nihilism' in R Adhar (ed), *Research Handbook on Law and Religion* (Northampton MA, Elgar Publishers, 2018).

[58] *Mozert v Hawkins County Board of Education*, 827 F 2d 1058 (1987) at 1063.

justify its refusal to tolerate such fundamentalist views? Regulation of religion in that sense betrays religious beliefs, which will be at odds with the compromising stance liberals expect of believers and with liberalism, as the commitment to tolerance is in contradiction with the rejection of and intolerance towards illiberal views. The accommodation of the religious request would therefore follow from the impossible regulation of religion by the liberal state.

### iv. Solutions: The Accommodationist versus the Separatist

Fish is right to point out these tensions between religious views and liberalism. Liberalism will struggle with those who refuse to cooperate. Liberal authors diverge on how to solve these difficult cases. According to accommodationists such as Stanford constitutional law professor Michael McConnell, religious fundamentalists should benefit from rights to opt out. McConnell reasons as follows:

> When scrutinizing a law or governmental practice (...), the courts should ask the following question: is the purpose or probable effect to increase religious uniformity, either by inhibiting religious practice (...) or by forcing or inducing a contrary religious practice (...), without sufficient justification?[59]

McConnell thus emphasises the connections between religious freedom and pluralism. Echoing the ECtHR's quote above, he aptly underlines that a generous conception of religious freedom is an indispensable condition for diversity within democracy. *How* open to diversity and *how* generous must courts be, however? The answer depends on the chosen baseline. Should it be unfettered (religious) diversity, subject to what is necessary to achieve the state's legitimate interests, as argued by McConnell, or a public liberal order subject to a principle of self-restraint?

### v. A Principle of Non-intervention

If, like McConnell, the starting point is unfettered religious diversity, the state ought not to exclude religious requests in light of their content, even where this is extreme. Any state evaluation of the value of religious positions would stand in the way of liberalism's commitment to freedom of conscience. The correct posture for the state would be non-intervention.[60] A more morally-laden approach, says McConnell, would degenerate into a form of political correctness inimical to individual freedom. Respect for diversity would thus guarantee state neutrality, which, in turn, would guarantee individual liberty. McConnell

---

[59] MW McConnell, 'Religious Freedom at a Crossroads' (1992) 59 *The University of Chicago Law Review* 115.

[60] MW McConnell, 'Why Is Religious Liberty the "First Freedom"?' (1999–2000) 21 *Cardozo Law Review* 1243.

acknowledges that equality, tolerance and neutrality are key commitments of the liberal state. However, the extension of these commitments onto private persons and organisations would not reinforce, according to him, but betray these very commitments:

> In the case of liberalism, this would not simply be an overextension. It would be an inversion. When government insists that all citizens be neutral, tolerant and egalitarian, it ceases to be liberal.

Accordingly, the liberal state should tolerate even the intolerant citizens for McConnell. The fundamentalist mother, whose objection to the school syllabus lies not in a particular allegedly coercive aspect of the programme but in the very exposure to other points of view, would therefore have a right to opt her daughter out of classes. Undeniably, McConnell's system of thoughts allows a wide expression of religious views and encourages pluralism. However there is some contradiction in valuing diversity and nonetheless allowing some citizens to retreat from diversity altogether. At the very least, but this would fall outside the scope of McConnell's demonstration, there is an argument that granting an exemption to the fundamentalist mother in the *Mozert* case might contravene children's rights to and the state's legitimate interest in education. Consequently, even assuming that unfettered religious liberty is the correct baseline, the *Mozert* case might still qualify as an illustration of the limits which the liberal state may legitimately impose on religious freedom. More fundamentally, one may question whether unfettered religious liberties is the correct baseline.

## *vi. The Liberal Public Order as the Baseline*

American lawyer and law professor Kathleeen Sullivan clearly thinks that it is not. The correct baseline, she contends 'is not unfettered religious liberty, but rather religious liberty insofar as it is consistent with the establishment of the secular public moral order'.[61] What is interesting for my purposes in Sullivan's view is that this liberal public moral order is not a form of faith but an overarching system of beliefs.[62] I will explore in section II below in what way liberalism can indeed avoid being one form of faith amongst others. For now, taking Sullivan at her word, this idea of liberalism as an overarching system of beliefs proves very fruitful. It offers a remedy to liberalism's alleged partiality and responds to Fish (above) and others[63] who see liberalism as embedded in the disagreements it claims (in vain) to impartially adjudicate. If liberalism is indeed an *overarching* system of beliefs, it would have the necessary higher ground to raise above

---

[61] KM Sullivan, 'Religion and Liberal Democracy' (1992) 59 *The University of Chicago Law Review* 195, 198.

[62] ibid, 201.

[63] See, for example, M Sandel, *Liberalism and the Limits of Justice* (Cambridge, Cambridge University Press, 1982).

conflicting systems of thoughts and legitimately solve particular tensions. The thorny question, of course, is to determine on what grounds liberalism might claim this overarching status. Liberalism has no inherent legitimate claim to neutrality. Nor does secularism.[64]

Sullivan, however, does not base her position on the spurious ground that this would be 'neutral,' 'but on the ground that the First Amendment committed the United States to a certain public philosophy'.[65] The justification for this higher status, in other words, is not philosophical or moral but political and constitutional. McConnell disagrees with her reading of the First Amendment. However, the crux of the disagreement between McConnell and Sullivan seems to revolve more around Sullivan's notion of a secularised public space[66] than on the idea of a liberal overarching framework. Sullivan considers that the US Establishment clause forbids any state support of religious practices. Even purely symbolic support of religious celebrations, through the display of nativity scenes or merely indirect support through the tax system, would violate the Establishment clause, she argues. If state support for religion were only prohibited when it violated conflicting rights to religious freedoms, the two US Religion clauses would become blurred. The Establishment clause protecting against state meddling with religion on the one hand and the Free Exercise clause protecting citizens' individual conscience on the other would lose their specificity and be assessed in the same way, in terms of their impact on individual conscience.[67] McConnell disagrees. He argues that it is historically wrong to interpret the US Constitution as a Charter for a secular order. The Constitution, according to him, would forbid only measures that increase religious homogeneity (ie foster conversion or lapses), not support of religion as such.[68] Construed in the strict sense suggested by Sullivan, the Establishment Clause would induce a climate of suspicion towards religion, which would betray constitutional purposes and framers' intent.

My aim here is not to join this debate on the correct interpretation of the US Clauses. Rather, what I would like to underline here is that both authors acknowledge that the constitutional liberal order is the correct framework for their dispute. Unlike Fish, McConnell recognises that the liberal state may legitimately regulate religious freedom. What he takes issue with is the suggestion that this regulation should, in the US context, entail the establishment of a 'naked public sphere', that is a public sphere devoid of any religious signs and connotations. I will return to this debate in a different, European context in subsequent chapters. For now, it is

---

[64] On this, see J Rawls, 'The Idea of an Overlapping Consensus' (1987) 7 *Oxford Journal of Legal Studies* 1.

[65] See McConnell's summary of Sullivan's position, 'Crossroads' (n 59) 190.

[66] Sullivan, 'Religion' (n 61) 198–201.

[67] On the tensions between these two clauses, see K Greenawalt, *When Free Exercise and Nonestablishment Conflict* (Cambridge MA, Harvard University Press, 2017).

[68] McConnell, 'Crossroads' (n 59) 168–69.

important to note that the idea of a liberal overarching framework is amenable to a wide range of views, including views that are very supportive of religious liberties. When McConnell, in Sullivan's words, chooses unfettered religious liberty as his baseline, he is not suggesting that the liberal state may never legitimately restrict the exercise of religious freedom rights, but that the state should abstain from evaluating the content of the religious beliefs in question, even when they are illiberal and intolerant. In other words, if McConnell's argumentation does contain an accusation of partiality against liberalism, it targets particular instances of regulation and does not invalidate the liberal state's broader claim to regulation. Like Sullivan and contra Fish, McConnell situates his reflections in the context of the political. Whilst he refutes any moral superior standing of liberalism, he accepts the idea of a shared political space and believes that the liberal political order can 'protect the full and equal rights of religious believers and communities to define their own way of life (…) and to participate fully and equally with their fellow citizens in public life'.[69]

Going back to the question at the beginning of this section – are religious freedom and liberalism inevitable enemies? – the answer would therefore be 'no'. Fish is right to locate morality in religious and other personal systems of thoughts but this does not make liberalism illegitimate. Its claim to regulation does not rest on a moral position but on a political claim. Its legitimacy is democratic.[70] It relies on democracy's procedural qualities as an inclusive, open-ended discursive process.[71]

## C. Conclusion to Section I

In this section, I have examined the connections between religious freedom, democracy and liberalism, focusing on theories that have cast doubts on the importance of these connections. Under an analogous-to-secular approach, the importance of religious freedom for democracy and liberalism is undermined. Religious freedom may still in effect be allowed to flourish: special vulnerabilities from which minority religion members may suffer and innocuous expressions of religious beliefs would, for example, certainly feature in this approach. However, liberalism's protection of religion, under an analogous-to-secular conception, is always indirect. It can only occur when and to the extent that an underlying secular value worthy of protection requires the state's intervention. In this approach, religious freedom is not conceptually of value for liberal democracies. Religious citizens are entitled to rights out of concerns for fairness, equality, non-discrimination, but not because *religious*

---

[69] ibid, 117.
[70] See J Habermas, 'Postscript to Between Facts and Norms' in M Deflem (ed), *Habermas, Modernity and Law* (London, Sage Publications, 1996) 137: 'the democratic process bears the entire burden of legitimation'.
[71] Habermas, *Between Facts* (n 6) fn 5.

freedom matters. Indeed, if religious freedom did matter, there is a suggestion that the liberal state would fail in its duty of neutrality towards conceptions of the good by unduly singling out religion. Contrary to the analogous-to-secular approach, I have suggested that liberal democracies may have something to learn from religious voices and that the concept of religious freedom is compatible with liberal neutrality. If liberalism is understood as an overarching framework, rather than one competing version of the conception of the good life, its regulation of religious freedom would not be a violation of neutrality, even when religious freedoms are regulated for what they are: *religious* requests.

If a more holistic conception of religious freedom is compatible with liberal neutrality, will liberal regulation of religious freedom be compatible with believers' own moral frameworks? According to the most radical of accommodationists, liberalism can never provide the devout, in Nagel's words, with a reason for tolerance.[72] The religious devout person will always turn to their own religious system and remain unpersuaded by liberal arguments. The devout person by definition will be intolerant just as liberalism, by definition, will be intolerant of the intolerant religious devout person. Like authors who endorse the analogous-to-secular view, accommodationists are sceptical of the connections between democracy, liberalism and religious freedom, but for opposite reasons. Whereas the analogous-to-secular conception doubts that religious freedom per se matters for democracy and liberalism, Fish, and accommodationist authors more generally, doubt that liberalism and democracy matter for religious freedom. In this latter conception, only religious frameworks could truly make sense of and establish religious freedom and in all (or at least the most difficult of) cases, accommodation of rights to opt out would be required.

On the contrary, I have suggested that democracy is the foundation of liberalism and that the democratic liberal order can support religious freedom. Unlike Fish, my starting point is that a shared political space amongst people with diverse views is not 'mission impossible' but a real and promising possibility. In the section to follow, I will therefore explore how democracy, liberalism and religious freedom can support one another and how, consequently, religious freedom may be an asset for believers as well as 'for atheists, agnostics, sceptics and the unconcerned'. I will argue that respect for pluralism is the key condition to healthy connections between religious freedom, democracy and liberalism.

## II. WHY PLURALISM MATTERS FOR DEMOCRACY AND RELIGIOUS FREEDOM

The preceding section has shown that liberal authors have widely differing views on religious freedom. Authors who adopt the analogous-to-secular view would like to dispense with it; they would dilute, disaggregate or dissolve it in secular

---

[72] Nagel, 'Moral Conflict' (n 1) 229.

equivalents. Accommodationists see it, on the contrary, as fundamental: religious freedom would be the first freedom of the liberal state.[73] Finally, separatists would relegate it to the private sphere. I have suggested that the most radical line of separation within liberal (and non-liberal) authors lies in the importance they accord, if any, to religious freedom in law. The analogous-to-secular view denies its importance whereas accommodationists, unsurprisingly, and perhaps more surprisingly separatists,[74] value the concept. Common features emerge from the reasoning of authors who value the concept of religious freedom in law. They all acknowledge that the liberal state may legitimately *limit* religious expressions in certain circumstances and they all acknowledge that religious citizens may legitimately expect a degree of self-restraint from the liberal state – although they will differ hugely on where to set the limits and where to exercise the self-restraint.[75]

In this section, I would like to explore this idea of limit and self-restraint further. Drawing on the work of political theorist professor Stephen Holmes, I will argue that self-restraint can be enabling both for democracy and for religious freedom. This self-restraint, I will argue, is to be welcomed as evidence of the importance conferred to pluralism. Going further, with renowned late American philosopher John Rawls, I will argue that a generous and inclusive concept of religious freedom contributes to maintaining this pluralism and thereby invigorates democracy (section A) and that the concept of public reason, understood in its revised version, can invigorate rather than diminish democratic debate (section B). Ultimately, as a conclusion, I will present three features, which, I submit, are at the core of an inclusive type three form of secularism[76] and a democratic approach to religious freedom: a method of avoidance; a principle of inclusion; and a principle of revision.

## A. Self-restraint, Religious Freedom and Pluralism

In this section I examine, drawing on the work of Holmes, one aspect of the connections between religious freedom and democracy, namely the notion of self-restraint. Interestingly, in Holmes' work, self-restraint not only benefits religious believers, whose religious autonomy it thus protects from interference from the state, it also preserves democratic debate from controversies. My aim here is not to embrace and defend Holmes' framework, but to take away from his work the idea that religious freedom and democracy can be mutually beneficial.

---

[73] McConnell, 'First Freedom' (n 60) 1243.

[74] See R McCrea, 'The Consequences of Disaggregation and the Impossibility of a Third Way' in C Laborde and A Bardon (eds), *Religion in Liberal Political Philosophy* (Oxford, Oxford University Press, 2017) 69.

[75] I take the objection that the notion of self-restraint is relative and that it is therefore the criteria used to draw the limits of intervention that do the work, not the idea of self-restraint. However, through these criteria, a notion of self-restraint does emerge.

[76] On the types of secularism, see Ch 2.

*i. Democratic Rule as Self-restraint*

According to Holmes, the core of democracy is not freedom but self-restraint.[77] It is because 'rulers too need to be ruled'[78] that the notion of constraints best characterises democracy. As an analogy, Holmes very vividly refers to Ulysses, who bound himself on a mast in order to resist the sirens' enchanting songs.[79] Likewise, rulers in democratic regimes choose to bind themselves to constitutional masts in order to resist tyrannical impulses. However constitutional constraints, Holmes goes on, are not merely safeguards against tyranny. Beyond this crucial negative function, constitutions 'establish rules that help put democracy into effect'.[80] In other words, they also serve a positive function. They encourage a democratic culture of free public debate. In that sense, constraints are as much enabling as they are restricting. This 'paradoxical insight that constraints can be enabling, which is far from being a contradiction, lies at the heart of liberal constitutionalism'[81] and of Holmes' work. The enabling effect of constraints benefits both the state and its citizens. For the state, 'a limited government can be more powerful than unlimited government'.[82] As Holmes goes on to explain: 'To purchase minority compliance, the electoral majority must assure the electoral minority that its most precious values and rights will not be violated'.[83] In exchange for this state protection, citizens and communities must accept restrictions too. Many of their views and tenets will not be allowed in their fullest expression. These self-imposed constraints benefit communities in a deeper sense than merely being a bargaining chip for peace. 'Rules restricting available options can enable individuals and communities to achieve more of their specific aims than they could if they were all left entirely unconstrained', says Holmes.[84]

Constraints would thus lead to a kind of work division and increase overall efficiency. Reasons for tolerance therefore begin to emerge for the religious devout person: to avoid civil unrest and enhance social efficiency. The same ideas of compartmentalisation and self-constraints can apply to religious freedom.

*ii. Gag Rules as Protective of the Public Sphere*

In his chapter on gag rules, Holmes extends these insights to religious freedom rights by making a case for a method of avoidance. The method of avoidance takes controversial religious issues off the public agenda, which unburdens and

---

[77] S Holmes, *Passions and Constraints: On the Theory of Liberal Democracy* (Chicago, The University of Chicago Press, 1995).

[78] ibid, 5.

[79] See J Elster, *Ulysses and the Sirens* (Cambridge, Cambridge University Press, 1979) 81–86, 88–103.

[80] ibid, 6.

[81] Holmes, *Passions* (n 76) xi.

[82] ibid, 21.

[83] ibid, 29.

[84] ibid, 173.

at the same time establishes the public forum. In that sense, religious freedom rights are not only protective of a private non-political sphere; they also protect the political sphere itself, by keeping divisive issues away. The method of avoidance, therefore, does not rely on a sacralised division between the private and public spheres. The division rests on strategic grounds, to shelter religious citizens from unwarranted intrusions (the negative dimension of religious freedom rights) and to unburden the public forum from controversial divisive issues (the positive dimension of religious freedom rights):

> Paradoxically, a religiously pluralistic country devoted to majority rule can be *united* by a deftly drawn *division* between public and private spheres. Compartmentalization can reinforce social cohesion. Other controversies, in this case, will be easier to resolve because religious schisms are not allowed to crystallise into political factions.[85]

The division between the private and the public spheres – emblematic of Holmes' core idea of self-restraint – thus seeks to reinforce both religious freedom and political deliberation.

## iii.  Holmes and Pluralism

Holmes' construction is intrinsically respectful of pluralism. It is because there is acknowledgment of and respect for the diversity of convictions amongst citizens that the method of avoidance emerges. If there were no underlying diversity, there would be no need for avoiding divisive issues. The method of avoidance also acknowledges religious diversity in a more profound sense. The method is, importantly, respectful of (religious) pluralism because it abstains from seeking uniformity. Its vision of the political is a deliberative model, which does not require an intrinsic shared identity. On the contrary, 'No "popular will" worth taking seriously has a mystical pre-existence'.[86] Unburdening the public agenda does not require a naked public square where mention of religion would be out of place but it presupposes a 'neutral territory – such as a classroom where children of all sects are debarred from stigmatizing others as un-American'.[87] Holmes' analysis of gag rules confirms the importance of religious freedom rights for democracy. Robust protection of religious freedom rights in the private sphere will also protect and reinvigorate democracy by unburdening the public agenda. Holmes thus supports my argument that religious rights are not only important for religious believers but are also a positive good for democracy. Let us explore more precisely, drawing on Rawls, how pluralism, religious freedom and democracy might interact.

---

[85] ibid, 206.
[86] ibid, 172.
[87] ibid, 224.

## iv. Rawls and Pluralism

In *Political Liberalism*, Rawls sets out to answer the following question: How is it possible that there may exist over time a stable and just society of free and equal citizens profoundly divided by reasonable though incompatible religious, philosophical and moral doctrines?[88] Diversity is thus the starting-point and root of Rawls' reflections on democracy and religious freedom. Rawls starts by observing the diversity of religious and philosophical doctrines or, in his words, the diversity of comprehensive doctrines, which he defines as sets of coherent, organised and recognised rules that single out especially significant values.[89] Rawls does not seek to deny or minimise this diversity:

> Political liberalism assumes the fact of reasonable pluralism as a pluralism of comprehensive doctrines, including both religious and nonreligious doctrines. This pluralism is not seen as a disaster but rather as the natural outcome of the activities of human reason under enduring free institutions.[90]

Pluralism, Rawls explains, is here to stay[91] and so it should. Our freedom of conscience depends on it. To justify this connection between pluralism and freedom of conscience, Rawls points to the absence of any reasonable criteria for selecting one comprehensive view above others: 'We recognize that our own doctrine has, and can have, for people generally no special claims on them beyond their own view on its merits'.[92] This endurance of pluralism lies in what Rawls calls the 'burdens of judgment'. The burdens of judgment express the recognition that 'many of our most important judgments are made under conditions where it is not expected that conscientious persons with full powers of reason, even after free discussion, will all arrive at the same conclusion'.[93] Given the burdens of judgment, disagreement is therefore reasonable.[94] Were we to use a particular comprehensive doctrine for political justification, we would necessarily impose our beliefs over the reasonable beliefs of others, and thereby violate their freedom of conscience. If terms of cooperation relied on a 'continuing shared understanding of one comprehensive religious, philosophical or moral doctrine', they 'could only be maintained by the oppressive use of state power'. To avoid this 'fact of oppression', the political, in Rawls' conception,

---

[88] J Rawls, *Political Liberalism*, 2nd edn (New York, Columbia University Press, 1996) 10, xxv.
[89] ibid, 59.
[90] ibid, xxiv.
[91] See ibid, 216.
[92] ibid, 60.
[93] ibid, 58.
[94] This conclusion does not imply that I have to recognise conflicting views as being reasonable. If I do not agree that Mormonism, for example, is reasonable, I may legitimately give reasons in support of my view. However, I cannot reasonably expect Mormons to defer to my view simply because, say, my own Christian tenets stand in opposition to Mormonism. I am grateful to Julian Rivers for prompting me to add this clarification.

cannot rely on a given comprehensive doctrine but can only emerge from an *overlapping consensus* on terms acceptable to all as free and equal.[95]

### v. The Principle of Legitimacy

This notion of overlapping consensus on terms acceptable to all leads to the principle of legitimacy. The principle of legitimacy, says Rawls, will guide the exercise of political power in 'accordance with a constitution the essentials of which all citizens as free and equal may reasonably be expected to endorse in the light of principles and ideals acceptable to their common human reason'.[96] This principle of legitimacy is the focus of the overlapping consensus in a society of citizens who are divided by reasonable disagreement but are free and equal. The principle of legitimacy requires that in discussing constitutional essentials and matters of basic justice, we are not to appeal to comprehensive religious and philosophical doctrines – to what we, as individuals or members of associations, see as the whole truth.[97] Like Holmes, Rawls thus postulates a division of the political and the personal. The autonomous conception of the political allows for a shared public space. For example, Quakers, as pacifists, might refuse to engage into war, yet still support the constitutional and legal regime under which the majority votes for going to war.[98] The separation of the personal (ruled by comprehensive doctrines) and the political (under the principle of legitimacy) enables toleration and democracy. In that sense, following Holmes,[99] Rawls takes controversial religious (and philosophical) issues off the public agenda. However, going further, Rawls acknowledges that this divide between the public and private spheres will not remove all controversies. The question of how to draw the boundaries,[100] for example, will remain contested and cannot be removed from politics.[101]

The quote above from the ECtHR in *Kokkinakis* powerfully illustrates this Rawlsian position. As Rawls' political liberalism rests on reasonable disagreement, pluralism is indeed 'indissociable from a democratic society'.[102] Further, as *Political Liberalism* expects citizens to recognise this underlying reasonable pluralism, freedom of conscience emerges as a fundamental principle rooted in

---

[95] Rawls, *Political Liberalism* (n 87) 133 ff.
[96] ibid, 137.
[97] ibid, 224.
[98] ibid, 393.
[99] Rawls explicitly refers to S Holmes', 'Gag Rules or the Politics of Omission' in J Elster and R Slagstad (eds), *Constitutional Democracy*; ibid, 15 (in fn 16).
[100] The feminist critique of how the public/public divide can entrench women's positions of vulnerabilities would, for example, be part of these healthy ongoing contestations. See, stating that the challenge of the public/private distinction is what the feminist project is about: R Gavison, 'Feminism and the Public/Private Distinction' (1992) 45(1) *Stanford Law Review* 1.
[101] Rawls, *Political Liberalism* (n 87) 152.
[102] *Kokkinakis* (n 2) para 34.

pluralism. The connections between democracy, religious freedom and pluralism thus lie at the heart of the Rawlsian framework. Paradoxically, a few authors have, however, accused Rawls of undermining religious pluralism in democracy. Their accusation targets Rawls' requirement of public reason.

*vi. The Requirement of Public Reason*

The condition of public reason expresses the requirement that I defend my proposals about the fair terms of social cooperation with reasons that are capable of being acknowledged in good faith as such by others. The requirement of public reason thus imposes constraints on political deliberation. Rawls rests the idea of public reason on a duty of civility[103] whereby citizens owe it to one another to justify their decisions on fundamental political issues by reference only to public values and public standards.[104] The concept of public reason[105] rests on the Rawlsian idea of reciprocity:[106] public reasons are not 'reasons we happen to share' but 'reasons that count for us because we can affirm them together'.[107] As we seek to justify political principles in arguments that others can also endorse, we thus show to one another respect as free and equal citizens.[108] Such a politically-driven conception of the person and of society reflects Rawls' ideal of citizenship – where all are free and equal. Indeed, it is because I see my fellow citizen as an equal that I feel the need to explain my views and put forward reasons, which she might reasonably be expected to accept. The notion of public reason is thus both a rule of omission, designed to unburden the public agenda, and a positive moral force, an instrument for a fair and inclusive society. Let us explore how public reason (which by definition supposes restraint in political deliberation) may nonetheless support pluralism and encourage a generous concept of religious freedom.

## B. Pluralism, Religious Freedom and Public Reason

In this section, I will examine and respond to an important critique of public reason. The charge is that Rawls' concept of public reason muffles religious views

---

[103] Rawls, *Political Liberalism* (n 87) 217.

[104] See L Wenar, 'John Rawls' in EN Zalta (ed), *The Stanford Encyclopedia of Philosophy*, Spring 2017 at plato.stanford.edu/entries/rawls/.

[105] For a presentation of the rationales of the concept of public reason, see J Quong, 'Public Reason' in EN Zalta (ed), *The Stanford Encyclopedia of Philosophy*, Spring 2013 at plato.stanford.edu/entries/public-reason/.

[106] Rawls, *Political Liberalism* (n 87) xlvi, 218, 226.

[107] C Larmore, 'Public Reason' in S Freeman (ed), *The Cambridge Companion to Rawls* (Cambridge, Cambridge University Press, 2002) 368.

[108] C Larmore, 'The Moral Basis of Political Liberalism' (1999) 96 *The Journal of Philosophy* 599, esp 608.

and thereby truncates public debate. What I call the expansive approach[109] takes issues with the constraints imposed by public reason and argues instead for a broader range of political reasons, inclusive of religious arguments. In his recent important book, NYU legal and political philosophy professor Jeremy Waldron criticises Rawls' public reason for 'distorting' and 'truncating' public discussion by failing to allow religious citizens to say what is important to them.[110]

## i. Waldron's Critique

Waldron's criticism of public reason stands at the crossroads of two lines of investigation: his work on equality and his analysis of Rawls' idea of an overlapping consensus. Waldron starts with the observation that the overlapping consensus by definition only reflects part of the reasons why each citizen supports the laws and institutions. He then deduces from this that the notion of public reason will misrepresent (or at least will only partially present) the particular complexity of a particular citizen's view. He concludes that the reasons left out will entail a loss, not only for the particular citizen whose view is truncated, but also a moral loss for public discussion: 'If the reasons that are excluded are morally significant reasons, then the complaint about their exclusion ought to be a complaint on behalf of the interests and considerations that the reasons draw attention to'.[111]

Underlying each step of his reasoning is Waldron's normative view of equality. According to Waldron, moral equality rests on four capacities that all humans have the potential to possess in some degree: reason, autonomy, moral agency, and the ability to love. His account of equality leads him to put greater emphasis on each citizen's individual perspective. More deeply, Waldron's stance on equality also leads him to broaden the notion of respect on which public reason rests. Waldron thinks that the most controversial aspect of public reason is the suggestion that 'voicing justificatory arguments outside the framework of public reason is not a civil or respectful way of dealing with one's fellow citizens'.[112]

In other words, Waldron challenges the three premises on which Rawls' concept of public reason rests: the idea of intelligibility; the idea of improved

---

[109] To varying degrees, the following authors, amongst others, have argued for an 'expansive approach' to public reason: K Greenawalt, *Private Consciences and Public Reasons* (New York, Oxford University Press, 1995); C Eberle, *Religious Conviction in Liberal Politics* (Cambridge, Cambridge University Press, 2002); P Weithman, *Religion and the Obligations of Citizenship* (Cambridge, Cambridge University Press, 2002); J Stout, *Democracy and Tradition* (Princeton, NJ, Princeton University Press, 2004); SD Smith, *The Disenchantment of Secular Discourse* (Cambridge MA, Harvard University Press, 2010); JK Vallier, *Liberalism and Public Faith: Beyond Separation* (New York, Routledge, 2014).

[110] J Waldron, *One Another's Equals: The Basis of Human Equality* (Cambridge MA, The Belknap Press of Harvard University Press, 2017) 211.

[111] J Waldron, 'Isolating Public Reasons' in T Brooks and M Nussbaum (eds), *Rawls' Political Liberalism* (New York, Columbia University Press, 2015) 130.

[112] ibid, 128.

political deliberation; and the idea of respect or duty of civility towards our fellow citizens.

### ii. The Intelligibility Argument

The exclusion of religious arguments (and other comprehensive views) from public reasons is often explained by the inability of non-believers to grasp the significance of religious arguments. Public reasons, says Rawls, are reasons that fellow citizens may reasonably be expected to accept. Religious arguments will normally not fall into that category because the underlying belief system on which they rely will not have any persuasive force for those who do not share these beliefs. Waldron challenges this conclusion on two grounds. First, he denies the assumption that religious arguments are wholly incomprehensible to non-believers. Second, he challenges the suggestion that the political should be defined exclusively in terms of deliberative persuasion. On the first ground, Waldron points to the familiarity of religious arguments for believers and non-believers alike. Western liberal political culture is saturated with references to Judeo-Christian theological concepts.[113] It is therefore likely, says Waldron, that religious arguments will resonate with a secular audience.[114] The unintelligibility argument, Waldron claims, is often exaggerated: 'the opponents of religious interventions simply underestimate the prospects of mutual intelligibility' because many 'have resolved to have nothing to do with religious thought and standing firm on that resolution, they demand to be spoken in only secular terms'.[115]

According to Waldron, the exclusion of religious arguments would not therefore rely on their unintelligibility but rather on the idea that a secular audience will not accept them. However, and here is Waldron's second objection to the intelligibility argument, limiting public reasons to reasons that all can accept is reductive. Political statements do not merely have a persuasive function. They also (usefully) serve as communicative acts, to explain our particular political stance.[116] Consequently, Waldron refutes the second premise that supports the concept of public reason: the idea that public reason facilitates political deliberation.

---

[113] J Waldron, 'Tribalism and the Myth of the Framework' in P Catton and G Macdonald (eds), *Karl Popper: Critical Appraisals* (London, Routledge, 2004). See also N Wolterstorff, *Justice: Rights and Wrongs* (Princeton, NJ, Princeton University Press, 2008) Pts I–II, tracing back the secular notions of equality and freedom and, more generally, the concept of rights, to Hebrew and Christian scriptures. For Islamic sources, see A Ahmed An-Na'im, *Islam and the Secular State: Negotiating the Future of Shari'a* (Cambridge, MA, Harvard University Press, 2008).

[114] Waldron, *One Another's Equals* (n 109); see also C Eberle, *Religious Conviction* (n 108) 255–60.

[115] J Waldron, 'Two-Way Translation: The Ethics of Engaging with Religious Contributions in Public Deliberation' (2012) 63 *Mercer Law Review* 845, 860.

[116] ibid, 856.

### iii. The Improved Political Deliberation Argument

As explained in the first section, the concept of public reason seeks to unburden the public forum from controversies and thereby improve – indeed enable – political deliberation.[117] For Waldron, this view comes at (too high) a cost: valid arguments will be lost in the process.[118] Ultimately, he argues that this loss impoverishes rather than benefits political deliberation. How can political deliberation benefit from this self-censorship, Waldron asks, if we are not sure that 'we have heard everything there is to be said in favour of the opposite position'?[119] Intellectual curiosity alone should prompt us to welcome religious arguments even if – and especially if – we are not believers. Waldron therefore reverses the perspective. Whereas in Rawlsian terms, the concept of public reason is justified from the perspective of the speaker, Waldron focuses on the point of view of the listener, as explained below.

### iv. The Duty of Civility Argument

In Rawlsian terms, the concept of public reason expresses the speaker's *duty of civility* towards his fellow citizens. By exercising self-restraint, the speaker shows his willingness to engage with his/her fellow citizens. However, shifting the focus to the listener, Waldron considers that good citizenship, on the listener's part, would imply an open ear to all arguments on a given issue. He therefore concludes:

> it is better and in the end more respectful for people just to call things as they see them, giving them the fullest possible account and bearing the fullest possible witness to the grounds on which they adhere to publicly important positions.[120]

It is also in the name of respect that American philosophy scholars Gerald Gaus and Kevin Vallier propose a revisionist and expansive account of public reason. Gaus and Vallier endorse the concept of public reason as a duty upon public officials but contend that it should not apply as an account of the duties of citizens.[121] In relation to citizens, they submit that convergence rather than consensus should serve as a sufficient justification for political deliberation.

---

[117] See also S Benhabib, *Situating the Self, Gender, Community and Postmodernism in Contemporary Ethics* (New York, Routledge 1992), who argues that 'deliberation, would be more meaningful if citizens were able to take part as fuller, concrete selves'.

[118] See also P Quinn, 'Political Liberalisms and Their Exclusions of the Religious' in P Weithman (ed), *Religion and Contemporary Liberalism* (Notre Dame IN, Notre Dame University Press, 1997) 149–52, who argues that appeal to (religious) arguments would, in some instances, usefully increase the pool of rationales from which to draw.

[119] Waldron, *One Another's Equals* (n 109) 213.

[120] ibid, 211.

[121] I do not need to examine here the debates raised about the scope of the public reason requirement. For a discussion, see J Quong, 'The Scope of Public Reason' (2004) 52 *Political Studies* 233.

Critical of the liberal emphasis on interpersonal justification,[122] they promote a convergence thesis under which laws are justifiable when citizens have their own different reasons for supporting them. The claim is that the convergence thesis would be more respectful of citizens: by allowing them to rely on comprehensive doctrines, it would give an account of citizenship more responsive to each citizen's particularity and integrity. More forcefully, some authors have hinted that the concept of public reason might encourage moral scepticism towards comprehensive doctrines[123] or at least, a certain bias against religious arguments.[124]

### v. Responses: Public Reason and Public Forum

Public reason does not suggest anything as to the truth or untruth of (religious) comprehensive doctrines. Far from encouraging moral scepticism, Rawls' political conception starts with the recognition that citizens legitimately have strong commitments rooted in their own diverse comprehensive doctrines. In fact, as shown in section II.A above, it is precisely this acknowledgment of reasonable pluralism which prompted the writing of *Political Liberalism*. Nonetheless, it is undeniable that the concept of public reason, as presented and criticised most recently by Waldron, will impose constraints on religious citizens. However, under the inclusive view of public reason, these constraints are attenuated. Under Rawls' revised inclusive view of the concept of public reason,[125] citizens may be allowed, under certain situations, to present their values as rooted in their comprehensive doctrines. The requirement for citizens to 'translate' these arguments into secular accessible reasons still applies but in deferred mode. It is sufficient, states Rawls under the 'proviso',[126] that at some point, religious citizens add proper public reasons to justify their position. Religious citizens may legitimately present the full extent of their religious commitments as long as at some point they can add a secular public reason to back their position. Religious citizens are also still free to put forward religious arguments to proselytise their religion under freedom of speech. The fear that the public reason requirement will prevent religious citizens from sharing their religious views and presenting the depth of their commitments must not, therefore, be exaggerated. Further elaborations of the requirement, following a Habermasian deliberative account of the concept,[127] have shown that the concept of public reason retains value and

---

[122] GF Gaus, *Justificatory Liberalism: An Essay on Epistemology and Political Theory* (New York, Oxford University Press, 1996) 10–12.

[123] D Enoch, 'Political Philosophy and Epistemology: The Case of Public Reason' in D Sobel et al (eds), *Oxford Studies in Political Philosophy, Volume 3* (Oxford, Oxford University Press, 2017).

[124] N Wolterstorff, 'Why We Should Reject What Liberalism Tells Us About Speaking and Acting in Public for Religious Reasons' in Weithman, *Religion and Contemporary Liberalism* (n 17).

[125] Rawls, *Political Liberalism* (n 87) 435 ff.

[126] ibid ii–iii, 249.

[127] See above.

need not bear unduly heavily on religious citizens. Christopher McCrudden[128] has noted that the use of public reason in the public forum may push the problem (of finding common intelligible grounds) aside rather than solve it. The use of public reason will be appealing to courts and useful for legal reasoning, McCrudden concedes:

> the adoption of 'public reasons' approach addresses the epistemological problem[129] by translating the way the religion formulates its arguments into ways that the court will find understandable (and acceptable) and therefore the epistemological problem does not arise *for the* court.[130]

However, McCrudden adds, the problem may then arise for the religion in question 'which is then faced with the task of resisting an unacceptable translation, thereby risking losing the court's sympathy, or itself converting its belief system into public reason terms'.[131] I believe that McCrudden is right but the difficulty he underlines does not concern religious citizens and communities alone. Whether believer or non-believer, each and every citizen will have to internalise the political values and work out how they fit into their own comprehensive doctrines. The public reason requirement does not weigh exclusively on religious citizens. The duty of translation (which forces religious citizens to translate their religious arguments into secular accessible public reasons) is thus not as one-sided as might first appear. As elaborated by the German philosopher Jürgen Habermas,[132] translation makes demands on both sides.

## vi. Habermasian Account of Public Reason

According to Habermas, public reason giving is a cooperative task, in which the non-religious citizen must likewise participate.[133] The speaker must strain to convey their points in ways that will communicate as much of their content to people who do not share their faith. However, the listener has a similar responsibility. They must strain to listen and try to understand what is being said, and draw on their own background and cultural resources in order to get a bearing on what is being argued. As Saint Louis University philosophy scholars James Bohman and William Rehg observe, 'the fundamental form of coordination through language requires speakers to adopt a practical stance oriented towards

---

[128] McCrudden, *Litigating* (n 9).

[129] The epistemological problem, in McCrudden's terminology, refers to the difficulty of understanding normative systems other than those to which we are ourselves committed, ibid, 87 ff. See section I above.

[130] ibid, 99.

[131] ibid.

[132] J Habermas, 'Religion in the Public Sphere' (2006) 14 *European Journal of Philosophy* 1.

[133] ibid, 11.

reaching understanding'.[134] It is this willingness to reach understanding, which characterises, for Habermas, 'communicative action'[135] and which can also aptly apply to remedy the dangers of the Rawlsian requirement of public reason. It is therefore possible, I submit, to adopt a deliberative political conception of public reason which minimises the loss against which Waldron warns. The alternative, it is to be feared, would not be more respectful of religious citizens or more enriching of political deliberation but would bring in more controversies and ultimately threaten the ideal of a shared public forum. However difficult the public reason requirement may be to achieve,[136] dispensing with it entirely is not the answer, as it would dissolve the foundational *vivre ensemble* into a mere fragile *modus vivendi*.

## C. Conclusion to Section II

Drawing on Rawls, I argue that the connections between democracy, pluralism and religious freedom are vital and rely on three features. The first feature is a method of avoidance, which guarantees the state's neutrality towards comprehensive doctrines; the second is a principle of inclusion, which guarantees equality and fair terms of cooperation between religious and non-religious citizens; the third and last feature is a principle of revision, which guarantees that the terms of legitimate diversity are subject to constant review. I submit that the combination of these three features best safeguards religious freedom rights both in their negative (the right of non-interference) and positive (the right to participation) dimensions. The method of avoidance both unburdens the public sphere and protects religious citizens from undue state interference. The principles of inclusion and revision ensure that a generous approach to religious freedom rights is adopted, thus allowing religious and non-religious citizens fair participation in public debate on the one hand and a more informed public debate itself, open to self-revision, on the other.

The *principle of inclusion* postulates a generous conception of religious expression so that the voice of the minorities, the marginal and vulnerable members of society may be heard and contribute to the political debate. Remember that the rationale of public reason is not (merely) to unburden the public forum of controversial religious issues for the sake of political deliberation. The deeper rationale consists of protecting everyone's status as free and

---

[134] J Bohman and W Rehg, 'Jürgen Habermas' in EN Zalta (ed), *The Stanford Encyclopedia of Philosophy*, Spring 2007, at plato.stanford.edu/entries/habermas/.

[135] J Habermas, 'Some Further Clarifications of the Concept of Communicative Rationality' in M Cooke (ed), *On the Pragmatics of Communication* (Cambridge, MA, MIT Press, 1999).

[136] See, however, refuting the difficulty of translating religious arguments into public reasons, Habermas, 'Public Sphere' (n 131) 10.

equal citizens. The argument is that this deeper objective is best achieved by an unburdening of the public forum, through the constraints of public reason. If all controversies were to enter into the public forum, minorities' (religious) views would not be better represented. On the contrary, they would get lost, crushed by the comprehensive views of the majority. An unburdened political deliberation is more likely to give a voice to minorities. However, in line with this deeper objective of equality, I argue for an inclusive conception of religious liberties, one that is indeed faithful to this liberal aim of giving a voice to the marginalised. Simultaneously, the hope is that this inclusive approach to religious freedom will ensure that religious views will be a vital part of the non-political background culture on which political consensus relies and thereby help rethink the terms of legitimate diversity.

Here it is useful to emphasise that the background culture (and the religious views within it) influences the political conception, just as the political conception reciprocally has an influence on the background culture. The political conception of justice is autonomous – it can be justified by appeal to political values alone. Yet this free-standing status of the political conception does not mean that it belongs to a parallel world, one in which political and non-political values never meet. The *legitimacy* of the political conception may stand outside of comprehensive doctrines but its *content* is embedded and inserted, like a module,[137] into the different comprehensive doctrines. Religious freedom and political rights do not, therefore, evolve in isolation. There is some 'slippage' between people's comprehensive views and the political conception, which allows (religious) citizens to endorse the political conception as well as their other views.[138] In other words, the ideal of a shared public forum not only advances political aims, it also enables each of us to rethink and debate what constitute legitimate terms of cooperation. This constant reviewing, under what I call the principle of revision, prevents a freezing of individuals into their present state;[139] it preserves society's capacity to change and, in Harvard philosophy professor Roberto Unger's words, it guarantees our 'deep freedom'.[140]

---

[137] Rawls, *Political Liberalism* (n 87) 387, 12–13, 145.

[138] ibid, 60.

[139] JP Sartre, *Being and Nothingness: A Phenomenological Essay on Ontology* (New York, Washington Square Press, 1984) 347–61. See on this idea, M Iser, 'Recognition' in EN Zalta (ed), *The Stanford Encyclopedia of Philosophy* Fall 2013 at plato.stanford.edu/entries/recognition/.

[140] RM Unger, *The Religion of the Future* (Cambridge MA, Harvard University Press, 2014) 314. The concept of deep freedom refers to our capacity to change our society: 'Deep freedom is therefore freedom, grasped and realized through change of institutions and practices: not just through a one-time change but through a practice that can generate future, ongoing change in the institutional order of society. Deep freedom is thus also freedom as understood within the bounds of what I earlier described as the conception of a free society. The idea of deep freedom develops through an interplay between the conception of a free society and the institutional arrangements required to make that conception real. The conception informs the making of the institutional alternatives. The making of the alternative prompts us to enrich and revise the conception'.

### III. CONCLUSION TO CHAPTER 4

In this chapter, I have made the case for a democratic approach to religious freedom, one that embraces (religious) diversity and is supportive of a shared democratic framework. In the first section, I have shown why religious freedom matters for citizens – religious and non-religious alike. Religious freedom ensures that the liberal democratic framework is fully inclusive. To eradicate the concept of religious freedom in law would inevitably undermine the importance of religious commitments, religious identity and religious voices in our diverse democracies. Even if in practice equivalent underlying secular interests might protect (most) of the religious interests at stake in religious freedom claims, on a conceptual level the disaggregation of religion in law into underlying secular interests would necessarily entail a dilution of the value of religion in democracies. The concept of religious freedom conveys claims of equality and liberty but, as the ECtHR has reminded us: 'It is also, in its religious dimension, one of the most vital elements that go to make up the identity of believers and their conception of life'.[141] Importantly, as I have argued in section I, the abolition of this religious dimension would come at a cost for both religious citizens and non-religious citizens. In the ECtHR's words, the concept of religious freedom 'is also a precious asset for atheists, agnostics, sceptics and the unconcerned'.[142]

The second section has demonstrated why the liberal democratic framework, conversely, matters for the protection of religious freedom. Paradoxically, the constraints imposed by the liberal democratic framework have a liberating effect on religious freedom, as they guarantee in return a posture of non-interference from the state. More deeply, the liberal framework may be respectful of pluralism – not only for the pragmatic reason that should the state interfere with (religious) pluralism, the underlying diversity of views would unduly burden the political, but also because pluralism is, more positively, seen as beneficial and enriching for democracy. The public reason requirement, which protects the liberal framework by ensuring overall intelligibility and genuine communication of arguments in the political sphere, should, in that light, be construed sufficiently flexibly to allow religious voices to take part meaningfully.

In sum, in the *vivre ensemble* I propose, religious liberties are recognised fully, both as rights of non-interference as well as a positive good for democracy, but in return religious citizens (like any other) are expected to endorse the idea of liberal reciprocity. Whilst this endorsement of liberal reciprocity imposes restraint on religious freedom (notably through the requirement of public reason), I have argued that these constraints are liberating. Not only are they strategically welcome for encouraging more fluid and less burdened political deliberation but, counterintuitively, they also support the political contributions

---

[141] *Kokkinakis* (n 2) para 31.
[142] ibid.

of religious citizens – by allowing their voices to be heard, both in political debates and in the necessary underlying ongoing discussions about the terms of legitimacy of our liberal *vivre ensemble*. In this perspective, the right to religious freedom can therefore importantly be seen as a form of membership of a political community, a way of participating in (rather than opting out of) the political. It is in that sense that the concept of religious freedom may support an inclusive type three form of secularism, as defended in preceding chapters.

In the Part to follow, I will tease out practical implications of this democratic approach to religious freedom, through case studies of contemporary tensions of religious freedom and conflicting interests, with a focus on Britain and France.

# Part II

# Case Studies: The Mended Vivre Ensemble

A domain so-called, or a sphere of life, is not [...] something already given apart from political conceptions of justice. A domain [...] rather is simply the result [...] of how the principles of political justice are applied, directly to the basic structure and indirectly to the associations within it. The principles defining the equal basic liberties and opportunities of citizens always hold in and through all so-called domains.

John Rawls[1]

IN PART I of this book, I have made a case for a type of secularism which is consistent with democracy, one under which religious freedom would not only be protected against state interference, but pluralism and religious freedom valued as a positive good, susceptible of enriching political debate and contributing to society.[2] I have suggested that this democratic-reinforcing role of religious freedom and secularism is necessary to avoid the divisions and exclusions triggered by the competing dichotomous narratives, which, by contrast, draw the contours of secularism/national values/religious freedom on identitarian lines and thereby separate those 'within' and those 'outside'. To avoid this divisive approach, and its resulting broken *vivre ensemble*, I have submitted in Chapter 4 that the connections between democracy, pluralism and religious freedom are vital and rely on three features. The first feature is a method of avoidance, which guarantees the state's neutrality towards comprehensive doctrines; the second is a principle of inclusion, which guarantees equality and fair terms of cooperation between religious and non-religious citizens and, the third and final feature is a principle of revision, which guarantees that the terms of legitimate diversity are subject to constant review.[3] In Part II, I would like to confront this paradigm with concrete cases. This confrontation has two aims: to offer *one* understanding, amongst other possibilities, of acceptable concrete solutions for a mended *vivre ensemble*, respectful of both context

---

[1] J Rawls, 'The Idea of Public Reason Revisited' in S Freeman (ed), *Collected Papers* (Cambridge, MA, Harvard University Press, 1999) 573, 588–99.
[2] See Ch 4.
[3] See Ch 4.

(as analysed in Chapters 2 and 3) and paradigm (as defended in Chapter 4). The democratic paradigm is inherently indeterminate, in the sense that its precise substance depends on the contextual deliberations of democratic actors. It is therefore only through the analysis of case studies that one can propose possible concrete solutions in line with earlier chapters and thereby make theoretically-grounded normative proposals for change of some current outcomes in France and Britain.

Second, Part II will reveal a crucial implication of the democratic paradigm proposed in Part I. The principles of inclusion and revision defended in Chapter 4, which guarantee equality and fair terms of cooperation between religious and non-religious citizens and postulate constant revision of the terms of legitimacy, also imply that law does not assign pre-political meanings to certain spheres of life or domains of activity. If it did, as Rawls' above quote eloquently expresses, certain spheres would potentially be exempt from political principles of equality, fairness and revision. To tease out this important implication, the chosen case studies in Part II will focus on tensions raised in the particular domain of the workplace and commercial relationships for the provision of goods and services.

This domain is particularly relevant for my purposes because it is indeed sometimes conceived as a pre-political sphere.[4] Unlike the sphere of education, which is part and parcel of the constitutional arrangements on state and religion, and which I have therefore touched upon in Chapters 2 and 3,[5] the workplace seems to offer a more autonomous field of enquiry.[6] In England, the Church of England is not closely associated to the employment sector – unless naturally the Church itself acts as an employer. Similarly, in France, laïcité does not traditionally apply to the private sphere. In the French private sector of employment law, no constitutional requirements of neutrality will therefore restrict employees' freedom of religion a priori. More forcefully, some see the commercial sphere as standing at a distance not only from constitutional arrangements, but also from the political, a conception that Part II will challenge. The choice of the workplace and commercial relationships for the provision of services also relies on another more concrete justification. Presuming then, as I will demonstrate, that the employment sphere is not apart from the political, hence not immune from 'the principles defining the equal basic liberties and opportunities of citizens', the question arises as to how to balance conflicting individual claims to these principles. It is in the workplace and commercial area that the trickiest tensions

---

[4] See above.

[5] For an analysis of the importance of education in the conception of laïcité in the French IIIrd Republic see Ch 2; and for the interactions between education and laïcité in the headscarf affairs in the 1980s see Ch 2, section II.A). On the interaction between education, church establishment, autonomy and inclusion, see Ch 3.

[6] Constitutional considerations will, however, be at the forefront in France in cases that concern public agents, bound by constitutional neutrality duties, see below.

between clashing claims to these rights and opportunities have arisen and continue to arise. Religious requests will emanate from employees who wish the *vivre ensemble* of the workplace to be more amenable to their religious beliefs. Reciprocally, employers or service providers might also wish to request from their employees and customers that they adopt behaviour compatible with their own (religious) beliefs so that they may run their business in a way that concords with their convictions. Both employees and employers (or service providers) may therefore seek to obtain, on religious grounds, restrictions to the other party's competing rights. In an employment context, tensions will crystallise as a conflict of rights between employers and employees. The promotion of inclusion of (religious) employers may come at the cost of the inclusion of (other)/(non-)religious employees, and vice versa. This horizontal clash of fundamental rights, therefore, also makes the choice of the workplace particularly interesting for my purpose of ensuring an inclusive environment to religious citizens. It also provides an opportune terrain in which to test another underlying question of this chapter head on – namely, at what point does a request for an exemption based on religious beliefs turn into a request to opt out from the overarching framework? Finally, this context is one in which a flurry of norms intertwine, adding to the search for a mended *vivre ensemble* within a particular workplace, a national dimension as well as a European one – both in the context of the European Union and within the framework of the Council of Europe. The study of English and French employment law and occupation cases adds to the usual combination of divergent national legal traditions, within a common human rights framework, under the European Convention on Human Rights, another layer of norms and principles, stemming from EU Council Directive 2000/78/EC of 27 November 2000 Establishing a General Framework for Equal Treatment in Employment and Occupation (the Directive).

In Chapter 5, I will tease out important issues through the analysis of two recent rulings of the Court of Justice of the European Union (CJEU) on religious discrimination in the context of the Directive: *Asma Bougnaoui v Micropole SA*[7] and *Achbita, Centrum voor Gelijkheid van kansen en voor racismebestrijding v G4S Secure Solutions*.[8] These rulings yield several lessons for the concept of religious freedom and the role of the courts in adjudicating disputes in this field. Whilst underlining the useful input of the rulings and of their accompanying Advocate Generals' Opinions, Chapter 5 will highlight a few problematic aspects in light of the paradigm proposed in preceding chapters. In Chapter 6, I will confront the *Achbita* ruling with contemporary cases, with a focus on European Court of Human Rights (ECtHR) cases, to suggest

---

[7] Case C-188/15 *Asma Bougnaoui v Micropole SA*, Judgment of the Court (Grand Chamber) of 14 March 2017, available at eur-lex.europa.eu/legal-content/GA/TXT/?uri=CELEX:62015CJ0188.

[8] Case C-157/15 *Achbita, Centrum voor Gelijkheid van kansen en voor racismebestrijding v G4S Secure Solutions*, Judgment of the Court (Grand Chamber) of 14 March 2017, available at eur-lex.europa.eu/legal-content/EN/TXT/?uri=CELEX%3A62015CJ0157.

ways forward. The ECtHR faces similar dilemmas to those before the CJEU. On the one hand, the aim to advance respect for fundamental rights across Member States pushes towards a gradually convergent reading of the meanings and qualifications of the rights protected under the European Convention framework. On the other, the Court is aware that a degree of discretion or margin of appreciation must also be afforded to Member States, if the ECtHR is to avoid a backlash against its decisions and to genuinely claim respect for national constitutional and legal traditions. I will reveal how the ECtHR's case law offers valuable insights on how to approach these contradictory aims in ways respectful of the democratic paradigm.

# 5

# *Lessons from* Achbita

IN ITS CONCOMITANT *Asma Bougnaoui v Micropole SA*[1] and *Achbita, Centrum voor Gelijkheid van kansen en voor racismebestrijding v G4S Secure Solutions*[2] rulings, the Court of Justice of the European Union (CJEU) clarified the extent to which employers could restrict their employees' right to wear religious symbols in the workplace. The *Bougnaoui* case concerned a design engineer, Ms Bougnaoui, employed by a French private IT consulting company, Micropole. Following some complaints by Micropole's customers about Ms Bougnaoui's headscarf, she was asked to remove it on visits to customers, and after she had refused, she was eventually dismissed. In the *Achbita* case, the employee concerned was working in Belgium as a receptionist for a security company, G4S. She was asked to remove her headscarf, which infringed the company's neutrality policy, and when she refused, she was eventually dismissed. In the (apparent) absence of a neutrality policy in place in *Bougnaoui*, the CJEU ruled that the prohibition of the Islamic headscarf constituted direct discrimination, under Article 2(2)(a) of the Directive of Council Directive 2000/78/EC of 27 November 2000 establishing a general framework for equal treatment in employment and occupation (the Directive). By contrast, the prohibition of the Islamic headscarf by virtue of a neutrality policy in *Achbita* was characterised as justifiable indirect discrimination, under Article 2(2)(b) of the Directive.[3] Despite, as I will show, other contradictions between the two rulings, the distinction drawn between direct and indirect discrimination makes sense on the facts.[4] In *Bougnaoui*, the dismissal directly relied on the employee's religion (to which the wearing of the *hijab* must be assimilated) whereas in *Achbita*, the impact on the religious employee's rights resulted from a rule which, although neutral, put religious employees (and especially Muslim female employees) at a particular disadvantage. Whether the discrimination is characterised as direct or

---

[1] Case C-188/15 *Asma Bougnaoui v Micropole SA*, Judgment of the Court (Grand Chamber) of 14 March 2017, available at eur-lex.europa.eu/legal-content/GA/TXT/?uri=CELEX:62015CJ0188.

[2] Case C-157/15 *Achbita, Centrum voor Gelijkheid van kansen en voor racismebestrijding v G4S Secure Solutions*, Judgment of the Court (Grand Chamber) of 14 March 2017, available at eur-lex. europa.eu/legal-content/EN/TXT/?uri=CELEX%3A62015CJ0157.

[3] *Achbita* (n 2) para 30.

[4] See, however, critical, J Weiler, 'Je Suis Achbita' (2017) 28 *European Journal of International Law* 989, at 1005 ff; see also A Hambler, 'Neutrality and Workplace Restrictions on Headscarves and Religious Dress: Lessons from *Achbita* and *Bougnaoui*' (2018) 47(1) *Industrial Law Journal* 149, 160.

indirect, it may be justified. The justification test in case of direct discrimination is, however, more strict: a difference of treatment based on one of the protected characteristics may only be justified if it corresponds to a genuine and determining occupational requirement, under Article 4(1) of the Directive.[5] Justification of an indirectly discriminatory measure, on the other hand, is only subject to the requirements of legitimacy, proportionality and necessity under Article 2(2)(b)(i) of the Directive.

The French Court of cassation's preliminary reference specifically invited the Court in *Bougnaoui* to clarify whether customers' preferences could amount to 'a genuine and determining occupational requirement', under Article 4(1) of the Directive. The CJEU's response is unequivocal: 'the concept of a genuine and determining occupational requirement' must be construed objectively in light of the activities concerned and cannot include 'subjective considerations, such as the willingness of the employer to take account of the particular wishes of the customer'.[6] In its *Achbita v G4S Secure Solutions ruling*, the CJEU stated that 'an employer's desire to project an image of neutrality towards both its public and private sector customers is legitimate, notably where the only workers involved are those who come into contact with customers'. The Court thereby followed the Opinion of the Advocate General Kokott,[7] who had framed the legal issues of the case in the light of Article 16 of the Charter of Fundamental Rights (CFR) on the freedom to conduct a business.[8] In that light, the neutrality policy, even if designed for the sake of satisfying particular wishes of customers, would, in its inherent expression of an employers' right to conduct a business, constitute a prima facie legitimate aim justifying the indirect discrimination suffered as a result by a few employees,[9] provided that it was enforced proportionately.[10] As regards the legitimacy of the neutrality policy, the key factor according to the CJEU is whether the policy has genuinely been pursued in a 'consistent and systematic manner'.[11] As to the overall proportionality assessment, the Court grants a wide margin of appreciation to Member States, again following Advocate General Kokott who, in her Opinion, underlined the constitutional status of laïcité as a part of Belgian national identity. This constitutional laïque context would justify that 'the wearing of visible religious symbols may

---

[5] AG Kokott had argued that a company's dress code would normally fall within the employer's 'degree of discretion in the pursuit of its business' and therefore could constitute an occupational requirement within the meaning of Art 4(1) of the Directive, which allows for derogations to non-discrimination provisions in case of 'genuine and determining' occupational requirements.

[6] *Asma Bougnaoui v Micropole* (n 1) para 40.

[7] Opinion of AG Kokott, 31 May 2017, in Case C-157/15 *Achbita, Centrum voor gelijkheid van kansen en voor racismebestrijding v G4S Secure Solutions NV*, EU:C:2016:382 at para 81.

[8] *cf* describing this approach as 'surprising', M Bell, 'Leaving Religion at the Door? The European Court of Justice and Religious Symbols in the Workplace' (2017) 17 *Human Rights Law Review* 784, 786.

[9] Opinion of AG Kokott (n 7) para 84.

[10] Opinion of AG Kokott (n 7) para 141.

[11] *Achbita* (n 2) paras 40–41.

legitimately be subject to stricter restrictions (even in the private sector and generally in public spaces) than in other Member States'.[12] One crucial factor, which the Court nonetheless urges national courts to take into account in the proportionality test, is whether the employee enjoys a customer-facing role. To ensure that the policy meets the requirement of proportionality, the court thus states that the policy ought to be limited to those workers who interact with customers.[13]

This chapter will highlight the main implications of *Achbita*. In a first section, I will argue that the comparison of the rulings of *Achbita* and *Bougnaoui* reveals contradictions. Contrary to the approach in the *Bouganoui* ruling and in Advocate General Sharpston's Opinion, the *Achbita* ruling and Advocate General Kokott's Opinion seem to retreat to a reasoning in terms of pre-determined political spheres, which reduces the importance of the '*principles of political justice*' in the employment sector to a minimum. In a second section, I will analyse the implications of the *Achbita* minimalist approach for the concept of religious freedom and judicial proportionality tests. I will argue that the *Achbita* ruling risks undermining the democratic-enhancement potential of religious freedom and of courts as fora for adjudicating in this area.

## I. SPHERES OVER PRINCIPLES

In this section, I will argue that, in *Achbita*, the Court implicitly adopts a reasoning in terms of spheres of competence. It places the private sphere of contractual autonomy (which includes employment relationships) as the natural baseline of legal regulation and consequently constrains judicial intervention to a minimum (section A). It also defines the national constitutional sphere as the natural framework and consequently construes the application of general political principles of equality restrictively, in light of the alleged greater neutrality requirements which would apply in a constitutional laïque setting (section B). Overall, these spheres of contractual and constitutional autonomy thus implicitly call in *Achbita* for a particular deferential attitude of the court towards neutrality policies of employers. Whilst one can understand the predicament of the CJEU, which, as a supranational court of an EU framework initially designed for commercial purposes, fears excessive encroachment both upon rights to conduct business and upon national identities,[14] one might still be sceptical of the reasoning in terms of pre-political spheres that ensues.

---

[12] Opinion of AG Kokott (n 7) para 125.
[13] *Achbita* (n 2) para 42.
[14] See T Tridimas, *General Principles of EU Law*, 3rd edn (Oxford, Oxford University Press, 2019).

## A.  The Contractual Sphere: The Non-interventionist Ordoliberal Baseline Argument

Recall that in *Achbita*, the CJEU considers that the wishes of customers might justify a neutrality policy, itself largely sufficient to justify restrictions to the religious freedom of employees with open-facing jobs even though the Court was adamant, in the concomitant *Bougnaoui* ruling, that customers' wishes could not justify a direct discriminatory measure.[15]

### i. *Contradiction between* Bougnaoui *and* Achbita

In *Bougnaoui*, Advocate General Sharpston eloquently underlined the risks of the employer using his prerogatives to transfer into the workplace, through customers' preferences, the prejudices that exist in society at large:

> Where the customer's attitude may itself be indicative of prejudice based on one of the 'prohibited factors', such as religion, it seems to me particularly dangerous to excuse the employer from compliance with an equal treatment requirement in order to pander to that prejudice.[16]

In *Achbita*, the wearing of the *hijab, too*, was seen as a problem only because the employee was in constant contact with customers who might object to her wearing signs of religious affiliation. Yet, because these customers' objections had been anticipated and entrenched in a general company neutrality rule by G4S, customers' preferences and prejudices, dismissed in the *Bougnaoui* ruling, were suddenly relevant. The CJEU suggests that the discrimination suffered by the G4S employee ought to be held to be justified. In a sense, however, Micropole had been more amenable to religious employees than G4S. It had feared customers' objections but did not dismiss the employee until those fears had materialised. G4S on the other hand had prevented from the start any possibility of a reconciliatory position. Put together, the two CJEU rulings therefore seem contradictory. Customer preferences might have no say under Article 4(1) of the Directive to justify a measure which amounts to direct discrimination but they may justify a measure which only indirectly discriminates against employees on the ground of their religion under Article 2(2)(b). Given that the only element that separates a direct discrimination scenario (as in *Bougnaoui*) from an indirect discrimination situation (as in *Achbita*) is the existence of a unilateral neutrality company policy,[17] the protection offered by the Directive against prejudice and intolerance

---

[15] This section reiterates many of the points made in my blog, M Hunter-Henin, 'Lessons from the European Court's Hijab rulings', available www.ucl.ac.uk/european-institute/news/2017/apr/lessons-european-courts-hijab-rulings.

[16] Opinion of AG Sharpston, 13 July 2016 in Case C-188/15 *Asma Bougnaoui and Association de défense des droits de l'homme (ADDH) v Micropole SA*, para 133.

[17] See Hunter-Henin (n 15) and *Asma Bougnaoui v Micropole* (n 1) para 34.

seems easy to circumvent. If the Directive is to offer a work environment free of prejudice, it is not clear why the existence of a company policy should be sufficient to defeat that aim.

## ii. The Ordoliberal Inspiration of Achbita

As University College London EU law scholar Oliver Gerstenberg astutely suggests, the CJEU is perhaps expressing a quasi-natural private law expectation,[18] whereby the right to religious freedom would be qualified by an ordoliberalism framework, one in which economic liberties are immune from interferences, and the Constitution mainly serves to protect the autonomy and freedom of economic exchanges.[19] Should the law recognise autonomous prerogatives for employers, under the right to conduct a business, as entrenched in Article 16 CFR, the follow-up question is whether it should be entirely up to the employer to determine what measures this business autonomy requires, or whether the Court should intervene to assess whether the chosen measure indeed furthers legitimate commercial interests. A reasoning in terms of spheres of competence, inspired by an ordoliberal stance, leans towards affording the employer a right of self-determination. According to Advocate General Kokott, the neutrality policy imposed by G4S

> is essential not least to avoid the impression that external individuals might associate with G4S itself or with one of its customers, or even attribute to the latter, the political, philosophical or religious beliefs publicly expressed by an employee through her dress.[20]

While superficially, this statement seems to indicate a verification of the need for neutrality policies, it actually does not explain why a security company might have a commercial interest in projecting an image of neutrality towards religion. No objective reason can be put forward to explain how Ms Achbita's *hijab* might have undermined G4S's corporate image as a security expert or why an image of neutrality was desirable in the first place. The *Achbita* ruling is therefore evocative of ordoliberalism, in which the workplace appears as an autonomous sphere, subject to minimal judicial review.

## iii. The More Moderate Stance of French Law

Leaning in that direction, the 2016 *El Khomri* Act, which reformed French labour law, has allowed company neutrality rules across all sectors as a general

---

[18] O Gerstenberg, *Euroconstitutionalism and Its Discontents* (Oxford, Oxford University Press, 2018) 134.
[19] See F Hayek, 'The Economic Conditions of Inter-state Federalism', V, n 2 (1939) *New Commonwealth Quarterly* 131, reprinted in F Hayek, *Individualism and Economic Order* (Chicago, University of Chicago Press, 1947).
[20] 'Opinion of AG Kokott (n 7) para 95.

employer's business prerogative, whether they affect issues of internal govern-ance of the company or external relations with customers.[21] The 2016 Act resembles Advocate General Kokott's position in *Achbita*, which reasons as if the employer was in the position of the state and could expect, like the state, an attitude of restraint from employees to ensure that customers do not doubt the company's impartiality. The 2016 Law, however, is both broader and narrower. If the 2016 Law, unlike *Achbita*, does not refer to contact with customers as a potentially relevant factor in the proportionality assessment of the restriction to employee's religious freedoms,[22] it authorises French judges to step in should the restriction rely purely on subjective considerations and be unrelated to the needs of the workplace.[23] By requiring a verifiable objective rationale, the 2016 Act departs from an ordoliberal philosophy, which would grant employers rights to self-determination in the workplace. In contrast with this legislative compro-mise, a few authors, in France and Belgium, have put forward proposals which construe rights to conduct a business as encompassing the right to enforce a (secular) ethos throughout their company, with minimal judicial review.

### iv. Employer's Prerogatives and Secular Ethos

Various legal bases might support such a widening of employers' prerogatives in France (and Belgium). A few authors have suggested an extension of laïcité to the private sphere of employment,[24] later condemned by the French Cour de Cassation.[25] Others have relied upon Article 4(2) of the Directive,[26] even though the article has not been entrenched into French law,[27] to argue that employers ought to decide whether their company should convey a secular ethos. Under Article 4(2):

> Member States may maintain national legislation in force at the date of adoption of this Directive or provide for future legislation incorporating national practices existing at the date of adoption of this Directive pursuant to which, in the case of occupational activities within churches and other public or private organisations the ethos of which is based on religion or belief, a difference of treatment based on a

---

[21] LOI n° 2016-1088 du 8 août 2016 relative au travail, à la modernisation du dialogue social et à la sécurisation des parcours professionnels, JORF n°0184 du 9 août 2016.

[22] See above, Introduction n 13 and for a discussion of proportionality see below, section II.

[23] 'Art. L. 1321-2-1.-Le règlement intérieur peut contenir des dispositions inscrivant le principe de neutralité et restreignant la manifestation des convictions des salariés si ces restrictions sont justifiées par l'exercice d'autres libertés et droits fondamentaux ou par les nécessités du bon fonctionnement de l'entreprise et si elles sont proportionnées au but recherché'.

[24] On these proposals, see S Hennette and V Valentin, *L'affaire Baby Loup, ou la nouvelle laïcité* (Paris, LGDJ, 2014).

[25] See *Baby Loup* (n 47).

[26] See below.

[27] Article 4(2) is a clause which only allows Member States to entrench existing practices. Article 4(2) explicitly provides that Member States can only avail themselves of this possibility if they have passed legislation or had legislation in place to that effect at the time of adoption of the Directive. France has not passed any legislation for that purpose.

person's religion or belief shall not constitute discrimination where, by reason of the nature of these activities or of the context in which they are carried out, a person's religion or belief constitute a genuine, legitimate and justified occupational requirement, having regard to the organisation's ethos. This difference of treatment shall be implemented taking account of Member States' constitutional provisions and principles, as well as the general principles of Community law, and should not justify discrimination on another ground.

Provided that its provisions are otherwise complied with, this Directive shall thus not prejudice the right of churches and other public or private organisations, the ethos of which is based on religion or belief, acting in conformity with national constitutions and laws, to require individuals working for them to act in good faith and with loyalty to the organisation's ethos.

French Professor Vincent Valentin, a specialist of law and laïcité, argues that Article 4(2) should include companies seeking to promote a laïque ethos.[28] In Valentin's construction, companies such as G4S Securities in the *Achbita* case would be entitled to enforce its policy as a secular ethos. Indeed any company wanting to adopt neutrality policies would fall under this new reading of Article 4(2).[29] However, rather than grounding these policies in economic interests, as expressed in the right to project a corporate image (which would then justify behaviour internally in line with that chosen image) as in *Achbita*, the rationale in Valentin's scheme lies in the employer's internal governance powers, independent of any economic interests.[30] In Valentin's scheme, the internal governance powers thus absorb and colour commercial interests and external relation issues. Rather than broadening the scope of Article 4(2), professor Louis-Léon Christians of the University Catholic Leuven supports a similar outcome by challenging the pertinence of the specific exception carved out by Article 4(2). Christians thus argues that the distinction between ordinary companies and companies pursuing a specific ethos is no longer workable. As ethical and commercial interests are increasingly blurred,[31] the corporate image, more than a marketing instrument designed to project a message to customers, would embody the very identity of the company,[32] and the law should therefore

---

[28] V Valentin, 'La notion d'entreprise de conviction "laïque"' in B Callebats and others (eds), *Les Religions et le droit du travail. Regards croisés d'ici et d'ailleurs* (Bruylant, 2019) 271. On this notion of companies with a laïc ethos, see also F Gaudu, 'L'entreprise de tendance laïque' (2011) 12 *Droit Social* 1186; J Colonna and V Renaux-Personnic, 'Affaire *Baby Loup*: La Cour d'appel s'oppose à la Cour de cassation' (2014) 007 *Gazette du Palais* 22. By contrast, see against such 'relegation of laïcité as an ethos', F Dieu, 'L'affaire *Baby Loup*: quelles conséquences sur le principe de laïcité et l'obligation de neutralité religieuse?' (2014) *JCP A* 2114; J Mouly, 'L'affaire *Baby Loup* devant la Cour de renvoi : la revanche de la laïcité?' (2014) *Recueil Dalloz* 65; P Adam, 'Affaire *Baby Loup* : vues du sommet' (2014) *Revue du droit du travail* 607.

[29] Valentin, 'La notion d'entreprise de conviction "laïque"' (n 28) 174.

[30] Valentin refers to 'un choix d'organisation' (n 28) 278.

[31] See L-L Christians, 'Les mutations du concept d'entreprise de tendance. Essai de prospective juridique sur les futures entreprises post-séculières' in Callebats et al, *Les Religions et le droit du travail* (n 28) 253.

[32] See DF Flake, 'Image is Everything: Corporate Branding and Religious Accommodation in the Workplace' (2014) 163 *University of Pennsylvania Law Review* 699, 754.

recognise that all employers pursue a certain work ethos.[33] In Christians' scheme, it is thus the commercial interests and external relations powers of the employer that are stretched to include the prerogative to impose a secular ethos through neutrality clauses. Albeit loosely subjecting this power to external relations, *Achbita* is close to these proposals in that it also confers legitimacy, in principle, to decisions made by the employer in the sphere of the workplace.

> An employer's desire to project an image of neutrality towards both its public and private sector customers is legitimate, notably where the only workers involved are those who come into contact with customers.[34]

The *Bougnaoui* ruling, on the contrary, following Advocate General Sharpston's Opinion, prioritised fundamental principles over spheres:

> In the context of age discrimination, the Court has held that the principle of non-discrimination must be regarded as a general principle of EU law which has been given specific expression in the Directive in the domain of employment and occupation.[35] The same must apply as regards the principle of non-discrimination on grounds of religion or belief.[36]

Therefore, whereas the clashing rights appear in *Achbita* under an ordoliberal lens, favourable in principle to employers' prerogatives, the perspective in *Bouganoui* encourages a more careful scrutiny of competing rights. Such inconsistency between the *Achbita* and *Bougnaoui* rulings can hardly be resolved by an appeal to the particular deference owed to French and Belgium secularism.

## B. The National Sphere: Alleged Deference to the Constitutional Laïque Context

In *Achbita*, the Court's non-interventionist stance is also justified by reference to the laïque constitutional context of the case. The Court hereby follows Advocate General Kokott, who underlined that:

> In Member States such as France, where secularism has constitutional status and therefore plays an instrumental role in social cohesion too, the wearing of visible religious symbols may legitimately be subject to stricter restrictions (even in the private sector) and generally in public spaces, than in other Member States the constitutional provisions of which have a different or less distinct emphasis in this regard.[37]

Despite being acknowledged by commentators of the case as uncontroversial, I would like to stress here that this observation is paradoxical. Laïcité does not

---

[33] See Christians (n 31) 253.
[34] See text to n 7 above.
[35] See C-447/09 *Prigge and Others*, EU:C:2011:573, judgment of 13 September 2011, para 38.
[36] Opinion of AG Sharpston (n 16) 62.
[37] Opinion of AG Kokott (n 7) para 125.

apply in France in the private sector or public spaces unrelated to the state. This paragraph will demonstrate that the appeal to the concept of laïcité, far from marking a deferential attitude, takes sides in national debates and encourages a certain (controversial) trend towards an extensive reading of the concept.

### i. An Extension of Laïcité Requirements to the Purely Private Sphere

In France, in a purely private law context, laïcité and its resulting neutrality requirements do not apply.[38] The principle of laïcité only relates to the public sphere of employment, ie the sphere controlled by the state.[39] This sphere is extensively defined under French law: it will extend to public agents who have but a loose and temporary connection with the state and will cover private companies as long as they are entrusted with a mission of public service under the control of the state. Neutrality requirements will, under French law, consequently bind all employees working for a public law company or a private company in charge of a public service mission,[40] regardless of the status of the employee in question as civil servant, public agent or private law employee and independent of the tasks assigned to the employee concerned. In a 2013 decision, the Cour de cassation spelled out that the tasks assigned to the employee and her lack of contacts with customers did not have any bearing on the solution. The employee, a private law agent working for a CPAM (*Caisse d'assurance primaire maladie*), a Health National Insurance Centre, was required to refrain from wearing religious symbols at work, because her employer was fulfilling a mission of public service under the control of public authorities.[41] Similarly and a fortiori, public agents will always be tied by neutrality requirements because their employer, as a public body, will always fall on the public side of the divide.[42] It is easy to

---

[38] Under French law, restrictions may be imposed by the employer on employee's rights but, under Art L.1121-1 of the French Employment Code, only if they are justified by the particular task performed by the employee in question and if the restrictions are proportionate to that justification. Moreover, if the restrictions are directly or indirectly discriminatory, according to Art L.1321-3, incorporated by the French law of 27 May 2008, in pursuance of the Directive, restrictions of a discriminatory nature must be justified by an essential requirement and be proportionate to the goal sought (L.1321-3 of the Employment Code).

[39] Naturally, a wider definition of the public sphere may be opportune in other contexts. For example, the feminist critique has adopted a wider definition of the 'public' as a sphere, where power and authority are exercised (and are regarded as the natural province of men). See H Charlesworth, C Chinkin and S Wright, 'Feminist Approaches to International Law' (1991) 85 *American Journal of International Law* 613, 626. For my purposes, the relevant definition of the public sphere is the sphere controlled by the state.

[40] On the notion of public service mission, see M Hunter-Henin, 'Living together in an age of religious diversity: Lessons from Baby Loup and SAS' (2015) 4(1) *Oxford Journal of Law and Religion* 94.

[41] French National Health Insurance Centres are controlled by public authorities that have the power, should they see fit, to dissolve their board of administration: see CE 30 March 2005 *Union régionale des syndicats CFTC de la Réunion, Juris-data* n 264541.

[42] CE 28 June 1963 arrêt *Narcy, Grands arrêts de la jurisprudence administrative* 293 and CE 22 February 2007 arrêt *APREI (association du personnel relevant des établissements pour inadaptés), Grands arrêts de la jurisprudence administrative* 294.

imagine a scenario in which non-discrimination on the ground of religion, as provided for under the Directive, may thus conflict with the principle of laïcité and its ensuing neutrality requirements. One may thus query the weight that French law confers on the presence or absence of decision-making powers by public authorities in determining the extent of the religious freedom enjoyed by employees. From the point of view of the employee, the decisive character attributed to this factor may be difficult to apprehend, especially when a sudden change occurs in the control of the company. Should the structure of a company evolve over time to welcome the involvement of public authorities, French courts have confirmed that employees would then suddenly need to abide by strict religious neutrality requirements,[43] a solution possibly problematic under the Directive. However, in *Achbita* and *Bougnaoui* these considerations were not relevant, as public authorities were not in control.[44] Whether under Belgian or French law, laïcité was *not* applicable in the factual matrix of the *Achbita* case.

## ii. A Misplaced Deference to Laïcité

Had the Court in *Achbita* ruled in favour of the employee, it would not have clashed with laïcité. Private companies which serve the general interest but operate outside of the control of the state will not fall under the principle of laïcité, even if they receive substantial public funding.[45] A fortiori, purely private law endeavours such as those at stake in *Bougnaoui* and *Achbita*, which receive no financial state support and operate purely to serve commercial interests, lie totally outside of laïcité requirements. There was therefore no doubt that IT and security companies, such as those who employed Ms Bougnaoui and Ms Achbita, fell outside of the laïcité remit. If private citizens have been in the last ten years increasingly subjected to restrictions on their rights to manifest their religion in the French (and Belgian) public sphere, these legal developments have not relied on the concept of laïcité.[46] No particular deference, therefore,

---

[43] See for example, CE 6 April 2007 *Commune d'Aix-Marseille*, (2007) *Revue française de droit administratif* 812, conclusions by François Seners, which held that the change in the controlling bodies of an organisation carried a change in its nature.

[44] This conclusion is not undermined by the fact that G4S provided reception services for customers in both the public and private sectors. In both cases, control of the reception services provided remained within the control of G4S, a purely private company.

[45] According to the case law of the French Conseil d'Etat, a mission of public service requires an activity of general public interest carried out under the control of public authorities. Indirect control may be sufficient to meet the criteria but financial contribution alone – however substantial – will not: CE 28 June 1963 arrêt *Narcy*, *Grands arrêts de la jurisprudence administrative* 293 and CE 22 February 2007 arrêt *APREI* (*association du personnel relevant des établissements pour inadaptés*), *Grands arrêts de la jurisprudence administrative* 294.

[46] The special committee set up to consider the issue of the wearing of the full veil concluded that the concept of laïcité was not relevant to the issue and the government's text which led to the 2010 French legislative ban on the covering of the face in the public sphere did not rely on the notion. See M Hunter-Henin, 'Why the French Don't Like the *Burqa*: *Laïcité*, National Identity and Religious Freedom' (2012) 61 *International Comparative and Law Quarterly* 1.

was owed to constitutional laïque traditions in *Achbita*. In the purely private law *Baby Loup* case,[47] the dismissal of a private nursery employee who had refused to remove her *jilhab* was held legitimate and proportionate by the French Cour de cassation but only because ostentatious religious signs were construed as potentially harmful for children's freedom of conscience. However debatable the suggestion that the wearing of a religious sign could harm children might have been,[48] the rationale limited the scope of the legitimate restriction to the childcare sector. By contrast, the *Achbita* ruling applies to all employment sectors. By seemingly adopting a deferential approach, the CJEU is therefore giving support to the most virulent interpretations of secularism.

## C. Conclusion to Section I

In this section, I have criticised the reasoning, implicit in *Achbita*, whereby political principles of equality and opportunities should have less of a reach in certain spheres. I have argued that the notion that the commercial sphere would not only entitle employers to make policy decisions in the workplace but would also confer on the decisions made an a priori legitimacy reflects an ordoliberal interpretation of employment law. Such approach, I submit, is detrimental to democracy. Chapter 4 has made a case for a deepening democratic effect of the connections between pluralism and religious freedom and set out the conditions for such beneficial effect to occur. One of these, following a principle of inclusion, consists in giving a voice to the marginal and minority members of society. In practice, the principle of inclusion would therefore require that all competing interests are given a priori equal consideration and weight. On the contrary, the ordoliberal inspiration (arbitrarily) places commercial interests as the 'natural' baseline. In doing so, it inhibits democratic participation and dialogue by constructing rights to conduct business as rights to opt out from '*principles defining the equal basic liberties and opportunities of citizens*'. As a result, it muffles opposing interests and denies the possibility of a shared *vivre ensemble*. This ordoliberal critique of *Achbita* may require nuance, however. After all, if, as argued, *Achbita* (wrongly) considers that neutrality policies decided by the employer are *in principle* legitimate, it still leaves room for a proportionality test. In the section to follow, I will argue that the proportionality test that emerges from *Achbita* does not address the abovementioned democratic flaws, because it emphasises consistency over proportionality.

---

[47] Cass Ass Plén 25 June 2014 (2014) *Recueil Dalloz*, 1386, underlining the vulnerability of the nursery children with whom the applicant had contacts.
[48] See Hunter-Henin (n 46).

## II. CONSISTENCY OVER PROPORTIONALITY

In this section, I will compare the ECtHR decision of *Eweida v UK* and the CJEU *Achbita* ruling and suggest from the contrast that the guidelines issued in the *Achbita* ruling on how to carry out the proportionality test give insufficient importance to religious freedom. On 15 January 2013, the ECtHR released a decision on four cases concerning employees' religious freedom in England.[49] Two of the four cases (*Eweida* and *Chaplin*) involved employees' requests to wear religious signs in the workplace, whereas the other two (*Ladele* and *McFarlane*) related to employees' requests to be exempted on religious grounds from working with same-sex couples.

### A. Introductory: The *Eweida* Case

In the *Eweida* decision, Mrs Chaplin and Ms Eweida, respectively employed by a public hospital (Royal Devon and Exeter NHS Foundation Trust) and a private airline company (British Airways) had requested the right to wear a visible Christian cross over their uniform. In the other two cases included in the decision, Mr McFarlane, a counsellor for a private company, Relate, and Ms Ladele, a registrar in Islington, had requested exemptions to avoid counselling same-sex couples or celebrating same-sex unions. In all of the four cases, the ECtHR held that the applicants had suffered an interference with their right to religious freedom, protected under Article 9(1) of the European Convention on Human Rights (ECHR) but in three out of four of the cases, the Court held that this interference was legitimate and proportionate, under Article 9(2). In respect of Mr MacFarlane and Ms Ladele, the Court considered that the employer was entitled to deny their request for exemption in order to protect competing equality rights of same-sex couples and that the interference was proportionate to that aim. As regards Ms Chaplin's claim, the Court held that her employer's refusal pursued the legitimate aim of protecting the health and safety of patients whose wounds might come into contact with the cross and get infected or who might grab the cross and injure themselves or others with it. The refusal by British Airways to allow Ms Eweida to wear a cross similarly pursued a legitimate aim, held the Court – the aim of protecting the company's corporate image – but unlike the other three cases, the Court, in *Eweida*, ruled that the restriction imposed as a result on Ms Eweida's religious freedom rights had been disproportionately enforced. Several factors pointed, according to the Court,

---

[49] For an analysis (in French) of the impact of the decision on English law, see M Hunter-Henin, 'Impact de l'arrêt *Eweida* de la Cour européenne des droits de l'homme sur le droit anglais' in B Callebat and others (eds), *Les Religions et le droit du travail. Regards croisés, d'ici et d'ailleurs* (Brussels, Bruylant, 2018) 281.

to a conclusion of disproportionality in *Eweida*: the cross which Ms Eweida wished to wear was discreet; other employees had been allowed to wear religious signs, such as Sikh turbans and Muslim *hijabs*, provided that they respected the company's colour scheme and, finally, British Airways had ultimately changed its company dress code and allowed crosses and other religiously connoted jewellery. In the *Eweida* case itself, the employee's right to wear a visible Christian cross over her uniform thus ultimately outweighed the airline company's right to decide on the corporate image.[50] The outcome contrasts with the *Achbita* ruling in which the employee's request to wear a Muslim *hijab* was denied because it clashed with the employer's commercial interests, as entrenched in a company neutrality policy.

Regardless of and beyond this difference in outcome, the ECtHR's decision in *Eweida* arguably better acknowledges the importance of religious freedom in the workplace. Its starting point is to underline the value of religious freedom and their manifestation in the workplace:

> Given the importance in a democratic society of freedom of religion, the Court considers that, where an individual complains of a restriction on freedom of religion in the workplace, rather than holding that the possibility of changing job would negate any interference with the right, the better approach would be to weigh that possibility in the overall balance when considering whether or not the restriction was proportionate.[51]

Consequently, the onus weighs on the employer to establish that restrictions to religious freedom pursue a legitimate aim and are proportionate to that aim.

By contrast, by emphasising consistency over proportionality, Advocate General Kokott's Opinion in the *Achbita* ruling also places on religious employees the duty to justify any change in their religious practice:

> We should not rush into making the sweeping assertion that such a measure makes it unduly difficult for Muslim women to integrate into work and society. Ms Achbita's case in particular makes this readily apparent. Ms Achbita worked as a receptionist for G4S for approximately three years without wearing an Islamic headscarf at work and was thus fully integrated into working life as a Muslim woman, despite the headscarf ban. It was not until after more than three years of working for G4S that she insisted on being allowed to come to work in a headscarf and, as a result, lost her job.[52]

The consistency argument, I will argue, unduly burdens religious employees (section B) whilst unduly reducing the review of employers' restrictive decisions to a mainly procedural test (section C).

---

[50] *Eweida and Others v the United Kingdom* App no 48420/10 (ECtHR 2013) para 95.
[51] *Eweida* (n 50) para 83.
[52] Opinion of AG Kokott (n 7) para 124.

## B. Burdens of the Consistency Argument for Religious Employees' Claims

In his powerful editorial on *Achbita*, New York University EU law professor Joseph Weiler[53] notes that 'the comparison between *Eweida* and *Achbita* is nothing less than embarrassing'. As Weiler elaborates, there is, in *Eweida*, an acknowledgment of the competing rights. In *Achbita*, the acknowledgment is far more ambiguous. I submit that this ambiguity can be traced back to an emphasis on consistency over proportionality.[54] In relation to the framing of the religious freedom claim itself, this insistence on consistency imposes on religious employees a requirement to justify any changes in their religious practice. The fact that Ms Achbita had not for over three years felt the need to wear a headscarf seems to be held against her, or at least to warrant further exploration. The presumption seems to be that, subject to satisfactory explanation, this change in attire is capricious and wrongly betrays the employer's legitimate expectations. The reasoning is reminiscent of the (then) House of Lords' decision in the *Begum case*,[55] which held that a school was entitled to deny the request of a school pupil to derogate from the school uniform policy because, amongst other reasons, there had been inconsistencies in the pupil's behaviour. The pupil had for two years agreed to abide by the school uniform rules without any complaints before suddenly requesting the right to wear a less revealing form of uniform. Rather than assuming that the student's change of mind was somewhat fickle, one could have argued that Miss Begum's change of mind about the proper form of dress to wear coincided with her reaching puberty.[56] In adulthood, it is also common for women to change their religious attire once they get married,[57] or become mothers.[58] Suggesting, as Advocate General Kokkot does, that religious employees need to justify a change in their behaviour is, I submit, problematic. Naturally, courts cannot just accept any employees' claim at face value. It is legitimate to require the beliefs invoked to reach a certain threshold, 'a certain level of cogency'.[59] In that assessment, consistency may seem a useful criterion by which to establish the sincerity and cogency of the claim.[60]

### i. Consistency as Proof of Sincerity and Cogency: A Dangerous Criterion

English courts have held in R *(Williamson and Others) v Secretary of State for Education and Employment and Others* that 'The [religious] belief must relate

---

[53] Weiler, 'Je Suis Achbita' (n 4) 991.

[54] This is not the reason given by Weiler, who develops another line of argumentation based on a failure of the CJEU to properly distinguish between religious manifestation and religious practice.

[55] R *(Begum) v Governors of Denbigh High School* [2006] UKHL 15, at para 7.

[56] M Malik, 'Religious Freedom and Multiculturalism. R *(Shabina Begum) v Denbigh High School*' (2008) 19(2) *King's Law Journal* 377.

[57] See Weiler, 'Je Suis Achbita' (n 4), referring to the Jewish Hassidic community, in which women cover their hair once they are married.

[58] See, for an illustration, the facts of the *Baby Loup* case.

[59] *Campbell and Cosans v United Kingdom* (1982) 4 EHRR 1.

[60] See A Hambler, 'Establishing sincerity in religion and belief claims: a question of consistency' (2011) 13 *Ecclesiastical Law Journal* 146.

to matters more than merely trivial. It must possess an adequate degree of seriousness and importance … it must be a belief on a fundamental problem'.[61] In other words, not all claims will necessarily fall under the category of protected beliefs for the mere reason that the employee asserts that they rely on religious grounds. Let us take the English case of *Khan v Vignette Europe Ltd* as an illustration.[62] In that case, Mr Khan, a Muslim telemarketing employee who had been dismissed by his employer for having downloaded pornographic material on his work computer, had belatedly requested an adjournment of the court hearing on his case for religious reasons. After two requests of adjournment for other reasons had been denied, Mr Khan claimed that he wished to 'enjoy a period of mental and spiritual purity' during Ramadan,[63] which might be compromised by the pornographic material integral to the facts of the case. In that case, the English courts could arguably have held that the claim that his alleged religious reluctance to be confronted with pornographic material stood in contradiction with his recent interest in pornography.[64] Similarly, courts may question the sincerity of a claim where religious beliefs are suddenly invoked to obtain an advantage from the employer (such as an extra day off) in the absence of any other signs of religious commitments.

The consistency argument as a factor for establishing the sincerity of the employee's claim should, however, be used parsimoniously and cautiously. Should courts scrutinise employees' behaviour in order to determine whether they are faithful to religious tenets in all respects, they would venture into discussion of religious scholastics for which they are ill-equipped, and indirectly limit protection to orthodox religious readings. The consistency argument must also take into account the fact that in their lives, people live their religious faith with more or less intensity. Even the facts of the *Khan* case in that respect could warrant a generous interpretation for the claimant. If indeed the applicant behaved differently in times of special religious significance, his behaviour in ordinary times would prove nothing, however inconsistent with his claim. People may, moreover, change their religious practice as they grow older, depending on their evolving personal circumstances. Advocate General Sharpston was very sensitive to this time dimension of religious practice and observance.[65]

---

[61] [2005] UKHL 15, at para 23, per Lord Nicholls.

[62] [2010] UKEAT 0134/09/1401 (14 January 2010).

[63] ibid at para 38. On the case, see A Hambler, 'Khan v Vignette Europe Ltd' (2010) 164 *Law and Justice* 103.

[64] Instead, the courts (Employment Tribunal and Employment Appeal Tribunal) held that the beliefs were protected but on the facts were outweighed by the employer's interests.

[65] Opinion of AG Sharpston (n 16) para 29, 'It is often (perhaps, generally) the case that not all of a particular religion's compendium of religious practice is perceived by someone who adheres to that religion as absolutely "core" to his or her own religious observance. Religious observance comes in varying forms and varying intensities. What a particular person treats as essential to his or her religious observance may also vary over time. That is because it is relatively usual for levels of personal belief, and hence of personal observance associated with that belief, to evolve as a person passes through life. Some become less observant over time; others, more so. Amongst those who do adhere to a particular faith, the level of religious observance may likewise fluctuate over the course of the religious year. An enhanced level of observance – which the practitioner may feel it appropriate to

Hinting, on the contrary, that change is in itself a reason to doubt the sincerity of the claim or to afford it less weight in the proportionality exercise would prompt state courts to unduly interfere with the assessment of the legitimacy of religious beliefs. The ECtHR has asserted many times that it is not up to Member States to assess the legitimacy of particular religious beliefs.[66] If change matters in *Achbita*, it may be again because the contractual framework appears to be the matrix in which to assess each party's respective rights. In that contractual perspective, unilateral changes of behaviour are indeed unreasonable per se, as they defeat the expectations created by the initial agreement between the parties. However, the ECtHR rejected this contractual framing of religious freedom in *Eweida* precisely because it undermines (and potentially eliminates) the importance of religious convictions, by allowing employees to consent to leave them outside of the workplace.

## ii. The 'Contracting Out' Approach

In the past, following the so-called 'contracting out' or 'specific situation rule' approach, English courts had suggested that employees could be deemed to have contracted their religious rights out of the workplace, either by agreeing to explicit contrary requirements in their contract of employment, or, implicitly, by subjecting themselves to workplace regulations and policies.[67] The justification of this approach relied upon the consent given by the employee to the restriction as well as the possibility, should the employee wish to change her mind, to resign and change jobs.[68] In *Eweida*, the ECtHR clearly condemns such reasoning.[69] Similarly, Advocate General Sharpston underlined that religious requirements cannot be politely discarded during working hours.[70] By contrast, the notion of consent still seems to lie at the heart of the *Achbita* ruling. Consent (and choice) even imbue the apprehension of religious manifestation itself. The emphasis on employer's rights in the Advocate General's Opinion seems, *in fine*, to rely on the idea that manifestation of religion is a matter of choice, rather than identity.[71] As such, employees' rights to manifest their religious faith are

---

manifest in a variety of ways – may therefore be associated with particular points in the religious year, whilst a "lesser" observance may seem adequate to the same person at other times'.

[66] See *Hassan and Tchaouch v Bulgaria* App no 30985/96 (ECtHR Grand Chamber, 26 October 2000) para 78.

[67] See European Commission's decision in *Ahmad v United Kingdom* (1982) 4 EHRR 126 App no 8160/78 (ECmHR, 1 March 1981).

[68] See *Stedman v United Kingdom* App no 29107/95 (ECmHR, 9 April 1997), in which the right to resign was held to be a sufficient guarantee, even in the absence of consent to the restriction.

[69] See the quotation in fn 63 (para 83).

[70] Opinion of AG Sharpston (n 16) para 118.

[71] On this issue of characterisation of religion as a matter of 'choice' or 'identity', see also PW Edge, 'Religious rights and choice under the European Convention on Human Rights' (2000) 3 *Web JCLI*; I Solanke, *Discrimination as Stigma: A Theory of Discrimination Law* (Oxford, Hart Publishing, 2016) Ch 2 and A Hambler, *Religious Expression in the Workplace and the Contested Role of Law* (Abingdon, Routledge, 2015) 63–67.

deemed to be intrinsically easier to amend and curtail than employers' competing interests.

> Unlike sex, skin colour, ethnic origin, sexual orientation, age or a person's disability,
> the practice of religion is not so much an unalterable fact as an aspect of an individ-
> ual's private life, and one, moreover, over which the employees concerned can choose
> to exert an influence. While an employee cannot 'leave' his sex, skin colour, ethnicity,
> sexual orientation, age or disability 'at the door' upon entering his employer's prem-
> ises, he may be expected to moderate the exercise of his religion in the workplace,
> be this in relation to religious practices, religiously motivated behaviour or (as in the
> present case) his clothing.[72]

Such a view of religious freedom also has an inhibitive effect on the proportionality test. In the paragraphs that follow, I will indeed demonstrate how the
guidelines issued in *Achbita* tend to mainly reduce the proportionality test to a
verification of procedural consistency, which unduly favours the employer.

## C. Proportionality Test Reduced Mainly to Procedural Consistency

Having dealt (wrongly, as I have argued)[73] with the issue of the legitimacy of the
neutrality policy and the importance to be conferred to the employee's conflicting claim to religious freedom, the Court still had to carry out a proportionality
test.[74] Under the proportionality test, the Court, any court, would be expected
as Weiler aptly puts it:

> to articulate why the values embedded and reflected in the legitimate purpose of the
> measure necessary to achieve such legitimate purpose outweigh the values embed-
> ded and reflected in the protected liberty which is affected and compromised by that
> measure. It is the ensuing balance that defines the hierarchy of values by which our
> societies wish to define themselves and, indeed, are often a marker of normative
> differences among such.[75]

Let us then consider whether the divergence between *Eweida* and *Achbita* might,
to an extent, rely on factual considerations, rather than on a differing evaluation
of these values.

### i. Factual Divergence between Eweida and Achbita

As pointed out by Advocate General Kokott,[76] the *hijab*, which Ms Achbita
wished to wear, was more conspicuous than the cross at the centre of the *Eweida*

---

[72] Opinion of AG Sharpston (n 16) para 116.

[73] See section II.B above, in relation to the neutrality policy and section II.A above, in relation to
the employee's claim.

[74] For a discussion of religious discrimination and religious freedom claims in England and
proportionality requirements, see L Vickers, *Religious Freedom, Religious Discrimination and the
Workplace*, 2nd edn (Oxford, Hart Publishing, 2016) Ch 3.

[75] Weiler, 'Je Suis Achbita' (n 4) 996.

[76] Opinion of AG Kokott (n 7) para 118.

dispute, which the ECtHR described as 'discreet'. Moreover, British Airways had not applied its dress code consistently, since it had allowed other religious clothing, such as the turban and *hijab*.[77] These two considerations enable Advocate General Kokott to distinguish the facts of *Achbita* from those of *Eweida* and suggest that the conclusion of disproportionality reached in *Eweida* might not be transferable to the facts of *Achbita*.

> In its judgment in *Eweida*, the ECtHR considers there to have been a violation of Article 9 ECHR not least because the undertaking concerned had previously permitted, or at least tolerated, the wearing of visible religious symbols by individual employees.[78]

### ii. Critical Analysis of the Proportionality Considerations in Achbita

Whilst the requirement of consistency in the enforcement of a restriction between various religious groups is an important consideration, it seems here to become the main consideration so that a policy neutrality requirement may be deemed proportionate, provided it is enforced neutrally. Two further considerations underlined by Advocate General Kokott, however, could potentially reverse such conclusion: should the neutrality policy restrict a discreet symbol or the rights of an employee who has no contact with customers,[79] national courts might then still well decide that the infringement caused to religious freedom is disproportionate. These two considerations are themselves problematic, however. The reference to the size of the symbol risks burdening certain religions more heavily than others. As Advocate General Sharpston warned, 'it is difficult to conceive how a male Sikh could be discreet or inconspicuous in his observance of the requirement to wear a dastar. He either wears the turban mandated by his religion or he does not'.[80] Moreover, it stumbles on the same criticism as the consistency argument: it encourages courts to assess the legitimacy of particular religious beliefs. Indeed, if courts are to a priori treat more favourably discreet symbols, they will tend indirectly to hold that moderate forms of religious expression are intrinsically more legitimate than ostentatious ones. A small scarf will thus be more acceptable than a *hijab*, which covers the head and neck and a fortiori, than a *jilhab*, which covers the whole body, except for the hands and face, or the *burqa* or *niqab*, which also cover the face. This does not mean that the conspicuous nature of a symbol can never be relevant. The more ostentatious, the more likely it is for example to interfere with the performance of the employee's duties and with other legitimate interests. However, the conspicuous nature of a religious symbol should not by itself be sufficient

---

[77] *Eweida* (n 50) para 94.
[78] Opinion of AG Kokott (n 7) para 103.
[79] *Achbita* (n 2), paras 37–38.
[80] Opinion of AG Sharpston (n 16) para 33.

to establish that the request to wear it is disproportionate. The same reasoning in my view applies to the argument of contact with customers. The mere fact that the employee has a customer-facing role should not be sufficient to establish the proportionality of the restriction of her religious freedoms; otherwise, as argued above, the court would open the door for customers' prejudices to dictate employees' rights (and obligations) in the workplace.

## D. Conclusion to Section II

In this section, I have highlighted two obstacles raised in *Achbita* to a thorough balancing of competing interests between employees' religious freedom and employers' commercial prerogatives. One is the way that religious freedoms are assessed through the prism of choice/contract and consent. As a result, they seem more malleable and adjustable than commercial interests, hence intrinsically carry less weight in the proportionality test than the competing interests of the employer. This approach, I submit, unduly introduces a hierarchy in favour of business rights.[81] The other obstacle, in *Achbita*, to a thorough proportionality test is the fact that beyond the procedural requirement of a consistent enforcement and neutral phrasing of the policy, the court does not require the employer to justify objectively why and to what extent the restrictions to religious freedom might be necessary. Naturally, the court in *Achbita* was only issuing guidelines for national courts. Besides, the EU Directive only sets minimum standards, leaving Member States free to increase the level of protection should they see fit. In a situation of clashing rights, increasing the level of protection of the rights of one party will have an impact on the conflicting rights of the other, however, so it is not entirely clear how this concept of increased protection might play out.[82] Moreover, as argued in this section, the very placing of religious freedom under a contractual lens risks minimising the importance of religious manifestation in the workplace. This uncertainty explains why, following the *Achbita* ruling, the UK government felt the need to offer prompt reassurance that the ruling would not affect the more robust protection currently offered in the UK to religious employees.[83]

---

[81] For a discussion on an emerging hierarchy, against religious freedom, but in the context of a clash between religious freedom and right to equality, compare L Vickers, 'Religious Discrimination in the Workplace: An Emerging Hierarchy?' (2010) 12 *Ecclesiastical Law Journal* 280; A McColgan, 'Class Wars? Religion and (In)equality in the Workplace' (2009) 38(1) *Industrial Law Journal* 1.

[82] See E Spaventa, 'Fundamental Rights Protection in the EU Composite Constitutional system' (2018) 55 *Common Market Law Review* 997.

[83] HC Deb 15 March 2017, vol 623, col 415 (Caroline Dinenage MP, Minister for Women and Equalities). For further discussion, see F Cranmer, 'Urgent Commons Question on CJEU Rulings in *Achbita* and *Bougnaoui*', *Law & Religion UK*, 15 March 2017, www.lawandreligionuk. com/2017/03/15/urgent-commons-question-on-cjeu-rulings-in-achbita-and-bougnaoui/.

### III. CONCLUSION TO CHAPTER 5

The recitals of Directive 2000/78 declare that 'Employment and occupation are key elements in guaranteeing equal opportunities for all and contribute strongly to the full participation of citizens in economic, cultural and social life and to realising their potential'. The Directive is thereby respectful of Rawls' statement: 'The principles defining the equal basic liberties and opportunities of citizens always hold in and through all so-called domains'. The workplace under the Directive is not a sphere immune from political principles but, on the contrary, a democratic space, that is, a space where the basic principles necessary for a democratic society need to flourish. As argued in preceding chapters, amongst these basic principles, a principle of inclusion is featured. Whilst the exact content of legal solutions depends on contextual deliberations and cannot therefore be defined in the abstract or set in stone, it is possible to exclude some – those that betray the principle of inclusion. This chapter has suggested that a few aspects contained in the *Achbita* ruling are problematic in that respect. Section I has argued that the ordoliberal inspiration underlying the reasoning of the Court in *Achbita* sets the sphere of employment aside and undermines the political principle of inclusion and the general goal of non-discrimination set out under the Directive. The same holds for the misplaced deference to the laïque constitutional context. Whilst one may understand that the Court is eager to grant consideration both to commercial interests and national constitutional traditions, carving out spheres of a priori competence to employers and national authorities – as it does – unduly undermines conflicting interests and blocks self-revision. As section II has demonstrated, such a starting point then inhibits the proportionality test in two ways: it frames religious freedom as a matter of choice and thereby implicitly puts more of the onus of adaptation onto the religious employee; and it dilutes the justificatory burden that weighs upon the employer.

Overall this chapter has, therefore, drawn a few (negative) lessons from *Achbita*. In light of the paradigm defended in earlier chapters, *Achbita* fails in two respects. Instead of reinforcing the democratic value of religious freedom, it legitimises a priori the possible exclusion of religious voices from the workplace. Instead of ensuring that the terms of legitimacy are constantly open to review and discussion, it limits dialogue. By restricting the balancing of competing interests through pre-determined political spheres, which evolve in parallel and separately from one another, each sphere risks closing itself to the others. Having thus outlined the negatives, I will seek in the chapter that follows possible concrete ways forward.

# 6

# *Beyond* Achbita: *Possible Ways Forward*

I N THE PRECEDING chapter, I have identified ways of adjudicating religious freedom requests in the workplace, which are not compatible with the democratic paradigm advocated for in earlier chapters. More precisely, Chapter 5 has demonstrated that compatibility with the principles of revision and inclusion promoted in Chapter 4 in order to foster a goal of enriching pluralism entails that the workplace and commercial relationships should not be immune from political principles. To ensure that the commercial and employment domains are not cut off from the political, the preceding chapter has highlighted the following three pitfalls. First, courts should refrain from treating the commercial and employment sphere as if it were a pre-political domain, a sphere of competence in its own right. Second and similarly, supranational courts should not grant Member States unfettered discretion. Third, and more generally, courts should avoid closing down the dialogue by muffling voices on one side of the debate. Chapter 5 has amply underlined the negative implications and, more broadly and fundamentally, the democratic deficit of a reasoning based on the above flaws. This chapter, more positively, will now seek to propose suggestions for alternative ways forward. In this chapter focused on case law, I will underline the role of courts in producing these outcomes and, thereby, in contributing to the enforcement of the principle of legitimacy. As discussed in Chapter 4, the principle of legitimacy, following late American philosopher John Rawls, guides the exercise of political power in 'accordance with a constitution the essentials of which all citizens as free and equal may reasonably be expected to endorse in the light of principles and ideals acceptable to their common human reason'.[1] This chapter will show that courts have a role in that process, as they remind actors of these shared fundamental principles, reasonably acceptable to all. They thus provide a framework for balancing conflicting claims.

From the preceding chapter, two main methodological negative lessons have emerged: courts should avoid excessive deference towards national authorities on the one hand, and a minimalist procedural proportionality review on the other. In this chapter, I will draw from contemporary cases possible guidelines on what measured deference towards national Member States and a stricter

---

[1] J Rawls, *Political Liberalism*, 2nd edn (New York, Columbia University Press, 1996) p 137.

proportionality test might look like. Section I will distinguish between excessive deference (which amounts to delegation of decision and curtails dialogue) and legitimate consideration of national constitutional traditions (which leaves dialogue open). Contrary to the assumed uniformity of reference to laïcité in *Achbita* with an earlier European Court of Human Rights (ECtHR) decision in *Ebrahimian v France*,[2] I will draw on a detailed comparison between the two cases to suggest that the reasoning adopted by the ECtHR in that respect is preferable. Section II will then draw on a comparison between *Achbita* and two other more recent rulings of the Court of Justice of the European Union (CJEU) on religious employers, in *Egenberger*[3] and *IR v JQ*,[4] to argue that to avoid undue deference towards the employer's assessment of the facts, the court should require objective considerations, specifically related to the tasks assigned to the employee in question. Section III, finally, will open up to US debates to discuss, in comparison with European developments, the extent to which there may be room for religious requests by service providers and employees, which clash with equality rights.

The goal of this chapter is thus to offer suggestions for possible outcomes to recent cases which would be in line with the democratic paradigm proposed in Part I, ones that would be mindful of context, open to revision and inclusive of minority marginal voices, and thereby allow pluralism and religious diversity to have a democratic-deepening effect.

## I. LAÏCITE: DEFERENCE RATHER THAN DELEGATION

In *Ebrahimian v France*, an employee had been working under a temporary contract as a social assistant in the psychiatric wing of a public hospital in the north of Paris. Following her refusal to remove her headband,[5] she was eventually dismissed. The French courts upheld the decision. According to French courts, the employer's request was legitimate, on the basis of the neutrality requirements, which bind public agents and the chosen sanction – dismissal – despite being the most serious disciplinary sanction available, was proportionate because of the vulnerability of the members of the public involved.[6] The ECtHR

---

[2] *Ebrahimian v France* App no 64846/11 (ECtHR Fifth Section, 26 November 2015).

[3] Case C-414/16 *Vera Egenberger v Evangelisches Werk für Diakonie und Entwicklung*, Judgment of the Court (Grand Chamber) of 17 April 2018, ECLI:EU:C:2018:257, available at eur-lex.europa.eu/legal-content/EN/TXT/?uri=CELEX%3A62016CJ0414.

[4] Case C-68/17 *IR v JQ*, Judgment of the Court (Grand Chamber) of 11 September 2018, ECLI:EU:C:2018:696, available at curia.europa.eu/juris/document/document.jsf?text=&docid=205521&pageIndex=0&doclang=EN&mode=lst&dir=&occ=first&part=1&cid=10157040.

[5] Even though the dispute in court places the principle of neutrality in opposition to the employee's right to wear un 'voile' (which does not translate as 'veil' but as 'headscarf'), the fact summary refers to a 'coiffe', namely a more discreet band or hat covering the hair.

[6] The administrative tribunal had underlined the vulnerability of patients and held that neutrality requirements were all the more necessary given the contacts between the applicant and patients in a state of vulnerability and fragility. See *Ebrahimian v France* (n 2) para 61.

held that the dismissal amounted to an interference with the employee's rights under Article 9(1) of the European Convention on Human Rights (ECHR) but that the interference pursued a legitimate aim, namely the 'protection of the rights and freedoms of others', and was proportionate to that aim, under Article 9(2) of the Convention. Consequently, the majority of the ECtHR held that there had been no violation of Convention rights. Whilst recalling the criticisms, which this ECtHR's decision has provoked, I will add a more approving note. In section A, I will analyse why the deference displayed by the ECtHR in *Ebrahimian* has (rightly) raised concerns. In section B, I will argue that nonetheless, the deference of the ECtHR in *Ebrahimian* – albeit extensive – may, contrary to the deference displayed in *Achbita*, be compatible with the democratic paradigm I have advocated.

## A. *Ebrahimian*: An Extensive Deference to Laïcité

In *Ebrahimian*, French courts (following an initial sanction for procedural irregularity of the dismissal process)[7] upheld the employer's dismissal decision on two grounds. First, they relied on the particular duties of neutrality, which are incumbent on public agents in France for the sake of the constitutional principle of laïcité,[8] as construed by the Conseil d'Etat in its 2000 opinion in *Demoiselle Marteaux*[9] and since then, as explicitly entrenched under a 2016 Law on the Deontology, Rights and Duties of Public Agents.[10] Second, the French courts noted that the wearing of the headscarf had triggered complaints by patients, and hence had disturbed the harmony of the department.[11] Several arguments militated against the application of neutrality duties in this case however. First, it was not clear whether the opinion of the Conseil d'Etat offered at the time a sufficiently well-established principle to make the risk of dismissal foreseeable and constituted a solid legal basis for the dismissal decision.[12] Second, beyond this issue of timing, the extension of neutrality principles to all public agents, albeit in line with the Conseil d'Etat's opinion and consistent with a subsequent

---

[7] By virtue of a decision of the Administrative Court of Appeal in Paris of 2 February 2004, *Ebrahimian v France* (n 2) para 12.

[8] *Ebrahimian v France* (n 2) para 26.

[9] CE 3 May 2000 avis, M*lle Marteaux*, n° 217017.

[10] The 2016 Act inserted neutrality duties into Art 25 of the 1983 Law, which lists all the obligations incumbent upon civil servants and public agents in France: Loi n.83-634 du 13 juillet 1983, as amended by Loi n.2016-483 du 20 avril 2016 relative à la déontologie et aux droits et obligations des fonctionnaires. See also the administrative regulation, which clarified issues of interpretation: Circulaire du 15 mars 2017 relative au respect de la laïcité dans la fonction publique. The title of the 2016 Law only refers to civil servants but Art 32 of the 1983 Law (as modified by the 2016 Law) explicitly extends neutrality requirements to civil servants and public agents, to which the regulation assimilates private agents undertaking a mission of public service.

[11] *Ebrahimian v France* (n 2) para 11. For a criticism of that rationale, see section A.ii below.

[12] For a discussion of this point, see *Ebrahimian v France* (n 2) para 51.

decision by the Cour de cassation of *Mme Abibouraguimane v CPAM de Seine Saint Denis*,[13] later endorsed by a legislative reform,[14] is problematic. If Member States are to guarantee the principle of pluralism, core to both the ECtHR's jurisprudence[15] and to the democratic approach advocated in this book,[16] such sweeping constraints on employees' religious freedom are arguably too broad, unless subject to a strict proportionality review.[17] It has rightly been observed that such a strict proportionality review was precisely lacking in *Ebrahimian*, whether before French courts or before the ECtHR.[18]

### i. Misplaced Proportionality Test

Where the principle of laïcité imposes neutrality requirements upon employees, French law postpones (and limits) proportionality requirements to the sanction phase.[19] Restrictions to employees' religious rights are in effect acceptable regardless of their proportionate enforcement, as long as the sanctions, which apply in case of refusal by the employee to abide by these restrictions, are proportionate. This deferral of the proportionality test in itself dilutes the proportionality requirements because it allows disproportionate restrictions to religious freedom as long as the sanctions faced by religious citizens who do not respect the restrictions are not excessive. However light and proportionate the sanction in case of non-compliance, it does not make the duty to comply in itself proportionate. As argued elsewhere,[20] should a religious restriction itself be a proportionate response to competing concerns, heavy sanctions imposed against individuals infringing the restriction may make the scheme disproportionate, but the reasoning cannot logically be turned around. Heavy sanctions may be the downfall of a justified restriction but light sanctions cannot save an unjustified restriction. Yet the ECtHR itself has at times been attracted to such reasoning. In its decision not to find a violation based on the French ban on the *burqa*, in *SAS v France*,[21] the ECtHR thus held that because of the alleged

---

[13] Soc 19 March 2013, (2013) *Recueil Dalloz* 777; comments by Jérôme Porta, 1026.

[14] See Art 32 of the 1983 Law, as modified by the 2016 Act (n 10).

[15] *Kokkinakis v Greece* App no 14307/88 (ECtHR Chamber, 25 May 1993) para 31.

[16] See above.

[17] For a critique of the decision in that light, see the interesting note by S Garahan, 'A Right to Discriminate? Widening the Scope for Interference with Religious Rights in *Ebrahimian v France*' (2016) 5 *Oxford Journal of Law and Religion* 352.

[18] E Brems, 'Ebrahimian v France: headscarf ban upheld for entire public sector', 27 November 2015, available at strasbourgobservers.com/2015/11/27/ebrahimian-v-france-headscarf-ban-upheld-for-entire-public-sector/; Garahan, 'A Right to Discriminate?' (n 17).

[19] Conseil d'Etat Demoiselle Marteaux (n 9); and Circulaire 2017 (n 10), according to which: sanctions should vary according to the role of the employee, the ostentatious or discreet nature of the religious symbol, the presence or absence of contacts with the public and the vulnerability of the public concerned.

[20] M Hunter-Henin, 'Living Together in an Age of Religious Diversity: Lessons from Baby Loup and SAS' (2015) *Oxford Journal of Law and Religion* 94, 117.

[21] *SAS v France* App no 43835/112014 (ECtHR 1 July 2014).

light sanctions[22] provided for[23] and the limited focus of the ban (targeting only fully-face covering garments),[24] the French ban on the full covering of the face in public places,[25] was legitimate and proportionate. Neither of the two reasons put forward by the ECtHR in *SAS* to justify the proportionality of the *burqa* ban – the ostentatious nature of the religious symbol and the lightness of the sanctions – applied in *Ebrahimian*, however. The applicant did not wear a veil covering her face, or even a regular headscarf, but merely a discreet scarf over her hair.[26] Nor could the lightness of the sanction save the restriction in *Ebrahimian*.

## ii. Why the Alleged Lightness of the Sanction Should be Irrelevant in a Proportionality Test

The lightness of the sanction, questionable in the *SAS* case, seems totally absent in *Ebrahimian*. It is difficult to imagine a harsher sanction in an employment law context than dismissal. Reminiscent of the reasoning adopted by the Cour de cassation in the *Baby Loup* case,[27] the French courts in *Ebrahimian* nonetheless justify the selection of the most serious disciplinary sanction by pointing to the fragility of the members of the public involved. The administrative tribunal had underlined the vulnerability of patients and held that neutrality requirements were all the more necessary given the contact between the applicant and patients in a state of vulnerability and fragility.[28] The ECtHR accepted the reasoning without questioning the assertion that religious symbols would put patients' equality rights into jeopardy. As criticised by the partly dissenting opinion of Judge O'Leary, the Court here comes very close to taking the French government's arguments at face value:

> In France, the neutrality of the public service is recognized as a constitutional value. Nevertheless, such recognition does not release the Court from the obligation under Article 9 § 2 to establish whether the ban on wearing religious symbols to which the applicant was subject was necessary to secure compliance with those principles and, therefore, to meet a pressing social need.[29]

---

[22] A maximum fine of €150 or/and the obligation to attend a citizenship course.

[23] *SAS v France* (n 21) para 152.

[24] *SAS v France* (n 21) para 151.

[25] Loi n. 2010-1192 *interdisant la dissimulation du visage dans l'espace public* of 11 October 2010, JO 12 October 2010.

[26] See *Ebrahimian v France* (n 2) para 38.

[27] Cass Ass Plén 25 June 2014 (2014) *Recueil Dalloz* 1386, underlining the vulnerability of the nursery children with whom the applicant had contacts. For an analysis, see M Hunter-Henin, 'Religion, Children and Employment: The Baby Loup Case' (2015) 64(3) *International Comparative and Law Quarterly* 717.

[28] See *Ebrahimian v France* (n 2) para 61.

[29] See, in stronger terms, the dissenting opinion of Judge De Gaetano: 'The thrust of the judgment is to the effect that the *abstract* principle of *laïcité* or secularism of the State *requires* a blanket prohibition on the wearing by a public official at work of any symbol denoting his or her religious belief. That abstract principle becomes in and of itself a "pressing social need" to justify the interference with a fundamental human right'.

In other words, the Court would here go too far as it would relieve the French authorities from having to prove that the restriction to religious freedom was necessary to achieve the policy and constitutional value of neutrality of the public service. Moreover, in the Court's reasoning, the proportionality requirements contained under Article 9, para 2 of the ECHR seem to fade away under the margin of appreciation granted to French authorities. As noted by Belgian human rights professor, Eva Brems:

> The Court does not really undertake its own autonomous assessment of the proportionality of the interference, but rather examines whether the national authorities have adopted an acceptable approach. This style might be called quasi-procedural, as it remains limited to examining the types of arguments that were taken into account, without critically examining their relevance in the concrete case.

Despite these real concerns, I will argue in section B below that the deference displayed by the ECtHR in *Ebrahimian* may, unlike the reference to the constitutional laïque context in *Achbita*, be compatible with the paradigm I have defended in Chapter 4. I will show that the deference towards national authorities in *Ebrahimian*, contrary to the discretion left to constitutional traditions in *Achbita*, leaves room for further revision and dialogue on the proper scope of the restrictions that may be imposed for the sake of laïcité, and hence can be reconciled with the principle of revision promoted in earlier chapters.

## B. From *Ebrahimian* to *Achbita*: From Deference to Laïcité to Delegation to National Authorities

In this section, I will argue that the deference to laïcité is more acceptable in *Ebrahimian* than in *Achbita*. My argument relies on two factors: first, contrary to the facts of *Achbita*, the principle of laïcité was indeed applicable in *Ebrahimian*. Second, the reasoning of the ECtHR does not offer a complete carte blanche to French national authorities. Unlike *Achbita*, it does not amount to a delegation of competence.

### i. Ebrahimian: *Laïcité within its Remit*

There is no need to explain again the contours of French laïcité.[30] Suffice to recall here that as a public agent employed by a public hospital, Ms Ebrahimian undeniably fell under the neutrality requirements stemming from the principle of laïcité. In light of the public law context of the case, the decisive factor seems indeed to have been, in *Ebrahimian*, that the principle of laïcité triggered a wide margin of appreciation for France. One may discuss whether the ECtHR afforded French authorities too much leeway but it seems undeniable that some

---

[30] See above, Chapter 5, section I.B.

deference towards constitutional traditions was legitimate. In *Ebrahimian*, one may understand that the ECtHR did not wish to intrude upon the interpretation of the fundamental constitutional principle of laïcité. The ECtHR stated that it does not fall within its remit to assess the legitimacy of the French constitutional model.[31] On the other hand, no such constitutional deference was owed to constitutional traditions in *Achbita*, as the principle of laïcité did not apply. As explained in the preceding chapter, the principle does not extend to purely private law endeavours.[32] Paradoxically, by invoking the constitutional laïque context outside of its remit, the Court in *Achbita* is therefore not stepping back from national debates, but taking sides in national controversies and supporting trends in favour of an extension of laïcité beyond its legal limits.[33] Moreover, whereas *Achbita* simply refers back to constitutional traditions, the ECtHR, in *Ebrahimian*, adds justifications for its deference, which, in the future, may allow for a reassessment of the margin of appreciation enjoyed by France.

### ii. Scope for a Revised Reassessment

Reading between the lines, the ECtHR's reasoning in *Ebrahimian* potentially restricts further extensive interpretations of laïcité. The ECtHR quotes approvingly two features, which, according to French law, as the Court sees it, justify the application of neutrality requirements in this case, namely: the status of public agent of the employee in question; and the specific nature of the relevant workplace, as a public hospital. The two features highlighted by the ECtHR to justify its stance of deference may not sit as comfortably as asserted with the Court's own previous case law, which so far has focused on educational sectors and civil servants.[34] Importantly for our purposes, these two factors may not match the French position perfectly either, given that French law extends religious requirements beyond public agents to private agents working for private companies entrusted with a mission of a public service, and bases religious restrictions on the employer's position and mission, regardless of any consideration of the employee's status and rights. The two factors highlighted in support of the Court's deference towards French restrictions in the name of

---

[31] *Ebrahimian v France* (n 2) para 68: 'La Cour est consciente qu'il s'agit d'une obligation stricte qui puise ses racines dans le rapport traditionnel qu'entretiennent la laïcité de l'État et la liberté de conscience, tel qu'il est énoncé à l'article 1er de la Constitution (paragraphe 21 ci-dessus). Selon le modèle français, qu'il n'appartient pas à la Cour d'apprécier en tant que tel, la neutralité de l'État s'impose aux agents qui le représentent'.

[32] Chapter 5, Section 1.B.i.

[33] Chapter 5, Section 1.B.ii.

[34] See for example *Kurtulmus v Turkey* App no 65500/01 (ECtHR 24 January 2006) (university professor); *Leyla Sahin v Turkey* App no 47774/98 (ECtHR 10 November 2005) (university student); *Dogru v France* App no 27058/05 (ECtHR 4 December 2008) (secondary school pupil); *Dahlab v Suisse* App no 42393/98 (ECtHR 15 February 2001) (state primary school teacher). See how the reasoning of the Court in *Kurtulmus* already goes beyond the educational sector, whereas the justification put forward in *Dahlab*, for example, seemed confined to the educational public sector.

laïcité therefore open up questions and possibilities. They are as much a reason for the Court to approve the French position in *Ebrahimian*, as they are grounds to justify disapproval in future cases in which restrictions might apply beyond the educational and hospital sectors and/or beyond public agents. The decision in *Ebrahimian* thus opens the way for compromises and a gradual convergence towards a more contextual approach. By contrast, as I have shown, the reference to laïcité in *Achbita* has an opposite effect.

### C.  Conclusion to Section I

In this section, I have contrasted the appeal to laïcité by the CJEU in *Achbita* and by the ECtHR in *Ebrahimian*. Whereas the former referred to laïcité beyond its limits, the ECtHR reasoned in a public law context in which, from a constitutional French perspective, laïcité was incontestably applicable. While the former does not add limits or justification to its (misplaced) deference towards national constitutional traditions, the ECtHR mentions two rationales which, in future, might warrant a reassessment of the margin of appreciation granted to France. I submit that the ECtHR's approach is more in line with the democratic paradigm I have defended in Part I. In its approach, the CJEU comes close to a delegation of competence to national authorities, again reasoning as if certain spheres might be immune from the application of fundamental political principles of fairness and opportunities of participation. Moreover, unlike the ECtHR, it does not open up possibilities for future revision of the terms of legitimacy but closes down dialogue. In the sections that follow, I will seek to address the second problematic aspect of *Achbita*, identified inthe preceding chapter, namely its emphasis on consistency over proportionality. I will suggest that a more effective proportionality review would be more in line with the democratic paradigm defended in Part I and offer concrete criteria which might guide the courts when carrying out such proportionality assessments.

### II.  PROPORTIONALITY RATHER THAN AUTONOMY

In *Egenberger*,[35] a job applicant applied to the German Evangelisches Werk for a post, which consisted of drafting a report on the United Nations International Convention on the Elimination of All Forms of Racial Discrimination. She complained that her lack of religious beliefs was the only reason she had been turned down and that she had therefore been victim of discrimination on the ground of religion (or lack of). In the case of *IR v JQ*,[36] a Catholic doctor, JQ, complained of unfair dismissal after the hospital he was working for dismissed

---

[35] *Egenberger* (n 3).
[36] *IR v JQ* (n 4).

him for having remarried in a civil ceremony following divorce from his first wife, with whom he had had a Catholic wedding. In the eye of the Church, the first marriage was indissoluble and the second marriage was therefore a violation of the Catholic ethos which the hospital was seeking to promote. In response, the employer argued that the requirement of Church membership (in *Egenberger*) or allegiance to the Catholic ethos in one's private life (in *IR*) was a genuine occupational requirement under Article 4(2) of the Directive, which allows employers to impose restrictions upon employees' rights for the sake of a (religious) work ethos. The question raised in these two cases of *Egenberger* and *IR* was whether the determination of what amounts to such genuine, legitimate and justified occupational requirement within the meaning of Article 4(2) could be left to the religious employer. The CJEU ruled that the right to self-determination of religious employers could not circumvent employees' right to effective judicial review as to the existence of the genuine, legitimate and justified occupational requirement and its proportionate enforcement. In this section, I will compare and contrast the effective right of judicial review conferred by the CJEU to employees in *Egenberger* and *IR* with the principle of minimum judicial intervention endorsed by the CJEU in *Achbita*. Confronting the two approaches, I will suggest that *Egenberger* corresponds to a more (welcome) contextual and demanding form of review than the non-interventionist stance adopted in *Achbita* (section A). I will then turn to the case law of the ECtHR to provide illustrations of the concrete criteria which courts might consider in carrying out such proportionality test (section B).

## A. The Rejection of the Church Autonomy Argument in *Egenberger*

### i. Autonomy Does Not Entail Self-determination

Under German law, churches traditionally have a privilege of self-determination. This view, now subject to European challenge, is deeply embedded in German constitutional norms: 'Religious societies shall regulate and administer their affairs independently within the limits of the law that applies to all. They shall confer their offices without the involvement of central government or local authorities'.[37] Accordingly, the German Federal Constitutional Court (*Bundesverfassungsgericht*) had bestowed on religious organisations competence to determine when a particular restriction on the ground of religion amounted to a genuine, legitimate and justified occupational requirement, and was thus justified under Article 4(2) of the Directive. Under German case law, judicial

---

[37] Grundgesetz Art 140, which refers to Art 137 of the Weimar Constitution (Weimarer Verfassung WRV) on religious societies (Religionsgesellschaften): 'Die Freiheit der Vereinigung zu Religionsgesellschaften wird gewährleistet. Der Zusammenschluß von Religionsgesellschaften innerhalb des Reichsgebiets unterliegt keinen Beschränkungen. Jede Religionsgesellschaft ordnet und verwaltet ihre Angelegenheiten selbstständig innerhalb der Schranken des für alle geltenden Gesetzes. Sie verleiht ihre Ämter ohne Mitwirkung des Staates oder der bürgerlichen Gemeinde'.

review of the religious organisation's assessment was limited to a review of mere plausibility. A more stringent review (it was thought) would encroach upon the religious autonomy granted to churches to define their own religious identity. By contrast, the CJEU in *Egenberger* insists that autonomy of religious organisations must be conceived as internal rather than external to the overall balancing framework:

> The objective of Article 4(2) of Directive 2000/78 is thus to ensure a fair balance between the right of autonomy of churches and other organisations whose ethos is based on religion or belief, on the one hand, and, on the other hand, the right of workers, inter alia when they are being recruited, not to be discriminated against on grounds of religion or belief, in situations where those rights may clash.[38]

In *Egenberger*, the Court insists that religious autonomy of churches cannot deprive individuals of their right to judicial review. In *Egenberger*, the CJEU suggests that the occupational activity of the employee in question was key to determining the equilibrium between the interests at stake. The Court holds that to be considered 'genuine':

> professing the religion or belief on which the ethos of the church or organisation is founded must appear necessary because of the importance of the *occupational activity* in question for the manifestation of that ethos or the exercise by the church or organisation of its right of autonomy.[39] (emphasis added)

The Court adds that the connection between such occupational activity and the employer's religious ethos must be ascertained objectively and must *also* satisfy the principle of proportionality.[40] Whilst judicial review as to the legitimate existence and proportionate enforcement of a religious work ethos falls upon national courts, the CJEU thus delivers strict guidelines to national courts. The employer's religious work ethos will only prevail over competing employees' rights when restrictions are *objectively* required to further that ethos and *specifically* connected to the tasks assigned to the employee concerned.

### ii. *The Requirement of a Connection between the Work Religious Ethos and the Employee's Tasks*

In *IR*, the Opinion of Advocate General Wathelet[41] prompted the Court to carry out a close scrutiny of the employer's claim that the company was promoting

---

[38] *Egenberger* (n 3) para 51.

[39] *Egenberger* (n 3) para 65.

[40] *Egenberger* (n 3) para 69: '(...) the genuine, legitimate and justified occupational requirement (article 4(2) of Directive 2000/78) refers to is a requirement that is necessary and objectively dictated, having regard to the ethos of the church or organisation concerned, by the nature of the occupational activity concerned or the circumstances in which it is carried out, and cannot cover considerations which have no connection with that ethos or with the right of autonomy of the church or organisation. That requirement must comply with the principle of proportionality'.

[41] Opinion of AG Wathelet, delivered on 31 May 2018, Case C-68/17 *IR v JQ*, available at curia. europa.eu/juris/document/document.jsf;jsessionid=674F992E08328FF0B4C1A9F75DAB3D1A?

a religious ethos and that the restrictions imposed upon the employee in question were necessary and justified for the sake of that ethos. The statement that the goal of the company IR was to enforce the work of CARITAS (the international confederation of Catholic charitable organisations) was not sufficient to establish the existence of a religious ethos, according to Advocate General Wathelet:

> It will therefore be necessary to determine whether the practice of the hospitals managed by IR falls within the doctrine of the Catholic Church in that those services are provided in a way that distinguishes them clearly from the services provided by public hospitals. That determination must address ethical questions in the healthcare sphere with particular importance in the doctrine of the Catholic Church and, in particular abortion, euthanasia, contraception and other measures to regulate procreation.[42]

In other words, the existence of a religious ethos cannot be self-proclaimed but has to correspond specifically to the way in which the company delivers its services. Similarly, the claim that a given employee must suffer restrictions to their fundamental rights for the sake of that ethos has to rely on reasons specifically related to the particular tasks assigned to the employee in question. Several factors in *IR* pleaded, according to AG Wathelet's Opinion – which the CJEU followed – against the existence of tight enough a connection between the employer's religious ethos and the tasks assigned to the employee, JQ. First, JQ was performing his role as a doctor just as any other doctor would do. The provision of healthcare services and patient care or his administrative tasks as the Head of Department in the department concerned were not intimately linked to the religious ethos that his employer was promoting.[43] Moreover, his marital situation (and more precisely the fact that he had remarried after divorce) did not have any impact on the performance of his tasks. However crucial, therefore, the principle of indissolubility of marriage may be within Catholic tenets, the employer must prove that respect of the principle is relevant for the employee's tasks. One can imagine, therefore, that had the doctor expressed views supportive of abortion or euthanasia, such connection would have existed, for a doctor might well encounter situations involving abortion or euthanasia requests. By contrast, a doctor would not be involved in giving advice on his patients' marital situations, nor would a doctor normally embody a model to follow in respect of family life.

---

text=&docid=202426&pageIndex=0&doclang=en&mode=lst&dir=&occ=first&part=1& cid=14351872.

[42] Opinion of AG Wathelet (n 41) para 46.

[43] See, endorsing this point, *IR v JQ* (n 4) para 58: 'Adherence to that notion of marriage does not appear to be necessary for the promotion of IR's ethos, bearing in mind the occupational activities carried out by JQ, namely the provision of medical advice and care in a hospital setting and the management of the internal medicine department which he headed'.

### iii. Comparison with the British Position

This interpretation of the facts echoes to an extent the British[44] position which, pursuant to the Directive, allows for general exemptions from non-discrimination provisions,[45] as well as a specific exemption where 'the employment is for purposes of an organised religion'.[46] In the latter case, the Equality Act 2010 provides two exceptions. Paragraph 2 of Schedule 9 to the Equality Act 2010 contains an exception for religious requirements relating to sex, marriage and sexual orientation, and paragraph 3[47] contains an exception for requirements to be of a particular religion or belief. Paragraph 2 allows religious requirements for the sake of promoting a religious work ethos provided the application of the requirement engages the compliance principle or non-conflict principle. Under the compliance principle, the requirement is applied so as to comply with the doctrines of the religion; under the non-conflict principle, because of the nature or context of the employment, the requirement is applied so as to avoid conflicts with the strongly-held religious convictions of a significant number of the religion's followers. The test adopted by the CJEU in *IR* is potentially more demanding and objective, however, than the alternative non-compliance or non-conflict British test. Unlike the British tests,[48] the *IR* test *always* directs courts to take account of the nature or context of the employment and clearly gives precedence to the objective connection between the requirement and the tasks assigned to the employee, playing down the impact of the requirement for the doctrines of the religion in question or its importance for the followers.[49]

---

[44] Northern Ireland falls under a distinct regime: Fair Employment and Treatment (Northern Ireland) Order 1998 and Equality Act (Sexual Orientation) Regulations (Northern Ireland) 2006.

[45] Equality Act 2010, Sch 9, Pt 1.

[46] ibid, Sch 9, para 2. On the phrase, 'employment for the purposes of an organised religion', see *R (on the application of Amicus – MSF Section) v Secretary of State for Trade and Industry* [2004] EWHC 860 (Admin).

[47] Paragraph 3 would comply with CJEU guidelines. It states that: 'A person (A) with an ethos based on religion or belief does not contravene a provision mentioned in paragraph 1(2) by applying in relation to work a requirement to be of a particular religion or belief if A shows that, having regard to that ethos and to the nature or context of the work – (a) it is an occupational requirement, (b) the application of the requirement is a proportionate means of achieving a legitimate aim, and (c) the person to whom A applies the requirement does not meet it (or A has reasonable grounds for not being satisfied that the person meets it)'.

[48] English case law in practice seems, however, to be compliant with the guidelines issued by the CJEU. For an illustration, prior to the Equality Act 2010, based on the Employment Equality (Sexual Orientation) Regulations 2003, reg 7(3), in which the exception granted to religious institutions was read down and subjected to an objectively assessed interpretation of the tests now in the Equality Act 2010, Sch 9, see *R (on the application of Amicus – MSF Section) v Secretary of State for Trade and Industry* [2004] EWHC 860 (Admin). More generally, for a survey of the English case law in this field see F Cranmer, *Religion and Belief in United Kingdom Employment Law* (Brill, 2017) esp at 48.

[49] For the difficulty of reconciling an objective test with the language used in the British provisions: R Sandberg and N Doe, 'Religious Exemptions in Discrimination Law' (2007) 66(2) *Cambridge Law Journal* 302; see also J Waltman, 'Church autonomy, sexual orientation and employment policy in Britain: a legislative history of the employment provisions of the Equality Act 2010' (2013) VII(1) *Politics and Religion* 173.

The latter point explains the second reason put forward by the Advocate General for rejecting the employer's claim.

### iv. A Connection Independent of Employees' Faith and the Impact on Followers

Another factor which countered the employer's position, according to the Advocate General – here again followed on that point by the CJEU – was the fact that:

> membership of the Catholic Church is not a required condition for the role of Head of the Internal Medicine Department and that IR recruits non-Catholics for roles with medical responsibility and entrusts managerial duties to them.[50]

Can duties of loyalty differ depending on the faith of the employee? The Advocate General considered that the variations in the restrictions imposed upon employees show that the tasks are not inherently close to the employer's religious ethos, thus dismissing the employer's argument that a violation of Catholic tenets is more of a blow when the violator is himself/herself a Catholic. If the religious Catholic ethos had been crucial for these tasks, the employer would have only appointed Catholics to these roles. This reasoning, which the Court endorsed,[51] undermines the discretion of the employer to impose a work ethos in the workplace. Despite the existence of a genuine religious work ethos, despite the clear contractual commitment undertaken by staff to respect it and the foreseeability that non-compliance with key church teachings would lead to sanctions, the employer will no longer be able to eliminate considerations of employees' competing rights through the exercise of contractual prerogatives. In each individual case, a careful and fresh balancing of competing rights will need to be carried out, in context.

If such contextual approach might increase litigation and uncertainty, in the short term at least, arguably, however, the focus on the specific connection between the religious ethos and the tasks assigned to the employee allows courts to steer away from religious scholastic discussions. Indeed, it will no longer be the importance of the given religious prescription for the religious faith in question that will be decisive, which would require venturing into religious tenets, but its importance for the performance of the employee's work – an assessment that the courts will be much more comfortable and equipped to make. Nonetheless, there is a concern that such a strict proportionality review would give too much unconstrained power to the judiciary. Far from deepening democracy, this new way of conceptualising church autonomy would confer unchecked power on judges. In the paragraph that follows, I will point to the case law of

---

[50] Opinion of AG Wathelet (n 41) para 67.
[51] *IR v JQ* (n 4) para 59: 'Positions of medical responsibility entailing managerial duties, similar to that occupied by JQ, were entrusted to IR employees who were not of the Catholic faith and, consequently, not subject to the same requirement to act in good faith and with loyalty to IR's ethos'.

the ECtHR to alleviate this concern. Whilst the insistence upon a contextual effective judicial review might increase uncertainty, it is to be hoped that, as case law grows and more guidelines emerge, stability and predictability will ensue. As analysed in the next paragraph, the ECtHR's jurisprudence has already yielded helpful guidelines in this area.

## B.  Guidelines from the ECtHR's Case Law

### i.  *Overview of ECtHR Cases*

In the German cases of *Schüth* and *Obst*,[52] the ECtHR ruled on the compatibility with Article 8 rights to privacy and family life of a decision by a religious employer to dismiss a Catholic Church organist (Schüth) or the Director of Public Relations for Europe of the Mormon Church (Obst) for extramarital relationships. In the Spanish case of *Fernández Martínez*,[53] the ECtHR reviewed the compatibility of a decision not to renew the employment contract as religious education teacher of a priest, following the publication of an article which had widely revealed the fact that the priest was married with five children and was a member of a movement for 'optional celibacy' for priests. In *Travaš v Croatia*,[54] the applicant, a theology professor teaching Catholic religious education in two state schools, was fired after the archdiocese, having discovered that the applicant had remarried in a civil ceremony following divorce, had consequently removed its canonical mandate. The reasoning of the ECtHR in these cases is strikingly close to the CJEU's approach in *Egenberger* and *IR*. Just like the CJEU,[55] the ECtHR reiterated the discretion afforded to national authorities[56] but, just like the CJEU,[57] the ECtHR immediately added that such margin of appreciation does not invalidate individual applicants' rights to an effective judicial review.[58] Like the CJEU,[59] the ECtHR has emphasised that judicial review of restrictions to employees' rights for the sake of a work religious ethos must include the verification that there exist objective and specific connections between the work religious ethos at stake and the particular tasks assigned to the employee in question:

> Whilst it is true that, under the Convention, an employer whose ethos is based on religion or on a philosophical belief may impose specific duties of loyalty on its

---

[52] *Obst v Germany* App no 425/03 (ECtHR 23 September 2010); *Schüth v Germany* App no 1620/03 (ECHR 2010 and ECtHR 3 February 2011); *Siebenhaar v Germany* App no 18136/02.

[53] *Fernández Martínez v Spain* App no 56030/07 (ECtHR Grand Chamber, 12 June 2014).

[54] *Travaš v Croatia* App no 75581/13 (ECtHR 4 October 2016).

[55] On the basis of Art 17 TFEU, see above section II.A.

[56] *Schüth v Germany* (n 52) para 65: 'The Court reiterates that it is in the first place for the national courts to interpret and apply domestic law (see *Griechische Kirchengemeinde München und Bayern e.V. v. Germany* (dec.), no. 52336/99, 18 September 2007)'.

[57] *Egenberger* (n 3) para 55, see above section II.A.

[58] *Schüth v Germany* (n 52), para 69.

[59] See *IR v JQ* (n 4).

employees, a decision to dismiss based on a breach of such duty cannot be subjected, on the basis of the employer's right of autonomy, only to a limited judicial scrutiny exercised by the relevant domestic employment tribunal without having regard to the nature of the post in question and without properly balancing the interests involved in accordance with the principle of proportionality.[60]

On that basis, the ECtHR held that the dismissal of an organist amounts to a violation of Article 8 of the Convention whereas it considered the interference with the applicants' rights justified and proportionate in the cases of *Obst*, *Fernández Martínez* and *Travaš*. A close comparative analysis of the cases will therefore provide useful clues as to the concrete criteria to take into account in a proportionality assessment.

### ii. *Comparative Analysis of* Obst *and* Schüth

Whereas Michael Obst, as head of the Mormon Church's public relations in Europe, was a representative of the Church's ethos,[61] Bernhard Schüth's tasks were confined to the music activities of the liturgy, and hence seemed further away from the church ethos. Whereas Obst was having a longstanding extra-marital affair, Schüth had formed a de facto new family life with his new partner following separation with his wife, so that the interference with Schüth's family life was greater.[62] Finally, whereas Obst could entertain job prospects elsewhere, Schüth's professional opportunities were limited. According to the Court, the seniority of Obst in his post[63] and his familiarity with the Mormon Church in which he was raised (should have) made him more aware than Schüth of the risks incurred for violating his employer's ethos, and his relatively young age (34 years old) made him less vulnerable than Schüth in case of dismissal.[64] The severity of the sanction of dismissal also seemed disproportionate in Schüth's case,[65] given that his prospects of finding another job were extremely limited in light of the predominant position of the Church in this sector.[66] The more recent cases of

---

[60] *Schüth v Germany* (n 52) para 69.

[61] See *Obst* (n 52) para 51: 'La cour d'appel du travail a clairement indiqué que ses conclusions ne devaient pas être comprises comme impliquant que tout adultère constituait en soi un motif justifiant le licenciement [sans préavis] d'un employé d'une Eglise, mais qu'elle y était parvenue en raison de la gravité de l'adultère aux yeux de l'Eglise mormone et de la position importante que le requérant y occupait et qui le soumettait à des obligations de loyauté accrues'.

[62] *Schüth* (n 52) para 67: 'The Court would first observe that, in their findings the employment tribunals made no mention of the applicant's *de facto* family life or of the legal protection afforded to it'. In effect, the Church's ethos would force the applicant to live a life of abstinence: ibid, para 71.

[63] Note that Schüth had also held a longstanding post as choirmaster (14 years) but the fact that it was not a post of responsibility seemed decisive to distinguish *Schüth* and *Obst*.

[64] *Obst* (n 52) para 48.

[65] See *Schüth* (n 52) para 73.

[66] See *Schüth* (n 52) para 39: 'Under section 2(3) of the Ecclesiastical Law on Religious Music of 15 June 1996 (*Kirchengesetz über den kirchenmusikalischen Dienst in der Evangelischen Kirche der Union (EKU) (Kirchenmusikgesetz)*), a church musician employed by the Protestant Church must in

*Fernández Martínez* and *Travaš* yield further clues as to how courts might carry out a contextual analysis of the competing rights at stake.

### iii. Analysis of the Cases of Fernández Martínez and Travaš

In *Fernández Martínez*, the applicant, a priest who – having received no reply to his request for a dispensation from the obligation of celibacy – had married and had had five children with his wife, was teaching religious education in a state secondary school. His position as a religious education teacher relied upon the decision of the relevant administrative authority, on the recommendation of the Diocese, to renew his yearly contract.[67] His marital situation had been well known and had never caused any difficulties until the publication of an article in which his situation, as well as his support for a movement for 'optional celibacy' for priests, became widely publicised. As a result, the Diocese removed their recommendation and the applicant's contract as a religious education teacher was not renewed. Whilst the interference with Father Fernández Martínez' family life seemed as great as the one suffered by Bernhard Schüth and his prospects of finding another post as restricted, the Court nonetheless held, by a small margin, that his dismissal was justified and proportionate. As a religious education teacher, he seemed closer to the Church ethos than Schüth was, as a Church organist and choirmaster.[68] Given his position as priest, the Court also underlined that the sanction against Fernández Martínez was foreseeable, even if the Church had been aware of and had tolerated his marital status for years. According to the Court,

> it is reasonable to presume that he was aware of the heightened duty of loyalty imposed on him by ecclesiastical law and could thus have foreseen that, despite the

principle be affiliated with a denomination which is a member of the Protestant Church of Germany or part of an ecclesiastical union therewith. Under section 21(2) of that Law, in conjunction with section 7(1) of the implementing law of 13 November 1997 (*Kirchengesetz zur Ausführung und Ergänzung des Kirchengesetzes über den kirchenmusikalischen Dienst in der EKU (Ausführungsgesetz zum Kirchenmusikgesetz)*, a person not fulfilling this condition may nevertheless be appointed, on an exceptional basis, to a post of church musician in secondary employment (*Nebenamt*) if he or she is affiliated with a Christian denomination that is part of the Labour Association of Christian Churches in Germany (*Arbeitsgemeinschaft christlicher Kirchen in Deutschland*), to which the Roman Catholic Church belongs'.

[67] In accordance with the provisions of a 1979 Agreement between Spain and the Holy See, implemented under Ministerial Order of 11 October 1982 on teachers of Catholic religion and ethics in secondary educational centres, 'religious education shall be taught by the persons who, every school year, are appointed by the administrative authority from among those proposed by the Ordinary of the diocese'. On the status of religious education teachers in Spain, see, more generally, J García Oliva, 'The Controversy Surrounding the Teaching of Denominational Religion in Spain' in M Hunter-Henin (ed), *Law, Religious Freedoms and Education in Europe*. Cultural Diversity and Law (Farnham, Ashgate, 2012) 183.

[68] *Fernández Martínez* (n 53) para 134: 'Indeed, from the point of view of the Church's interest in upholding the coherence of its precepts, teaching Catholic religion to adolescents can be considered a crucial function requiring special allegiance'.

fact that his situation had been tolerated for many years, the public display of his militant stance on certain precepts of the Church would be at odds with the applicable provisions of canon law and would not be without consequence.[69]

Fernández Martínez, moreover, seemed in a weaker position than Michael Obst, and a fortiori than Bernard Schüth, because his infidelities to the Church's ethos had not been divulged in secret or were known by a few, but had received media coverage.[70] Finally, although the dismissal produced harsh consequences, his entitlement to unemployment benefits softened the harshness of the chosen sanction and made it, according to the Court, proportionate.[71] The decisive factor seems, therefore, to have been – rather than the ministerial position of the employee as priest – the publicity that had surrounded his marital life:

> The Court finds that in choosing to accept a publication about his family circumstances and his association with what the Bishop considered to be a protest-oriented meeting, he severed the special bond of trust that was necessary for the fulfilment of the tasks entrusted to him.[72]

The doctrine, applicable in the US, whereby religious autonomy would be increased in respect of certain employees – ministers – especially devoted to the religious ethos in question seems therefore implicitly rejected.[73] The ECtHR will, however, recognise that certain tasks are particularly close to the Church's ethos and require special allegiance from employees performing them. In *Travaš v Croatia*, the Court thus held that the applicant, albeit a layman, had to abide by Catholic norms of behaviour because of his mission as a Catholic religious education teacher. Unlike in *IR*, where the CJEU considered that the applicant's personal life did not affect his mission as a doctor, the ECtHR in *Travaš* considered that the applicant's personal life had an impact on his teaching role:

> The question is rather whether a particular religious doctrine could be taught by a person whose conduct and way of life were seen by the Church at issue as being at odds with the religion in question, especially where the religion is supposed to govern the private life and personal beliefs of its followers.[74]

---

[69] *Fernández Martínez* (n 53) para 118. After about two years on unemployment benefits, the applicant found another job in a museum: ibid, para 20.

[70] *Schüth* (n 52) para 72: the applicant's case had not received media coverage, that, after 14 years of service for the parish church, he did not appear to have challenged the stances of the Catholic Church, but rather had failed to observe them in practice.

[71] *Fernández Martínez* (n 53) para 144.

[72] *Fernández Martínez* (n 53) para 135.

[73] Uncertainty, however, remains given that Fernández Martínez' current status as priest was ambiguous in light of his well-known transgressions (see *Fernández Martínez* (n 53) para 133) and that the contract of employment at stake did not involve his position as minister in the Church but his employment, upon recommendation of the Diocese, as religious education teacher in a secondary state school. On this aspect, see S Smet, 'Fernández Martínez v. Spain: The Grand Chamber Putting the Brakes on the 'Ministerial Exception' for Europe?', available at strasbourgobservers. com/2012/05/24/fernandez-martinez-v-spain-towards-a-ministerial-exception-in-europe/.

[74] *Travaš v Croatia* (n 54) para 97.

Ultimately, it is apparent that the ECtHR considered that outcomes in individual cases depend on a strict balancing exercise of the interests at stake. In *Schüth*, the Court thus ruled 'that a more detailed examination was required when weighing the competing rights and interests at stake'.[75] This careful balancing also lies at the heart of the Grand Chamber's decision in *Fernández Martínez*:

> a mere allegation by a religious community that there is an actual or potential threat to its autonomy is not sufficient to render any interference with its members' rights to respect for their private or family life compatible with Article 8 of the Convention. (...) The national courts must [conduct] an in-depth examination of the circumstances of the case and a thorough balancing exercise between the competing interests at stake.[76]

Even in *Travaš*, where the Church might be seen to enjoy a greater degree of latitude, the Court insisted on the importance for the state of carrying out a thorough proportionality test. In light of the possibility for the applicant to seek other employment in the education system by teaching courses of ethics and culture, the Court held that the dismissal had not been disproportionate.

This incursion into the case law of the ECtHR therefore reveals that a contextual proportionality review, focused on the connection between the restrictions upon employees' individual freedoms and the employees' tasks, provides a casuistic but objective tool with which to balance the competing interests at stake.

## C. Conclusion to Section II

In this section, I have analysed rulings from the CJEU in *Egenberger* and *IR*, as well as a sample of key cases from the ECtHR's case law on religious employers, to tease out what an effective proportionality review might look like. Through repeated decisions, which the CJEU might benefit from, the ECtHR has shown that objective criteria can gradually emerge and that *in concreto* balancing of the interests at stake does not ineluctably confer a final say on judges. Whatever one might think, therefore, of the outcome in a given case, I submit that the open-endedness and dialogical nature of the adjudication process would enrich democratic dialogue and is consistent with a democratic legitimacy which is no longer narrowly focused on parliamentary majoritarianism.[77] In that sense, a strict form of proportionality review, as embraced in the later rulings of the CJEU in *Egenberger* and *IR*, would serve the democratic paradigm I have defended in Part I. In the section to follow, I would like to open up to US debates

---

[75] *Schüth* (n 52) para 69; *Obst* (n 52) §§ 48–51.

[76] *Fernández Martínez* (n 53) para 131.

[77] It is impossible to refer to the extensive literature on the topic. For a few references, which move beyond parliamentary majoritism, see J Cohen, *Philosophy, Politics, Democracy. Selected Essays* (Harvard University Press, 2009); O Gerstenberg, 'Negative/positive constitutionalism, 'fair balance' and the problem of justiciability' (2012) 10 *ICON* 904, 914. *cf* Sabel and WH Simon, 'Destabilization

and consider the most delicate instances of clashing rights: those in which religious freedom requests potentially conflict with rights to equality of other protected categories, notably same-sex couples.

## III. RELIGIOUS FREEDOM AND EQUALITY RIGHTS

In recent controversies, the religious freedoms of employers or employees have clashed with equality rights of employees or customers. These clashes are novel and, in a way, startling because they pit minority rights against each other, rather than just being about clashes between minority and majority. Discrimination law, designed to protect vulnerable minority groups against prejudices or systemic bias of the majority, is therefore of limited help, as diverse protected characteristics under discrimination law are at stake, each pointing to opposite outcomes. Such cases, which place minority claims against each other,[78] are particularly delicate to resolve. Yet they are on the rise. Providers of services and employees have thus sought to refuse certain services to same-sex couples because they objected, for religious reasons, to being complicit in unions they regarded as sinful. In the *Ashers Baker* case,[79] a baker refused to bake a cake adorned with a pro-gay marriage message, whilst another baker, across the Atlantic, refused to bake one for a same-sex wedding.[80] Other wedding providers have raised similar objections. A US photographer in New Mexico, Ms Elaine Huguenin, refused to photograph the wedding of a same-sex couple;[81] florists, to provide flower arrangements[82] and Bed and Breakfast owners, to rent a venue for a same-sex wedding.[83] Outside of weddings, same-sex couples have also been refused a

---

Rights: How Public Law Litigation Succeeds' (2004) 117 *Harvard Law Review* 1015; MC Dorf and C Sabel, 'A Constitution of Democratic Experimentalism' (1998) 98 *Columbia Law Review* 267.

[78] In certain instances, protected characteristics may also overlap. The dismissal of a Muslim woman for wearing a headscarf may thus engage both discrimination on the ground of religion and on the ground of gender. On intersectional discrimination, see D Schiek and A Lawson (eds), *European Union Non-Discrimination Law and Intersectionality* (Routledge, 2011).

[79] *Lee v Ashers Baking Company Ltd & Others (Northern Ireland)* [2018] UKSC 49.

[80] *Craig v Masterpiece Cakeshop, Inc*, 370 P3d 272 (Colo).

[81] *Elaine Photography v Willcock*, 309 P 3rd 53 NM 2013, in which the New Mexico Supreme Court ruled against the photographer on 22 August 2013. The USSC declined to review the case on 7 April 2014.

[82] *Washington v Arlene's Flowers*, 2015 WL 94248 (Wash Super 2015), in which the Washington Supreme Court ruled against the florist. The florist petitioned for a writ of certiorari: *Arlene Flowers*, No 17-108 (US, 14 July 2017). On 25 June 2018, the US Supreme Court granted the petition for a writ of certiorari, vacated the judgment, and remanded the case to the Supreme Court of Washington for further consideration in light of the *Masterpiece Cakeshop* decision. On 6 June 2019, the Washington Supreme Court unanimously ruled against the florist again, see agportal-s3bucket. s3.amazonaws.com/uploadedfiles/Another/News/Washington%20State%20SC%20916152.pdf.

[83] The Illinois Human Rights Commission found that the same-sex couple had been discriminated against and appeal against the ruling of the Commission was dismissed on 8 June 2017 by the Fourth District of the Illinois Appellate Court. See *Wathen v Timber Creek Bed & Breakfast* www.aclu-il. org/en/press-releases/court-dismisses-appeal-case-finding-downstate-bed-breakfast-discriminated-against-gay. On the litigation since then to compel the B&B owners to comply with the penalties

double-bed room by B&B owners,[84] or been turned down by Catholic adoption agencies who refused to place children in their home.[85] Does it matter whether the objection emanates from a service provider or a public employee, such as a registrar who objects to celebrating a same-sex union?[86] Should it make a difference whether the objection arises in a purely commercial relationship, as in the abovementioned examples of wedding service providers, or in a not-for-profit context, as in the case of Catholic adoption agencies? Is it relevant that the objection comes from a service provider rather than from an employee, or from a public employee rather than an employee working for a private company? Should distinctions be drawn depending on the type of service provided, according to the degree of involvement required by the person who provides it or the ease with which same-sex couples might be able to find alternative providers? The democratic paradigm I have defended in Part I, whilst leaving many open questions in these instances, as the risks of excluding marginal vulnerable voices exist on both sides of the conflict, suggests ways forward.

In the United Kingdom, the landmark case in this area of conflicting rights is the case of *Ladele*,[87] in which a registrar in the Borough of Islington, North of London, had requested (in vain) an exemption, on religious grounds, to avoid celebrating same-sex unions. The case now stands as authority for allowing national (and local) state institutions to prioritise equality rights of same-sex couples over religious freedoms of (public) employees. In this section, I will argue that, whilst this principle is compatible with the democratic paradigm advocated for in earlier chapters, its application to the facts was questionable. Leaving room for competing views does not mean that the legislator is to refrain from expressing a preference towards one set of rights over others. However, this preference cannot preclude all balancing of competing interests. To avoid individuals suffering from the ambiguities stemming from changes in the law, any legislative preference should, I argue in section A, go hand-in-hand with predictability and proportionality. Otherwise, the expressed preference would in effect undermine any meaningful manifestation of conflicting interests and contradict the paradigm of enriching pluralism I have put forward. Even in the absence of any acknowledged legislative or constitutional preference for one set of interests, section B will warn, drawing on US cases, that courts should be attentive to hidden preference or bias. The condemnation of bias and disparaging treatment of religious beliefs is, I will argue, essential to the democratic

---

imposed upon them, see www.fordcountyrecord.com/news/judge-denies-paxton-b-b-s-motion-to-dismiss-lawsuit/article_8329885c-ae57-11e9-804c-37b1a2b8c46e.html.

[84] *Bull v Hall* [2013] UKSC 73.

[85] See www.churchmilitant.com/news/article/catholic-foster-care-adoption-agency-sues-state-of-michigan.

[86] *Ladele*; *Kim Davis, Miller v Davis*, No 15-5880, 2015 WL 1069 2640 6th Circ 26 August 2015.

[87] *Ladele v London Borough of Islington* [2009] EWCA Civ 1357, which led to the decision of the European Court of Human Rights in *Eweida v United Kingdom* [2013] ECHR 37.

paradigm advocated for in Part I, as it contributes to creating a more inclusive environment for religious providers and employees and thereby ensures that pluralism is not discouraged at the outset. Leaving aside considerations of legislative explicit or hidden preference or bias in favour of one set of rights, I will conclude with tentative thoughts about how to solve the complex conflict between purely private rights in specific instances.

## A. Balancing Private Interests in the Context of Legislative Ambiguities

I will open this section with the English case of *Ladele*. As I will show, the *Ladele* case does not state how to resolve the clash between the private competing interests to equality on the one hand and religious freedom on the other, but discusses the discretion and limits of legislative national and local authorities' powers in the context of competing private rights. On that latter question, the ECtHR grants Member States an extensive margin of appreciation. This paragraph will argue that this margin of appreciation is excessive on the facts. Having praised the ECtHR's reasoning for recognising an underlying conflict between private interests, this paragraph will argue that the Court should have ensured that the preference expressed by Islington Borough Council in favour of equality rights of customers fulfilled requirements of proportionality and procedural fairness. Such requirements, as I will argue, are indeed essential to fostering the dialogue I have advocated in earlier chapters.

### i. Presentation of the Ladele Case

When Islington Borough Council first recruited Ms Ladele, English law did not allow same-sex unions. Civil partnerships,[88] the first official legal union for same-sex couples under English law, only came into force in 2005 – 13 years after Ms Ladele's appointment by the Council and three years after her transfer to the department of celebration of unions. Ms Ladele felt that celebrating same-sex unions would violate her conscience and her religious conviction that homosexuality was a sin. At first, colleagues agreed to cover for her, under informal

---

[88] Same-sex unions were introduced under the Civil Partnership Act 2004 (in force since December 2005). Part 2 of the Act relates to England and Wales, Part 3 to Scotland and Part 4 to Northern Ireland. Civil partnerships are almost a replica of marriage, but for the name and a few distinctions. See P Tatchell, 'Why our new same-sex marriage is not equal marriage' 19 July 2013 The New Statesman: www.newstatesman.com/uk-politics/2013/07/why-our-new-same-sex-marriage-not-yet-equal-marriage. Civil partnerships have remained in force after the extension of marriage to same-sex couples. Following a successful challenge by an opposite-sex couple (*R (on the application of Steinfeld and Keidan) (Appellants) v Secretary of State for the International Development (in substitution for the Home Secretary and the Education Secretary) (Respondent)* [2018] UKSC 32), civil partnerships have been extended to opposite-sex couples: Civil Partnerships, Marriages and Death Registration Act 2019.

arrangements. However, once Ms Ladele had officially sent a written request for exemption to her employer, such informal arrangements soon became impossible. Indeed, Islington Borough Council decided to make her request public, provoking the outrage of her homosexual colleagues, two of whom then mounted a campaign against her. Eventually, a conciliatory solution was ruled out and Ms Ladele's dismissal became the only viable option. When the UK Parliament introduced civil partnerships into English law, it considered granting an exemption to registrars who might object, on religious grounds, to participate in the celebration of same-sex unions.[89] In the end, however, the amendment was rejected and Parliament did not grant any statutory exemptions to registrars. Instead, it allowed City Councils to grant individual exemptions as they saw fit. Islington Borough Council chose to endorse an equality policy fully and denied all exemptions. Ms Ladele argued in vain before English domestic courts that this position amounted to discrimination on the ground of religion.[90] The ECtHR then upheld English courts' solution, holding that:

> The aim pursued by the local authority was to provide a service which was not merely effective in terms of practicality and efficiency, but also one which complied with the overarching policy of being 'an employer and a public authority wholly committed to the promotion of equal opportunities and to requiring all its employees to act in a way which does not discriminate against others'.[91]
>
> ...
>
> In all the circumstances, the Court does not consider that the national authorities, that is the local authority employer which brought the disciplinary proceedings and also the domestic courts which rejected the applicant's discrimination claim, exceeded the margin of appreciation available to them. It cannot, therefore, be said that there has been a violation of Article 14 taken in conjunction with Article 9 in respect of the third applicant.[92]

Many of the criticisms levelled against the decision in *Ladele* revolve around the justification put forward by the ECtHR for the wide discretion granted to national authorities: the suggestion that a wide margin of appreciation was owed to national (and local) authorities because of the underlying *clash of private interests*.[93] By contrast, I will praise the ECtHR for recognising the existence of an underlying clash of private interests but criticise it for the extensive margin of appreciation granted as a consequence.

---

[89] Amendment proposed by Lady O'Cathain to the Equality Bill 2005, HL Deb 13 July 2005, vol 684, col 1147. For the position that exemptions should have a legislative basis, see M Malik, 'Religious Freedom, Free Speech and Equality: Conflict or Cohesion?' (2011) 17(1) *Res Publica* 21.

[90] Both the Employment Appeal Tribunal and the Court of Appeal held that the refusal amounted to justified indirect discrimination UKEAT/0453/08, para 130 and [2009] EWCA Civ 1357, para 75.

[91] *Eweida v United Kingdom* (n 87) para 105.

[92] ibid, 106.

[93] See below.

*ii. A Genuine Underlying Clash of Private Interests*

On one reading, Ms Ladele's claim should have been successful because it did not violate any rights of same-sex couples. Had Ms Ladele's request been accommodated, same-sex couples could still have had their unions celebrated.[94] The Court of Appeal had indeed observed that accommodating Ms Ladele would not have interfered with the provision of public service to same-sex couples.[95] In fact, same-sex couples would even have had the added benefit of having a celebrant sympathetic to their union. According to law and religion professor Ian Leigh, courts should usefully have recourse to a reverse test. Under that test, the relevant question to consider is: what rights would have been infringed had Ms Ladele's request been accommodated? The answer, Leigh then rightly notes, is none. No concrete rights to private and family life, as protected under Article 8 of the ECHR would have been violated, as same-sex couples would still have been allowed to secure celebration of their union. This proposed reverse test is pertinent under the European Convention framework as the restriction to Ms Ladele's religious freedoms is justified by the aim of protecting 'the rights of others'. More generally, however, it is possible to argue, under the positive value, which Part I has submitted should be conferred to pluralism, that equality interests should be construed more broadly. In that broader sense, equality interests would be at stake not only when the competing request would affect concrete rights to access a particular service, but also, more symbolically, when the competing request would seek to treat a certain category of persons differently, based on a protected characteristic such as gender, age or sexual orientation. Should a religious citizen be legally entitled to refuse a service to a person or couple because of their sexual orientation, law would then endorse the possibility of treating a certain category of people differently because of their personal characteristics.[96] Even if same-sex couples may easily have their union celebrated by another celebrant, or have the service they seek provided by another company, the very fact that law allows same-sex couples to be refused a service would arguably send the signal that they are not as worthy as other citizens and do not participate on the same terms. For that reason, the accommodation of requests for exemptions on religious grounds are less innocuous than might appear at first sight. Vice versa, however, the emphasis on Islington's commitment to equality principles[97] was arguably a way of hiding rather than solving underlying conflicting interests.

[94] *cf* underlining this fact and suggesting that as a result, Ms Ladele's conscientious objection should have been accommodated for: I Leigh, 'Damned if they Do, Damned if they Don't: the European Convention on Human Rights and the Protection of Religion from Attack' (2011) 17 *Res Publica* 55; see also I Leigh and A Hambler, 'Religious Symbols, Conscience, and the Rights of Others' (2014) 3(1) *Oxford Journal of Law and Religion* 2, 15.

[95] *Ladele v Islington Borough Council* [2009] EWCA Civ 1357, [2010] IRLR 211, para [44].

[96] See M Hunter-Henin, 'Impact de l'arrêt Eweida de la Cour européenne des droits de l'homme sur le droit anglais' in B Callebat, H de Courrèges and V Parisot (eds), *Les Religions et le droit du travail: Regards croisés, d'ici et d'ailleurs* (Brussells, Bruylant. 2018) 297; R McCrea, 'Religion in the Workplace: Eweida and others v United Kingdom' (2014) 77(2) *The Modern Law Review* 277.

[97] See for such emphasis, *Eweida v UK* (n 87) para 105.

### iii. Why a Commitment to Equality Did Not Remove Religious Freedom Interests

One may argue that by committing to an equality policy in that absolute fashion, Islington Borough Council was excluding religious employees from even raising requests on religious grounds. However, Islington Borough Council was thereby only exercising its latitude to decide whether or not to grant individual exemptions on religious grounds. While the Council may certainly be blamed for exercising its discretion in a stigmatising way,[98] the fact that it chose not to grant individual exemptions cannot in itself be criticised, for that was one of the very options which the Council was authorised to select. However, it is then up to the courts to ensure that the chosen option does not cause a disproportionate interference with employees' conflicting religious freedoms. Several factors in the case may have supported a conclusion of disproportionality. The fact that the duty to celebrate same-sex unions could not have been foreseeable at the time of Ms Ladele's recruitment, the hostility manifested towards her, the possibility for Islington to have been accommodating, etc, should all have weighed in favour of Ms Ladele at the proportionality test stage.[99] Instead, the ECtHR glossed over these considerations and upheld the pro-equality outcome reached by English courts on the basis of the wide margin of appreciation owed to Member States in instances of clashing rights.[100] Whatever one's preference between equality rights of same-sex couples and rights to religious freedom of those who object to homosexuality, the *Ladele* case therefore leaves the impression that Ms Ladele's religious freedom was sacrificed on the altar of equality when UK law itself had only embraced the principle of equality belatedly and far from wholeheartedly. Besides, there is an argument for considering that the disparaging treatment of Ms Ladele's convictions should in itself have triggered a decision of violation of her religious freedom and of discrimination against her, on the basis of religion.

### iv. Lack of Procedural Fairness in Ladele

The disparaging attitude on the part of the employer amounted for the first instance tribunal to discrimination on the ground of religion.[101] The decision was, however, reversed on appeal by the Employment Appeal Tribunal,[102] whose decision was then confirmed by the Court of Appeal[103] and upheld by the ECtHR. For the ECtHR,[104] outcomes derive from principles and a balancing of

---

[98] See below.
[99] Hunter-Henin, 'Impact de l'arrêt Eweida' (n 96) 299.
[100] *Eweida v UK* (n 87) para 106.
[101] *Eweida v UK* (n 87) para 28.
[102] UKEAT/0453/08, para 130.
[103] [2009] EWCA Civ 1357, para 75.
[104] *Eweida v United Kingdom* (n 87) para 99.

the competing interests at stake, independent of procedural considerations of fairness in the treatment of the religious employee's claim. Just as the efforts and willingness displayed by British Airways to accommodate Ms Eweida's religious claim were discarded,[105] the intransigence, even outright hostility of Islington Borough towards Ms Ladele did not, therefore, reciprocally, affect the outcome. If the ultimate goal, however, is to achieve an inclusive workplace, there is an argument that courts should sanction blatantly disparaging attitudes. As a final word on *Ladele*, I would like to stress that the enriching democratic effect attributed to pluralism in Part I does not postulate specific outcomes. My criticisms of the pro-equality stance reached in *Ladele* derive from procedural and proportionality requirements, not from an argument that the competing interests of same-sex couples were less prominent. For the same procedural and proportionality considerations, I will now express a few reservations about the decision reached in *Bull v Hall*.[106]

### v. Presentation of the Case of Bull v Hall

In *Bull v Hall*, Mr and Mrs Bull, two devout British Christian Bed & Breakfast owners, had a policy whereby only married couples could enjoy a double-bedded room. In compliance with that policy and their religious beliefs, they declined to honour a booking made for a double-bedded room by a same-sex couple in a civil partnership. The question arose as to whether their refusal was based on the customers' sexual orientation. If it did, the refusal of service would amount to direct discrimination and would be, as such, unlawful. If it did not, the refusal would only amount to indirect discrimination and justification could be put forward. The B&B owners' objection was not based on the couple's sexual orientation, strictly speaking, but on their unmarried status. Admittedly, given that at the time only heterosexual couples could marry, the basis for the objection would often overlap with sexual orientation. However, there was no exact coincidence because the hotel owners would also have denied a double-bedded room to unmarried heterosexual couples. Whilst acknowledging this possibility, the majority of the Court[107] nonetheless concluded that the hotel owners had directly discriminated against the same-sex couple.[108] As explained in Lord Toulson's concurring opinion:

> To treat civil partners differently from married persons on the ground that they are not married is to discriminate on grounds of their sexual orientation, no less than it

---

[105] On *Eweida*, see section I above.

[106] *Bull v Hall* [2013] UKSC 73. For a commentary on the Court of Appeal's decision [2012] EWCA Civ 83, see I Trispiotis, 'Alternative Lifestyles and Unlawful Discrimination. The Limits of Religious Freedom in *Bull v Hall*' (2014) *European Human Rights Law Review* 39.

[107] See Lady Hale's, Lord Kerr's and Lord Toulson's judgments. Contra, in favour of a finding of unjustified indirect discrimination, see Lord Neuberger's and Lord Hughes' judgments.

[108] *Bull v Hall* (n 106) para 31.

would be to treat a same sex married couple differently from an opposite sex married couple, for sexual orientation is the differential factor – civil partnership is for homosexual couples what marriage is for heterosexual couples.[109]

The UK legislator had created registered civil partnerships in order to extend to same-sex couples the possibility to enjoy and bear all the rights and duties of spouses.[110] As civil partners, the same-sex couple in the *Bull* case was, therefore, according to the Court, entitled to the same treatment as a married couple by the hotel owners.[111] I would argue, however, that it is inconsistent to reproach the hotel owners for symbolically treating civil partners differently to spouses when the UK legislature did just that by creating a status apart from marriage for same-sex couples alone.[112]

*vi. The Impact of Normative Ambiguities*

Nowadays, same-sex couples can marry in Britain[113] and though they can still choose to register a civil partnership instead, they can therefore no longer claim that civil partnership, albeit a replica of marriage, is the only route available to them to enjoy the rights and duties conferred on spouses. Consequently, should civil partners be denied a double-bedded room in Britain under a marriage-only policy, the denial would no longer be discriminatory at all. What is required, therefore, for the refusal to amount to direct discrimination is that the reason for the denial of service corresponds to the customers' protected characteristic (here sexual orientation). Without such a connection, the policy implemented by religious service providers would not be exclusionary of a vulnerable group. I would argue that the connection only existed in *Bull v Hall* because of the unequal treatment of same-sex couples by the UK legislator. One may therefore wonder whether the strong statement of Lady Hale in favour of equality in the case corresponds to the law as it then stood. Certainly, as Lady Hale points

---

[109] ibid, para 67.

[110] Civil Partnership Act 2004, see above n 87.

[111] *Bull v Hall* (n 106) para 26.

[112] See M Hunter-Henin, 'Unions de même sexe au Canada et au Royaume-Uni. Variations autour de la notion d'égalité. Réflexions de droit comparé à partir de l'affaire Wilkinson v. Kitzinger' (Same-Sex Unions in Canada and the United Kingdom. Comparative Reflections on Equality in light of Wilkinson v Kitzinger) (2007) 9 *Revue De La Common Law en français* 85. For an unsuccessful challenge to the separation between marriage and civil partnerships, see *Wilkinson v Kitzinger* [2006] EWHC 2022 (Fam). More generally, see R Dworkin, *Principles for a New Political Debate. Is Democracy Possible Here?* (Princeton, NJ, Princeton University Press, 2008).

[113] Marriage (Same Sex Couples) Act 2013 (in force since 13 March 2014) opened marriage to same-sex couples in England and Wales and the Marriage and Civil Partnership (Scotland) Act 2014 (in force since 16 December 2014) did the same for same-sex couples in Scotland. The Marriage (Same-sex Couples) and Civil Partnership (Opposite-Sex Couples) (Northern Ireland) Regulations 2019, issued on 19 December 2019 in pursuance of the Northern Ireland (Executive Formation etc) Act 2019, recently followed suit for Northern Ireland.

out, the legislator was probably moving in this direction.[114] It is not per se this expression of preference of the court for equality rights that is troubling, in my view, but its unpredictable application to the facts. Given that the UK Parliament had chosen at the time to avoid extending marriage to same-sex couples in order, principally, to avoid offending religious sensibilities, the tone of the court in *Bull v Hall*, as the defender of the allegedly clearly embedded fundamental principle of equality appears out of synchronisation with the actual state of the law. The argument should not be taken to mean that courts have to interpret statutes literally. The lack of legislative recognition of same-sex marriages at the time does not prevent courts from embracing a view of discrimination law favourable to equality on the basis of sexual orientation. The point I am making is simply that if courts do embrace a view, which goes beyond legislative positions, the fact that they are filling a 'normative legislative gap'[115] should be taken into account at the proportionality stage and weigh in favour of the party who had taken a different view.

This section has argued that normative ambiguities should weigh in the balancing of competing interests. Conversely, however, the clear preference expressed by the legislator in favour of one set of interests should not inhibit the balancing of competing interests at the proportionality stage. I am not, therefore, arguing conversely for a correlation between a clear legal endorsement of same-sex marriage[116] and a priority for equality rights in discrimination cases. On the contrary, that the law or Constitution protects and values same-sex marriage does not entail that opposite views on same-sex marriage are thereby illegitimate and unlawful.[117] The same reasoning applies (a fortiori) to the recognition of non-marital same-sex unions. The fact that same-sex unions had come to be entrenched under English law did not mean that conscience objections to same-sex unions were ipso facto illegitimate and unlawful. Yet, Lady Hale, writing for the majority in *Bull* stated:

> Now that, at long last, same sex couples can enter into a mutual commitment which is the equivalent of marriage, the suppliers of goods, facilities and services should treat them in the same way.[118]

---

[114] See C Stychin (2006) 'Family Friendly? Rights, Responsibilities and Relationship' in A Diduck and K O'Donovan (eds) *Feminist Perspectives on Family Law* (Routledge, 2007) Ch 2: 'Arguably, the ingeniousness of the Civil Partnership Act is the fact that it can produce a legal status of "civil partner" that does not depend upon marriage, but which displays all of the characteristics of a civil marriage. This is undoubtedly a strategy on the part of the Government to avoid what it perceives as the likelihood of backlash to same sex marriage in the UK. At the same time, it can fulfil its promise of equality by granting a legal status to committed same sex couples'.

[115] This expression is borrowed from J Seglow, 'Religious Accommodation Law in the UK: Five normative gaps' (2018) 21(1) *Critical Review of International Social and Political Philosophy* 109.

[116] In the US since *Obergefell v Hodges*, 576 US (2015).

[117] See J Raz, 'Free Expression and Personal Identification' (1991) 11 *Oxford Journal of Legal Studies* 303 at 321, arguing that law should allow rival ways of life.

[118] *Bull v Hall* (n 106) para 36.

Even assuming that Lady Hale's interpretation of the Civil Partnership Act was as favourable to equality interests as she declares, the conclusion that religious service providers must be denied exemptions to equality principles does not follow in my view. My main point here is, however, more modestly that the alleged consecration of the equality principle is far from being as clear as the Court presents it to be and that this ambiguity should have been acknowledged in the proportionality test. In the paragraphs that follow, I will open up to US debates to reinforce the conclusions reached in a European context, namely that an acknowledgment of competing interests and procedural requirements of fairness both matter.

## B. Balancing Private Interests in a US Context

This section will focus on two US cases: the first one, *Hobby Lobby*, concerns a clash between religious freedom and women's equality rights, and the other, the *Masterpiece Cakeshop* case,[119] a conflict between religious freedom and equality rights of same-sex couples. In the American case of *Burwell v Hobby Lobby*,[120] the company Hobby Lobby requested on religious grounds an exemption from the part of the medical insurance contributions owed by employers under the Affordable Care Act, which covered access to abortive contraception. The USSC granted the employer's request, on the assumption that there would be no harm for employees, because employees would supposedly be able to obtain the requisite coverage through alternative plans directly from insurance companies.[121] Despite this rationale of harm,[122] which seems to signal a balancing of competing interests, *Hobby Lobby*, as I will explain, implicitly and unduly prioritises religious freedom. In the US *Masterpiece Cakeshop* case, a baker from Colorado, Jack Phillips, refused to bake a cake for a same-sex wedding, because of his religious opposition to same-sex unions. The majority of the US Supreme Court held that the order of the Colorado Civil Rights Commission (Commission) against the baker must be invalidated because the Commission had expressed hostility towards the baker's religious beliefs.[123] The US Supreme Court's finding that the Colorado Commission's consideration of the claim 'was infected by antireligious bias' seemed on the facts, as

---

[119] USSC *Masterpiece Cakeshop Ltd, et al v Colorado Civil Rights Commission et al*, 584 US 16-111 (2018).

[120] *Burwell v Hobby Lobby Stores, Inc*, 134 S Ct 2751 (2014).

[121] ibid, 2759, 2782.

[122] On religious exemptions and harm, see FM Gedicks and RG Van Tassell, 'RFRA Exemptions from the Contraception Mandate: An Unconstitutional Accommodation of Religion' (2014) 49 *Harvard Civil Rights–Civil Liberties Law Review* 343; FM Gedicks and A Koppelman, 'Invisible Women: Why an Exemption for Hobby Lobby Would Violate the Establishment Clause' (2014) 67 *Vanderbilt Law Review En Blanc* 51.

[123] *Masterpiece Cakeshop* (n 119) 1732.

I will show, strained.[124] Beyond the inadequacy of the argument to the facts of the case, the condemnation of both bias and disparaging treatment of religious beliefs is, however, I will argue, laudable, as it contributes to creating a more inclusive environment for religious providers and employees and thereby ensures that pluralism is not discouraged at the outset.

Out of an analysis of these two US cases of *Hobby Lobby* and *Masterpiece Cakeshop*, this section will bolster two main methodological points, which have already emerged in a European context. The first one warns against an exclusion of one type of rights in favour of the other; the second one argues that procedural considerations may be relevant for fostering the democratic paradigm presented in Part I. In *Hobby Lobby*, a few American authors have sought to deny the existence of an underlying conflict of rights between employers and employees. On the one hand, some have argued that employees did not have any *droit acquis* to accessing the health care insurance scheme at stake in the case and could not therefore invoke any tangible harm as a result of their employers' request to (partly) opt out from contributions into the scheme. On the other hand, others have argued that by choosing a corporate form for their company, the employers had relinquished their rights to raise religious objections through their company's activities.

*i.* Hobby Lobby: *Against Denying Employees' Vested Rights to Equality*

A few US authors[125] have argued that Hobby Lobby employees had not lost any entitlements because they had no right to receive full health care coverage in the first place. The correct baseline, according to them, should be set before the Affordable Care Plan statute, which set up the contested employers' contributions to the health care plan. This point of reference would reflect the idea that government protective measures are but derogations in the context of a contractually regulated environment. On that view, the loss of a government employee benefit would never qualify as a harm. In the US, the Religious Freedom Restoration Act (RFRA)[126] strengthens such pro-employer positions when the employer's actions rely on religious grounds. RFRA creates a statutory right, subject to the

---

[124] D Cole, 'This Takes the Cake', *The New York Review of Books* (19 July 2018).

[125] See for example CH Esbeck, 'When Religious Exemptions Cause Third-Party Harms: Is the Establishment Clause Violated?' (2016) 59 *Journal of Church and State* 357, at 370. See also, suggesting that employees could only complain of a harm if the government, rather than lifting a religious burden on religious actors (eg the employer) and thereby creating harm to others (eg women employees), had itself shifted costs from religious citizens onto others: E Volokh, *Sebelius v. Hobby Lobby: Corporate Rights and Religious Liberties* (Washington DC, Cato Institute Press, 2014) 64. Refuting this distinction, see N Tebbe and others, 'When Do Religious Accommodations Burden Others' in S Mancini and M Rosenfeld, *The Conscience Wars: Rethinking the Balance between Religion, Identity and Equality* (Cambridge, Cambridge University Press, 2018) 8–10.

[126] Religious Freedom Restoration Act, Pub L No 103–141, 107 Stat 1488 (1993) (codified as amended at 42 USC §§ 2000bb–2000bb-4 (2006)).

traditional compelling interest test,[127] to regulatory exemptions for religiously motivated conduct.[128] The question in *Hobby Lobby* was whether for-profit business corporations might also qualify for a religious exemption under the RFRA. Reasoning against a natural baseline,[129] law professor Esbeck argues that the RFRA would entail that employees employed by religious employers would have no pre-existing entitlements until proven that the burden caused as a result to their religious employers' beliefs passed the test.[130] However, the notion that there is a natural baseline on which to ground legal reasoning is flawed. Any supposedly natural baseline is already a construction of the underlying interests in a given direction. Accordingly, as argued by law professor Nelson Tebbe, any 'meaningful comparisons can (therefore) only be made by considering the substantive commitments at play in a particular dispute'.[131] Reciprocally, I would argue that the choice of the corporate form should not be sufficient to exclude religious freedom claims by companies and their owners.

### ii. Against Denying Corporate Employers Religious Freedoms

In the *Hobby Lobby* case, a debate arose as to whether a corporate company could be entitled to religious rights.[132] Addressing the issue of the scope

---

[127] On the government compelling interest test, see SE Gottlieb, 'Compelling Governmental Interests: An Essential but Unanalyzed Term in Constitutional Adjudication' (1988) 68(5) *Boston University Law Review* 917.

[128] According to Section 3 of the Act: 'Government may substantially burden a person's exercise of religion only if it demonstrates that application of the burden to the person– (1) is in furtherance of a compelling governmental interest; and (2) is the least restrictive means of furthering that compelling governmental interest', 42 USC § 2000bb-I(b) (Supp V 1993).

[129] On this debate over the baseline argument, see RW Garnett, 'Accommodation, Establishment and Freedom of Religion' (2014) 67 *Vanderbilt Law Review En Blanc* 46, at 46–47; MO De Girolami, 'On the Claim That Exemptions from the Contraception Mandate Violate the Establishment Clause', *Law and Religion Forum* (5 December 2013), available at lawandreligionforum.org/2013/12/05/on-the-claim-that-exemptions-from-the-contraception-mandate-violate-the-establishment-clause/; N Tebbe and others, 'Hobby Lobby and the Establishment Clause, Part II: What Counts as a Burden on Employees?' *Balkinization* (4 December 2013), available at balkin.blogspot.com/2013/12/hobby-lobby-and-establishment-clause.html; E Volokh, 'Prof. Michael McConnell (Stanford) on the *Hobby Lobby* Arguments', *Washington Post* (27 March 2014), www.washingtonpost.com/news/volokh-conspiracy/wp/2014/03/27/prof-michael-mcconnell-stanford-on-the-hobby-lobby-arguments/; KC Walsh, 'A Baseline Problem for the 'Burden on Employees' Argument Against RFRA-Based Exemptions from the Contraceptives Mandate', *Mirror of Justice* (17 January 2014), mirrorofjustice.blogs.com/mirrorofjustice/2014/01/a-baseline-problem-for-the-burden-on-employees-argument-against-rfra-based-exemptions-from-the-contr.html.

[130] Esbeck (n 125) at 370. And for a critique, see M Schwartzman and others, 'The Costs of Conscience' (2017–2018) 106 *Kentucky Law Journal* 881, at 894.

[131] Tebbe and others (n 125) at 336. See also N Tebbe, *Religious Freedom in an Egalitarian Age* (Harvard University Press, 2017), esp 60.

[132] See M Tushnet, 'Do For-Profit Corporations Have Rights of Religious Conscience?' (2013) 99 *Cornell Law Review Online* 70, 77. See also MJ Horwitz, 'Santa Clara Revisited: The Development of Corporate Theory' (1985) 88 *West Virginia Law Review* 223–24; JD Nelson, 'Conscience, Incorporated' (2013) *Michigan State Law Review* 1573 and, in relation to *Hobby Lobby*, JK McFarlin, 'The Associational Hoax: Corporate Personhood and Shareholder Rights after Hobby Lobby and Citizens United' (2016) 3(2) *Business & Bankruptcy Law Journal* 251; S Bedi, 'Fully and Barely

of RFRA,[133] Justice Alito, writing the majority opinion, observed that 'it cannot be the corporate form *per se* that militates against ascribing religious protection under the Religious Freedom Restoration Act (RFRA) because non-profit corporations receive it'.[134] Justice Alito therefore pointed to the distinction between not-for-profit and for-profit organisations to argue that it need not always apply and that employers' religious ethos may in principle infuse their corporate company, whether the company is not-for-profit or for profit. By contrast, political science professor Jean L Cohen argues that the corporate form should always act as a shield; individuals cannot have it both ways.[135] If they choose to set up an autonomous entity legally distinct from its stockholders and consequently enjoy limited liability, they can no longer exercise their religious rights as if the corporate veil did not exist.[136] Underlying these debates is the broader issue of hijacking First Amendment freedoms to expand economic liberties in unprecedented ways.[137] Reaching a solution of compromise, taking on the corporate veil objection but reversing it, professor Steve Bainbridge[138] argued that there may be reasons for the owners to be able to claim a few benefits (such as limited financial liability) whilst still escaping some of the drawbacks (such as the inhibition of their own individual rights of conscience). The degree of intertwinement between the shareholders' religious beliefs and the corporation may justify, according to Bainbridge, a reversal of the corporate veil doctrine[139] and justify that in tightly-held companies, owners and employers may invoke their religious beliefs at the cost of their employees' competing interests. More generally, I would argue that making the recognition of religious rights dependent on the type of business model selected might be respectful of the coherence of each business model but would undermine the fundamental role of religious freedom by restricting ab initio their potential ambit in the commercial sphere to certain specific types of organisations. To ensure that the corporate world is not immune from 'the principles defining the equal basic liberties and opportunities of citizens', religious employers in my view should not therefore automatically lose all opportunities to promote a religious ethos when a

Clothed: case Studies in gender and Religious Employment Discrimination in the Wake of Citizens United and Hobby Lobby' (2016) 12(2) *Hastings Business Law Journal* 133.

[133] For a discussion of the scope of the RFRA, see D Laycock and OS Thomas, 'Interpreting the Religious Freedom Restoration Act' (1994–1995) 73 *Texas Law Review* 209.

[134] *Hobby Lobby* 134 S Ct 2751 (2014) at 18–19.

[135] JL Cohen, 'Freedom of Religion, Inc.: Whose Sovereignty?' (2015) 44(3) *Netherlands Journal of Legal Philosophy* 169, at 178.

[136] See also Justice Ginsburg's dissenting opinion arguing that by incorporating a business, an individual separates herself from the entity.

[137] J Barkan, *Corporate Sovereignty: Law and Government under Capitalism* (Minneapolis, University of Minnesota Press, 2013).

[138] SM Bainbridge, 'Using Reverse Veil Piercing To Vindicate the Free Exercise Rights of Incorporated Employers' (2013) 16 *Green Bag* 235.

[139] This would suggest that only 'closely held' corporations could be entitled to religious rights. See S Nadel, 'Closely Held Conscience: Corporate Personhood in the Post-Hobby Lobby World' (2017) 50 *Columbia Journal of Law and Social Problems* 417, 448.

corporate form is chosen to pursue it.[140] One first (negative) methodological lesson to draw, therefore, from the US case of *Hobby Lobby*, is that parties' claims should be recognised a priori. Courts should consider that each party potentially has suffered an infringement to their rights, and reject approaches that would lead to privileging one claim or the other outright. This directive, however, entails that all parties feel free to raise their claim and express their convictions in the first place. In other words, none of the parties should be the victim of disparagement as it could hinder their ability to reach the courts and, more importantly, would create a discriminatory and stigmatising climate in the workplace and commercial sphere, detrimental to the goal of enriching pluralism.

### iii.  A Non-disparaging Context: Masterpiece Cakeshop

In the US *Masterpiece Cakeshop* case,[141] the USSC did not address the substantive questions of free exercise of religion of the baker versus the equality rights of the same-sex couple who wished to purchase a wedding cake from him, but focused on procedural issues. It was not because the baker's religious freedom outweighed the customer's equality claim but merely because of the alleged hostility displayed by the Commission, which first considered the case, that the USSC ruled in favour of the baker. The hostility of the Commission emanated, according to the USSC, from differing treatment between similar cases as well as from comments by two of the commissioners. As for the comments made by the two commissioners,[142] it is not certain that they were motivated by hostility towards religion at all. Nor is it clear that there was any differing treatment from analogous previous cases.[143] In the previous cases, in which the Commission had ruled in favour of the bakers, the bakers had refused to bake cakes with messages demeaning gay persons and gay marriages. The analogy between the two types of cases decided by the Colorado Commission is fragile. Whereas the first cases involved a refusal to endorse a message on top of the cake, the message in the *Masterpiece Cakeshop*, if there was one, was inseparable from the wedding cake itself. The baker, Jack Phillips, had argued that the cake order inevitably carried a message supporting gay marriage, even if no explicit inscription or decoration to that effect featured on the cake. The very fact that the cake would be served as a wedding cake for a same-sex union, he argued, established

---

[140] This question of whether a corporate company can hold protected beliefs was considered by English courts in *Exmoor Coast Boat Cruises Ltd v Revenue & Customs* [2014] UKFTT 1103 (TC). The company's request to be allowed to file its tax returns on paper rather than online because of religious objections to electronic communications was turned down but because of the inconsistency of the objection, as the company used the internet to advertise the business. See, allowing the claim, *Blackburn & Anor v Revenue & Customs* [2013] UKFTT 525 (TC).

[141] USSC *Masterpiece Cakeshop, Ltd, et al v Colorado Civil Rights Commission et al*, 584 US 16-111 (2018).

[142] *Masterpiece* (n 141) at 1729.

[143] See *Masterpiece* (n 141) at 1749 (Ginsburg, dissenting).

that link, especially as wedding cakes are not a standard production but an artistic creation that implies personal involvement from its creator.[144] By awarding him a victory on merely procedural grounds, the Court distanced itself from this line of reasoning. Writing for the Court in the US *Masterpiece Cake* case, Justice Kennedy leaves open the question of whether the baker was indeed objecting to a message or to messengers, suggesting that similar facts might well lead to a different outcome in the future.[145] This purely procedural outcome is illustrative of a method of avoidance:

> Rather than rule definitively on perhaps the most controversial case of the year, the Court gave something to both sides, and by doing so managed to cobble together a seven-justice majority. In a starkly divided nation, it avoided a sharply divided result.[146]

For my purposes, the *Masterpiece Bakery* case is interesting in two respects. It highlights that procedural requirements may allow courts to retreat into a position of referee when tackling the substantial issues head on might create a backlash harmful to democratic dialogue. I submit that such an approach may at times be a legitimate way for courts to set the tone for a more appeased confrontation of arguments at a later stage. Moreover, procedural requirements have value in themselves. By compelling employers and institutions at a pre-judicial stage to consider competing interests fairly, they encourage a climate open to pluralism and dialogue. In concluding thoughts, I will examine the extent to which this directive of enriching pluralism may point towards some tentative outcomes.

### iv. Final Thoughts

In this final brief paragraph, I will examine the Northern Irish case of *Ashers Bakery*.[147] Mr and Mrs McArthur, two bakers who were devout Christians, had refused to make a cake decorated with the words 'Support Gay Marriage'. Mr Lee had ordered the cake with this special decoration for a party organised to mark the end of Northern Ireland anti-homophobia week and underline the importance of recent parliamentary debates for the recognition of same-sex marriage in Northern Ireland. Mr and Mrs McArthur did not object to providing a cake for Mr Lee because he was gay, nor did they refuse to bake him a cake

---

[144] Several features reinforced this artistic expressive argument. The logo for Masterpiece Cakeshop was an artist's paint palate with a paintbrush and baker's whisk. Behind the counter, Phillips had a picture that depicted him as an artist painting on a canvas. There was, moreover, evidence that Phillips took exceptional care with each cake – sketching the design out on paper, choosing the colour scheme, creating the frosting and decorations, baking and sculpting the cake etc.

[145] 'it is proper to hold that whatever the outcome of some future controversy involving facts similar to these, the Commission's actions here violated the Free Exercise Clause; and its order must be set aside'.

[146] Cole 'This Takes the Cake' (n 124).

[147] *Lee v Ashers Baking Co Ltd & Others (Northern Ireland)* [2018] UKSC 49.

because of the pro-gay event the cake was meant for. Their objection lay in the message that was to decorate the cake. As Lady Hale, writing for the UKSC said, the objection was to the message, not to the messenger.[148] The UKSC thus took a narrower definition of 'expression' than the one argued for by the US Colorado baker in *Masterpiece* Cakeshop,[149] and it is precisely because, on the facts of *Ashers Bakery* (contrary to *Masterpiece Cakeshop)*, this narrow definition of expression was relevant that the baker's refusal was held to be permissible. As indicated above, such instances of clashing rights do not yield easy answers. However, one can argue that denying the baker's request in such instances would have been detrimental to the pluralism advocated in earlier chapters and therefore approve the position of the UKSC in that case. Indeed, it is one thing to deny the baker the right to deny serving a category of vulnerable people, it is another to forbid him to express minority views on homosexuality or compel him to endorse the expression of views contrary to his own.[150] Naturally one can seek to draw further distinctions and suggest that a baker, like Mr Jack Philipps in the US *Masterpiece Cakeshop* case, was not refusing to serve a same-sex couple but a cake for a same-sex wedding and conclude that only the former should fall under discrimination law. Whatever the sexual orientation of the person ordering the cake, the baker would have refused his services. Vice versa, had a same-sex couple ordered a cake for their niece's birthday party, the baker would have willingly provided them with their order. Such finer distinctions would also be defensible under the democratic paradigm. However, the opposite view, which considers that denying a cake for the reason that it is meant to celebrate a same-sex union, is indissociable from a protected characteristic and thereby discriminatory on the basis of sexual orientation, hence unlawful, despite the baker's religious objections, would also be consistent with the democratic paradigm. These finer distinctions (or their absence) are thus to be negotiated in context, in light of particular circumstances, local and national backgrounds. By contrast, I would submit that the more general distinction drawn in *Ashers Bakery* between an objection to a message and an objection to the messenger is of imperative application in liberal democracies. Forcing a religious service provider to endorse a message he/she objects to would betray the goal of an enriching pluralism by denying any expression to minority views in commercial contexts.

---

[148] ibid, para 22.

[149] Recall that according to the latter, any cake would convey a message, whether accompanied by a particular inscription or decoration or not. Following such reasoning, other wedding providers might then also claim that their contribution is a work of art and that they can only participate if they have no deeply held objections to the event they are beautifying. A florist who artistically creates flower arrangements, a photographer who artistically portrays the day in a favourable light also arguably personally contribute to the event.

[150] See Hugh Collins' blog available at uklabourlawblog.com/2019/03/04/a-missing-layer-of-the-cake-with-the-controversial-icing-hugh-collins/.

## C. Conclusion to Section III

In this section, I have considered recent controversies opposing religious freedom claims to equality concerns of women and same-sex couples. Whilst the democratic paradigm defended in Part I leaves open the question of the precise outcome to reach in these delicate instances, I have drawn from recent developments, on both sides of the Atlantic, to produce further guidelines on how to approach the issues. This section has argued that changes and ambiguities in the law should be taken into account and weigh in favour of the party who relied on a different or past interpretation of the law in the proportionality stage. Moreover, the confrontation of the American case of *Masterpiece Cakeshop* and the English case of *Ladele* has underlined the importance of procedural fairness at the pre-judicial stage. Regardless of the assessment of the substantive claims, courts should arguably step in when a disparaging climate is tolerated in the workplace or in commercial relationships. The enriching democratic potential of pluralism can only flourish if courts ensure that outside of the courthouse too, diversity of views and identities can have a place. Flowing from this conclusion, the confrontation of the American case of *Hobby Lobby* and the British cases of *Ladele* and *Ashers Bakery* has demonstrated that the enriching potential of pluralism would call for a wide consideration of competing claims. I have therefore urged caution in relation to arguments that dismiss or undermine outright one set of interests. I have examined arguments for a restriction of particular interests, such as the suggestion that religious interests should be inhibited in light of the corporate form chosen to express them, or the commitment to equality embraced by the employer. On the other side of the spectrum, I have analysed arguments for restricting equality interests in these instances – in view of the lack of any concrete infringements of same-sex couples' rights or, more forcefully, of a legislative pre-delimitation in favour of religious freedom. All of these arguments, I suggest, are problematic, for they potentially curtail dialogue and undermine deliberation ab initio.

### IV. CONCLUSION TO CHAPTER 6

Having highlighted a few problematic aspects in the ruling of *Achbita* in Chapter 5, this chapter has explored possible ways forward. In a first section, I have suggested that a helpful distinction emerges from a comparison of *Achbita* and the ECtHR decision in *Ebrahimian*, between the problematic absolute and misplaced delegation of competence to national authorities identified in *Achbita* in the preceding chapter and the deference manifested by the ECtHR towards the French constitutional principle of laïcité. Section I has noted two crucial differences between the two respective approaches of the European courts. First, in *Ebrahimian*, unlike in *Achbita*, the principle of laïcité was actually applicable. Second, in *Ebrahimian*, unlike in *Achbita*, the deference towards the national constitutional context was accompanied by conditions which leave the door open for re-evaluation in the future. Section II has analysed in detail subsequent rulings of the CJEU, in *Egenberger* and *IR*, as well as relevant decisions of the ECtHR in order to tease out what a proportionality review might look like. I have demonstrated that a strict proportionality review, far from ineluctably conferring unrestrained judicial discretion, may follow objective criteria, as they gradually emerge from the case law. Amongst these objective criteria feature, for example: the consideration as to whether the religious ethos manifests itself in any concrete ways in the workplace; the evaluation of its impact on the performance of individual employees' tasks; the acceptance by the employer that employees who do not belong to that particular religion may nonetheless be appointed to the post in question; the extent to which the employee's functions may be deemed representative of the ethos promoted by the employer; the seriousness of the infringement caused to the employee's competing rights, notably his/her prospects of finding employment elsewhere; the publicity willingly given by the employee to his/her violations of the work ethos, etc. Finally, section III has explored instances of clashing rights between religious employers, employees or service providers and the rights to equal treatment of their employees or customers. Whilst precise outcomes depend on contextual evolving deliberations between stakeholders (including in the courtroom), I have suggested helpful guidelines, in line with the democratic paradigm defended in Part I. Courts should thus, I have argued, step in when necessary, to sanction a hostile and stigmatising climate in the workplace or commercial relationships and/or avoid a summary treatment of one set of interests.

The overall objective of the proposals made in Chapter 6 is to bolster the democratic paradigm defended in Part I. A deference towards national constitutional traditions confined within the limits of the principle of laïcité would not only offer a more accurate, hence more legitimate, basis for the margin of appreciation granted to Member States, it would enable European courts to maintain an informed dialogue with national authorities on the legitimate scope and consequences of the principle of laïcité. Likewise, a proportionality review would enable courts to gradually refine objective criteria as case law accumulates, and thereby engage in the ongoing discussion about where to draw a line between competing interests. Finally, as advocated in section III, an emphasis on procedural fairness at the pre-judicial stage, and a full consideration of all the interests at stake would ensure that the positive value recognised in pluralism is not undermined ab initio.

## V. CONCLUSION OF PART II

This second part has outlined potential pitfalls which would betray the democratic positive value that Part I has attached to pluralism. As shown in Chapter 5, a priori exclusion of religious voices from the workplace, undue and absolute deference to national authorities or the delimitation of legal solutions according to pre-determined political spheres, which evolve in parallel and separately from one another, all curtail dialogue and pluralism in arbitrary ways and I have argued that they should, therefore, be resisted. They fall short of the method of avoidance and principles of inclusion and revision advocated in Part I. Instead of guaranteeing the state's neutrality towards comprehensive doctrines, under the method of avoidance, they prioritise one set of interests, under the misguided idea of a 'natural baseline'. Instead of guaranteeing equality and fair terms of cooperation between religious and non-religious citizens, under the principle of inclusion, they muffle religious voices and, instead of guaranteeing that the terms of legitimate diversity are subject to constant review under the principle of revision, they close down dialogue.[151] Chapter 6 has offered possible alternative ways. It has argued for a deference towards national authorities, which would rely on an accurate assessment of national constitutional traditions, themselves open to further scrutiny and revision. It has made the case for contextual judicial proportionality review and shown how clashing private interests might receive full consideration in the courtroom and be protected from a disparaging and stigmatising climate outside of the court. These ways forward ground normative proposals to change certain approaches in contemporary controversies relating to religious freedoms in the workplace and commercial area. They lead us to question the diverging approach adopted by the CJEU in *Achbita* and the ECtHR in *Ebrahimian* towards laïcité and recommend that the CJEU aligns itself with the ECtHR model. Similarly, the ECtHR may serve as an inspiration in the way it carries out contextual proportionality review in its decisions in *Obst*, *Schüth*, *Fernández Martínez* and *Travaš*. It might be that the CJEU is already moving towards a stricter proportionality test, as indicated by the more recent rulings of *Egenberger* and *IR*. If radically divergent approaches were to be embraced, depending on whether the employer seeks to enforce neutrality policies (as in *Achbita*) or a religious work ethos (as *Egenberger* and *IR*), the divergence would be, as this chapter has shown, unjustifiable. Beyond these normative proposals, Part II has, more profoundly, sought to offer a different principled way of looking at these issues, in the hope that pluralism and religious freedom may no longer be seen as a threat but be conducive to a harmonious *vivre ensemble*.

---

[151] See Ch 4, section II.C.

# 7

# *Conclusion*

Freedom of thought, conscience and religion is one of the foundations of a 'democratic society' within the meaning of the Convention. It is, in its religious dimension, one of the most vital elements that go to make up the identity of believers and their conception of life, but it is also a precious asset for atheists, agnostics, sceptics and the unconcerned. The pluralism indissociable from a democratic society, which has been dearly won over the centuries, depends on it.[1]

H OW SHOULD WE think about recent controversies involving rights to religious freedom? This book has argued for a democratic conception of religious freedom, which embraces both its negative dimension, its protective function against state intrusion, and its positive dimension, its supportive function of pluralism, and ultimately of democracy. I have argued that the combination of the three features of avoidance, inclusion and revision can provide a backbone for this dual-dimension democratic-deepening understanding of religious freedom and usefully guide judges confronted to increasingly delicate cases opposing religious requests to clashing rights. As highlighted by the European Court of Human Rights' (ECtHR) statement, religious freedom matters not only for religious citizens, but also for democracy more generally, by offering a more democratic understanding of our *vivre ensemble*. Against current views of religious freedom, which neglect the connections either between religious freedom and democracy, or between religious freedom and pluralism, the democratic approach I advocate builds and reinforces these links. Under the method of avoidance, the state is to refrain from interfering with religious beliefs and thereby protect both the public sphere from intractable controversies and religious citizens' sense of identity and autonomy from undue interferences. Following the principle of inclusion, the state is to ensure that minority marginalised voices have opportunities to be heard on an equal footing. Finally, according to the principle of revision, both citizens and state institutions are expected to revise their commitments, in order to preserve the (ever renewed and revisited) horizon of a *vivre ensemble*.

---

[1] *Kokkinakis v Greece* App no 14307/88 (ECtHR Grand Chamber, 25 May 1993).

## I. FOR A DEMOCRATIC APPROACH TO RELIGIOUS FREEDOM

This book has defended this democratic approach of religious freedom both comparatively and normatively.

## A.  Comparative Demonstration

Comparatively, I have argued that a democratic-deepening interpretation of religious freedom is compatible with both the French laïque and the English church establishment contexts, but in ways and manifestations suited to each country and to their respective complex history of Church/state relationships. I have demonstrated that it is conceivable to expand the concept of laïcité into a democratic-deepening form of secularism. In fact, the French 1905 Law on the separation between the state and the Church contains, as I have shown, many traits which place laïcité in line with the democratic approach. In accordance with a method of avoidance, the 1905 Law delineated a political sphere free (at least in principle) from national or religious ideology, and sought to protect freedom of conscience in the private and non-state public spheres. By improving the fate of religious minorities, the 1905 Law also went some way towards a principle of inclusion, attentive to marginalised citizens. The challenges of Islam in modern times, instead of prompting a review of the terms of legitimacy, in line with the principle of revision, has instead provoked a retreat into illiberalism. These contemporary trends go against the democratic approach. Contrary to the method of avoidance, they define the state sphere exponentially and consequently trigger increasingly intrusive state regulation and prohibition of religious manifestation. Contrary to the principle of inclusion, they exclude marginal Muslim voices, which they depict as irremediably antagonistic to republican values. Contrary to the principle of revision, they ossify Republican and Muslim values into dichotomous narratives. I have shown that similar elements of compatibility with the democratic paradigm, tainted by illiberal contemporary streaks, characterise the English model. Because of its non-coercive nature and its protection of a democratic sphere immune to church influence, I have argued that English establishment, at the eve of the 20th century, had allowed a conception of religious freedom respectful of the method of avoidance and the principle of inclusion. Social divides have, however, hindered the reality of the principle of inclusion, whilst the narrative of 'fundamental British values', born out of fear of Islamic radicalisation, has veered towards a more communautarian vision of the *vivre ensemble*, contrary to the fluidity embodied by the principle of revision and to the openness expressed by the principle of inclusion. These contemporary trends deny the 'vital elements that go to make up the identity of (Muslim) believers and their conception of life'.[2] Instead of constructing

---

[2] *Kokkinakis v Greece* (n 1).

religious freedom as a 'precious asset for atheists, agnostics, sceptics and the unconcerned',[3] they picture it as a threat, to be contained and channelled in line with fundamental national values, or the requirements of living together, themselves construed as a reflection of fixed majority views. In contrast with these recent inward-looking trends, this book has argued that laïcité and Church establishment in England should (and can) each find within their rich history, elements of a generous interpretation of religious freedom, in line with the three features of avoidance, inclusion and revision advocated.

## B. Normative Demonstration

Normatively, this book has sought to vindicate this conception of religious freedom against two standard stances. The first stance expresses scepticism towards the full possibility of a common *vivre ensemble*. The second expresses scepticism towards the possibility and desirability of the category of religious freedom. The first position doubts the capacity of liberalism and religious frameworks to find (full) harmonious coordination. It consequently recommends either mutual indifference or priority for the religious position, which only the religious citizen could herself (legitimately) appreciate. According to the second stance, which I have named the 'secular-to-analogous' view, religious interests would only deserve protection when an underlying secular value worthy of protection requires the state's intervention. The secular-to-analogous approach may grant religious citizens many rights, but it will do so out of concerns for fairness, equality, non-discrimination, etc, never because *religious* freedom matters. On the contrary, I have argued that dispensing with the religious dimension of the request would come at a loss both for the religious citizens concerned and for democratic debate. The analogous view, in other words, fails to capture that religious freedom 'is also a precious asset for atheists, agnostics, sceptics and the unconcerned'[4] and consequently undermines the 'pluralism indissociable from a democratic society (which) depends on it'. On the contrary, the democratic approach emphasises the links between religious freedom, religious believers' sense of identity and pluralism. Specifically, I argue that following a method of avoidance, the state should not assess (or deny) the religious nature attached to a given claim. Following the principle of inclusion, it should embrace the religious claim put forward by religious citizens, as a *religious* claim, for this characterisation is, I have suggested, important for the claimant's sense of identity as well as for the richness of democratic debate. However, unlike the first stance, the democratic approach resists the temptation to confer any priority on religious interests. Conferring a priority on rights to religious freedom over competing

---

[3] ibid.
[4] *Kokkinakis v Greece* (n 1).

interests would certainly recognise that religious freedom is 'one of the most vital elements that go to make up the identity of believers and their conception of life'. However, it would fail to explain how religious freedom could be one of 'the foundations of a "democratic society"'[5] and be of any value to 'the atheists, agnostics, sceptics and the unconcerned'.[6] By contrast, I have argued that religious citizens – like everyone else – must accept the horizon of a *vivre ensemble*, of a shared constitutional liberal framework. As sceptics have rightly underlined, liberalism may not have any greater claim to neutrality or any higher moral ground. It is not superior on substantive grounds to religious frameworks. Its higher claim, however, stems from its political, procedural and constitutional position as an overarching framework. I have suggested that as an overarching framework in which competing views can be confronted, explained and balanced against one another, such a liberal constitutional framework is best placed, through its courts, to embody the requirements of the principle of revision. These requirements entail a constant dialogical engagement of competing interests with one another and an ongoing revision of the legitimate limits set to religious (and non-religious) interests.

In Part II, I have built on this paradigmatic democratic conception of religious freedom to put forward guidelines on how courts should address instances of competing rights and interests involving religious freedom, with a focus on disputes in the workplace and in the context of provision of services to consumers. As schematised in the tables below, I have identified several pathological traits which (I have argued) should be resisted, and several others which, in contrast, should in my view be adopted.

## II. CONSEQUENCES OF THE DEMOCRATIC APPROACH FOR THE COURTS

I have highlighted several practical consequences of the democratic approach for courts confronted with religious freedom cases.

### A. Clues Relating to the Assessment of the Religious Claim

In the assessment of the religious claim, I have argued that courts should rely on the claimant's subjective assessment, as prescribed by the ECtHR in *Eweida v UK*[7] and advocated by Advocate General Sharpston in *Bougnaoui*[8] and avoid dismissing the request outright by characterising the religious practice as erratic,

---

[5] ibid.
[6] ibid.
[7] *Eweida v United Kingdom* [2013] ECHR 37.
[8] Case C-188/15 *Asma Bougnaoui v Micropole SA*, Judgment of the Court (Grand Chamber) of 14 March 2017.

'contracted out' or extreme. Variations in the intensity of religious practice by the claimant, acquiescence to restrictive policies in specific situations, such as the workplace or the ostentatious nature of the religious symbol in question, should not therefore, per se, lead to a rejection of the religious freedom claim. The method of avoidance and principle of inclusion combine to dictate that courts do not meddle with the determination of which religious practices amount to acceptable religious manifestations but take on board the claimant's interest in expressing her religious faith, however conspicuous or inconsistent the manifestation may appear at first sight. This importance conferred to religious freedom portrays religion as part of the claimant's identity and ensures that religious citizens are not systematically compelled to choose between their religious commitments and participation in the workplace or in the provision of certain services. In line with the principle of revision, this recognition may nonetheless be accompanied by restrictions and limits, but following a careful proportionality test, not on the sole ground of the employee's consenting to leaving her religious freedom out of the workplace for example.

## B.  Against Delegation to Employers

The democratic approach therefore leads courts to scrutinise competing interests at play in the workplace, without deferring a priori to the employers' own assessment of the tensions. I have argued against delegating such powers of decision to employers. Neither the right to conduct a business under Article 16 of the EU Charter of Fundamental Rights or secularism, I have argued, may per se justify such delegation from courts to employers. In an ordoliberal inspiration, the Constitution would mainly serve to protect the autonomy and freedom of economic exchanges and judicial review of restrictions imposed on employees' fundamental (religious) freedoms for the sake of business would consequently be limited to verifying the consistency of their enforcement. I have made a case against this ordoliberal starting point, which can be detected in the ruling of the Court of Justice of the European Union (CJEU) in *Achbita*.[9] The ordoliberal inspiration, I have argued, betrays the method of avoidance – as the state fails to protect religious freedom against interferences from employers. It goes against the principle of inclusion, as mainstream religious manifestations and beliefs are more likely to be tolerated than minority practices. It, finally, falls foul of the principle of revision, as dialogue and engagement between protagonists is paralysed by the greater weight a priori granted to employers' decisions. Similarly, I have submitted that secularism does not support employers' requests to enforce neutrality policies in their companies. Such extensive reading of secularism

---

[9] Case C-157/15 *Achbita, Centrum voor Gelijkheid van kansen en voor racismebestrijding v G4S Secure Solutions*, Judgment of the Court (Grand Chamber) of 14 March 2017.

is, I have argued, unconvincing as it relies on two unproven assumptions: that neutrality in the workplace would be more protective of (vulnerable) customers' rights or commercial interests; and that a workplace free of religion and other ideological signs would qualify as a neutral sphere. On the contrary, I have argued that restrictions to religious freedom, under the principle of revision, should rely on tangible evidence of the competing interests which would be in jeopardy, and that the greater onus placed on religious employees under sweeping notions of neutrality should be acknowledged and addressed, as required under the principle of inclusion.

## C. For a Nuanced Deference to National Traditions

If courts are to avoid conferring a quasi carte blanche to employers, neither should they allow Member States unfettered discretion to decide the most delicate cases. As evident in the contextual anchoring of my proposal, constitutional national traditions are not to be ignored in supra-national courts' interpretation of the interests at stake. Consideration of national traditions reinforces the principle of revision by allowing a subtler contextual understanding of the competing claims. However, such refined understanding can only occur if supra-national courts invoke Member States' national traditions appropriately: when these are – and only when these are – applicable and with the complexities of the national controversies surrounding them. By contrast, I have argued that the reference to laïcité in Advocate General Kokkott's Opinion in *Achbita* was misplaced, as the principle of laïcité was not applicable, and undermined the principle of revision by taking sides in and closing down the debate in France on the proper contours of the concept.

## D. Comments on Proportionality

As the margin of appreciation of Member States and the employers' decision powers in my approach remain subject to judicial review, and the principle of inclusion urges judges to take all competing interests on board on an equal footing, the crucial test – from which concrete outcomes will flow – will be *in fine* a proportionality test. Under the proportionality test, courts will, as expected, seek to ascertain whether the restrictions imposed upon religious freedom are proportionate to the legitimate goal the employer is pursuing. No one single outcome ensues from such proportionality assessment, under the suggested avoidance, inclusion and revision features. Nor should one single outcome ensue. By definition, in line with the principle of revision, which postulates that the terms of legitimacy are constantly under review, concrete outcomes can only be transient. If one cannot and should not identify one single legitimate outcome in each given case, I have suggested that it is possible and desirable to exclude a few, which derive from a (in my view) flawed enforcement of the proportionality test. Such flawed instances correspond, for example, to misplaced proportionality tests, under which proportionality requirements do not apply to the contested restriction itself but to the sanction or consequences flowing from non-compliance with the restriction. As I have argued, such use of the proportionality test misses its target. The proportionality of the sanction proves nothing as to the proportionality of the restriction itself. Other flawed manifestations of the proportionality test relate to unproven assumptions as to the risks caused by a given religious practice to vulnerable people (children or patients). The conclusion that restrictions to religious freedom would be proportionate on the condition that they are limited to situations where the religious claimant is in contact with the vulnerable people in question collapses, because of its unproven premise. Finally, proportionality assessments are flawed when courts refrain at the outset from hearing all competing interests involved, for example when religious interests are discarded for the sole reason that they feature in a commercial corporate sector.

## E.  A Word on Brexit

Many of the recommendations I have made take place in the context of an EU Directive – EU Council Directive 2000/78/EC of 27 November 2000 Establishing a General Framework for Equal Treatment in Employment and Occupation (the Directive). Short term, Brexit is not likely to affect the comments made under the auspices of the Directive.[10] First, the relevant provisions of the Directive have been entrenched into a UK statute: the Equality Act 2010. Second, Article 126 of the (new)[11] Withdrawal Agreement 2019[12] provides for a transition period until the end of December 2020,[13] during which EU law will continue to apply.[14] Beyond the transition period, however, unless a successfully negotiated

---

[10] For a full assessment of the likely impact of Brexit on equality protection in UK Law, see C O'Cinneide, 'Values, rights and Brexit – Lessons to be learnt from the slow evolution of United Kingdom discrimination law' (2017) 30 *Australian Journal of Labour Law* 17.

[11] The 'new' Withdrawal Agreement replaces the Withdrawal Agreement which was negotiated by Theresa May's Government in November 2018 and rejected three times by the UK Parliament.

[12] The (new) Withdrawal Agreement was published on 19 October 2019. See assets.publishing.service. gov.uk/government/uploads/system/uploads/attachment_data/file/840655/Agreement_on_the_ withdrawal_of_the_United_Kingdom_of_Great_Britain_and_Northern_Ireland_from_ the_European_Union_and_the_European_Atomic_Energy_Community.pdf. It received Royal Assent on 23 January 2020.

[13] Under Art 126: 'There shall be a transition or implementation period, which shall start on the date of entry into force of this Agreement and end on 31 December 2020'. Under Art 132 of the (new) Withdrawal Agreement, the UK and EU can jointly agree, on a one-off basis, to extend that period by a further period of 'up to two-years' but the Conservative Manifesto for the 12 December 2019 General Election contains a pledge not to claim an extension beyond 31 December 2020: see vote.conservatives.com/our-plan.

[14] Art 127 of the (new) Withdrawal Agreement states that: 'Unless otherwise provided in this Agreement, Union law shall be applicable to and in the United Kingdom during the transition period'.

future relationship deal between the EU and the UK provides otherwise,[15] the UK would no longer be legally bound to abide by current levels of employers' right protection or so-called 'level playing field' commitments. By contrast, Annex 4 of the Protocol to the former Theresa May's Withdrawal Agreement had maintained these commitments, which meant that CJEU rulings up to the date of Brexit would have been treated as binding precedents.[16] Under the new version, the commitment is watered down, under paragraph 77 of the revised Political Declaration,[17] to a mere aspiration, since the Political Declaration has no binding force but merely contains terms, which 'the UK and EU will use their best endeavours in good faith to give effect to'.[18] If CJEU rulings, just like fundamental principles of EU law and provisions of the EU Charter on Fundamental Rights would no longer be binding on UK courts from 2021 onwards, UK judges would still be able to take them into account when they think it is appropriate. Moreover, as long as the UK stays in the Council of Europe, and remains subject to the European Convention on Human Rights framework,[19] the cross-fertilisation between EU and ECHR law[20] would probably indirectly maintain a degree of influence of EU law principles upon English law, especially upon statutes, such as the Equality Act 2010, which have originated from EU Directives.[21] Should the immediate[22] legal impact on equality protection remain limited, Brexit is nonetheless likely to increase the existing deep social, generational, regional and political divides across the UK, which the 2016 referendum vote has already revealed and heightened. Recommendations for a democratic

---

[15] It seems that a future relationship deal with the EU would entail that the UK commits to a level playing field. See Art 2 of *The Conclusions adopted on Friday 13th December by the EU Council on Article 50, in light of the results of the General Election*, EUCO XT 20027/19: 'The future relationship will have to be based on a balance of rights and obligations and ensure a level playing field' See, however, the statement by Boris Johnson that the UK Government does not intend to accept any alignment on EU rules: https://www.theguardian.com/politics/2020/feb/02/uk-refuse-close-alignment-eu-rules-boris-johnson-trade.

[16] EU (Withdrawal) Bill, HC Bill 5, Session 2017–9, cl 2.

[17] Under para 77 of the (new) Political Declaration: 'the Parties should uphold the common high standards applicable in the Union and the United Kingdom at the end of the transition period in the areas of state aid, competition, social and employment'. See TF50 (2019) 65 – Commission to EU 27, 17 October 2019, ec.europa.eu/commission/sites/beta-political/files/revised_political_declaration.pdf.

[18] Under Art 184 of the (new) Withdrawal Agreement.

[19] There have been discussions about repealing the Human Rights Act 1998 (which entrenches ECHR provisions into UK law) and replacing it with a British Bill of Rights: 'Plans to Replace Human Rights Act with British Bill of Rights Will Go Ahead Justice Secretary Confirms', *The Independent* 22 August 2016, available at www.independent.co.uk/news/uk/politics/scrap-human-rights-act-british-bill-of-rights-theresa-may-justice-secretary-liz-truss-a7204256.html. The 2019 Conservative Manifesto contains a confusing (but, at first sight, less radical) pledge to 'update' the Human Rights Act 1998.

[20] R Wintemute, 'Goodbye EU Anti-discrimination Law? Hello Repeal of the Equality Act 2010?' (2016) 27(3) *King's Law Journal* 387.

[21] However, there would no longer be anything to prevent the UK Government from pushing for a reform or repeal of the Equality Act 2010, which weakens the protection of workers' rights.

[22] Long term, the impact will be greater, as Brexit will cut off UK law from any future developments in EU law.

understanding of a *vivre ensemble* open to pluralism, and dialogue are therefore needed more than ever.

I hope that the proposals contained in this book will contribute to this aim and that in helping courts to solve contemporary controversies over religious freedom claims, they foster a more inclusive, tolerant and vibrant *vivre ensemble* for our societies, in England and France, as studied in this book, and beyond, in other western liberal democracies.

# Appendix

## Table of Pathologies

| Deference motive | Inspiration | Illustration | Legal basis | Consequences for religious believers | Limits | Reference |
|---|---|---|---|---|---|---|
| Delegation to company policies | Ordoliberal | *Achbita* | Art 16 CFR | 1. Contracting out possible<br>2. Inconsistency in religious practice suspicious<br>3. Conspicuous symbols more problematic | External relations only.<br>Consistency of enforcement | Chapter 5: Section I.A and Section II.A |
| | | Proposal by Professor Valentin | Art 4(2) Directive | | Consistency of enforcement | Chapter 5: Section I.A.iv |
| | Ordoliberal/ Corporate image | Proposal by Professor Christians | Art 16 CFR | | | |
| | Secularised neutrality | 2016 *El Khomri* Act | Art L. 1321-2-1 French Labour Code | | Objective reason required<br>Proportionate enforcement | Chapter 5: Section I.A.iii |

*(continued)*

*(Continued)*

| Deference motive | Inspiration | Illustration | Legal basis | Consequences for religious believers | Limits | Reference |
|---|---|---|---|---|---|---|
|  | Secularised neutrality | *Baby Loup* | Art L. 1121-1 and L. 1321-3 French Labour Code | Narrow definition of protected religious practices<br><br>1. Contracting out possible/Specific situation rule applicable<br>2. Inconsistency in religious practice undermines religious freedom claim<br>3. Conspicuous symbols more problematic | Child care sector only | Chapter 5: Section I.B.ii |
| Delegation to national constitutional identity | Fear of backlash | Opinion AG Kokott in *Achbita* | Art 4(2) TEU | Exponential expansion of restrictions<br><br>Misplaced divide between laïque and non-laïque systems | Minimum judicial review | Chapter 5: Section II.C |
| Delegation to national majorities | Fear of backlash | *SAS* | Margin of appreciation |  | Full-covering religious symbols only<br><br>Severe sanctions in case of non-compliance with restrictions not allowed | Chapter 6: Section I.A |

Table of Success Stories

| Inspiration | Illustration | Legal basis | Consequences for religious believers | Limits | References |
|---|---|---|---|---|---|
| Democratic approach to religious freedom | *Eweida* AG Sharpston in *Bougnaoui* | Art 9 ECHR Directive 2000 | 1. No contracting out 2. Inconsistency in religious practice not per se problematic 3. Religious symbols a priori legitimate regardless of size | Legitimate and proportionate restrictions allowed | Chapter 5: Section II, A and B |
| | *Egenberger, IR Schüth, Obst, Fernández Martínez* and *Travaš* | Directive Art 9 ECHR | Judicial scrutiny of competing rights | Restriction proportionate only if objectively and specifically justified | Chapter 6: Section II |

# Index

accommodationist approach   5, 9–13, 82
  educational curriculum, conflict with
      religious upbringing   11, 13
  epistemological and impartiality
      concerns   11–13, 14
  versus separatist   94
*Achbita (Samira) v G4S Secure Solutions*
      case (2017)
  Advocate General Kokott's Opinion   6,
      120, 121, 123, 124, 126, 131, 132,
      135, 136, 181
  analogous-to-secular view   6
  applicable to all employment sectors   129
  CJEU ruling   19–20, 120, 121, 126
  compared with *Ebrahimian*   144, 145
  compared with *Eweida*   131, 134, 135–136
  constitutional context   144
  contradiction with *Bougnaoui*   121,
      122–123
  facts of case   119
  *hijab*, customers' objections to   122, 123
  indirect discrimination   119, 120, 122
  laïcité inapplicable to   128
  looking beyond   139–175
  minimum judicial intervention
      principle   147
  neutrality policy, unilateral   119–123, 129
  ordoliberal inspiration of   123–124, 126,
      129, 180
  private law   128
  proportionality considerations   120, 129,
      136–137
  spheres of competence   121–129
  *see also Bougnaoui v Micropole* case (2017)
Adhar, Rex   33, 47, 58, 61, 62, 67
Ahmed An-Na'im, Abdullahi   106
Allen, Rebecca   73
analogous-to-secular view   5–9, 82, 83, 85, 98
  disaggregative approach   7–9
  under-inclusion/over-inclusion problem of
      analogous approach   6–7
Anderson, Elizabeth S   64
antisemitism   40, 41
anti-theory   93

Arthur, James   77
Asad, Talal   12
*Ashers Baking* case (2018)   157, 171–172
Audi, Robert   9, 62, 83
autonomy, religious *see* religious autonomy
avoidance method   2–3, 15, 101, 110
  non-interference principle   24, 110

Bader, Veit   65
Badinter, Robert   40
Bainbridge, Steve   169
Balibar, Etienne   18, 39, 57, 79
  *Secularism and Cosmopolitanism*   55
Barkan, Joshua   169
Barlas, Asma   83
Barry, Brian   87, 90
Bartlett, Jamie   77
Basdevant, Brigitte   37
Baubérot, Jean   27, 33, 35, 37, 38, 40, 55
Bedi, Suneal   168
Bell, David   36
Bell, John   45
Bell, Mark   120
Benhabib, Seyla   107
Bezci, Egemen B   33
Bhandar, Brenna   28
Birdwell, Jonathan   77
Birnbaum, Pierre   40
Bohman, James   109–110
Bolton, Paul   70
*Bougnaoui v Micropole* case (2017)
  Advocate General Sharpston's
      Opinion   121, 122, 126, 136, 179
  contradiction with *Achbita*   121, 122–123
  customers' preferences   119, 120
  direct discrimination   119, 120, 122
  facts of case   119
  genuine and determining occupational
      requirement   120
  private law   128
  *see also Achbita (Samira) v G4S Secure
      Solutions* case
Bowen, John   53
Bradley, Ian   58, 68

Brems, Eva   56, 142, 144
Brexit   182–184
Briand, Aristide   39
British Humanist Association   72
Brudney, Daniel   67
*Bull v Hall* (2013)   163–165
*burqa*
   ban on   48–49, 55, 56, 142
   right to wear in public   83
Buruma, Ian   51, 53
*Burwell v Hobby Lobby Stores* (2014)   20,
      166, 173
   argument against denying corporate
      employers religious
      freedoms   168–170
   argument against denying employees vested
      rights to equality   167–168

Calhoun, Craig   27
Callebat, Bernard   75, 161
Candar, Gilles   41
CARITAS (international confederation)   149
Catholic Church, England   70, 71
Catholic Church, France   31–42, 155
   marriage, indissolubility of sacrament   32
   Revolutionary hostility to   33, 34, 36,
      37–38, 47
   *see also* France; laïcité (French secularism);
      Law on Separation of Church and
      State (1905), France; separatist
      secularism (separation of Church
      and state)
Charter of Fundamental Rights (CFR)   120,
      180, 183
Chélini-Pont, Blandine   41
Christianity
   Christian cross, right to wear
      (*Eweida*)   75, 130–131, 134–136,
      158, 163, 179
   Church establishment, England *see*
      establishment, church (England)
   intolerant view, accommodation of   11
   and meaning of religion   9
Christians, Louis-Leon   125, 126
Church of England   58, 66, 69–71
   independence from politics   67–69
   *see also* England; establishment, church
      (England)
civil partnerships *see* same-sex couples,
      equality rights clashing with
      religious freedom
Clark, Kenneth   73

clash of civilisations   27
Clémenceau, Georges   41
Cochin, Auguste   34, 38
Cohen, Jean L   169
Cohen, Joshua   1, 16, 17, 64, 81, 156
Cole, David   167, 171
Collins, Hugh   15, 172
Combes, Emile   38
communautarian laïcité   44, 53–56
comparative approach   17–18, 177–178
   *see also* England; France
compliance principle   150
Comte, Auguste   38
Conseil d'Etat   31, 42–45, 50, 128
   *Demoiselle Marteaux* opinion   141
   Muslim veil, wearing of   48
   *Rapport*   38n, 39n, 40n, 43n, 49n
   separatist/inclusive interpretation
      of laïcité   45–48
Conseil d'Etat, separatist/inclusive
      interpretation   45–48
consistency argument, religious employees'
      claims
   burdens of   132–135
   consistency as proof of sincerity and
      cogency   132–134
   consistency over proportionality
      emphasis   130–137, 146
   contracting out approach   134–135
   procedural consistency, proportionality
      test reduced to   135–137
contextual approach   17–18
   England and *vivre ensemble*   58–79
   laïcité and democratic *vivre
      ensemble*   27–57
contracting out approach   134–135
contractual sphere   122–126
corporate veil doctrine   169
Cotterell, Roger   17, 18
Cottret, Bernard   34
Council of Europe   183
Court of Justice of the European Union
      (CJEU)   151, 156
   case law on religious symbols in
      workplace   19–20, 118, 120, 121,
      126, 129, 179
   *see also Achbita (Samira) v G4S Secure
      Solutions* case; *Bougnaoui v
      Micropole* case (2017); European
      Court of Human Rights (ECtHR);
      headscarf incidents (Islamic);
      Muslims

courts, views on religious minorities    11–12
Cranmer, Frank    66, 68, 137, 150
creationism    11
Cromwell, Oliver    58
cultural diversity    27
Cumper, Peter
customers' preferences, and Muslim
          dress    119, 120, 122

de Bellaigue, Christopher    50
de Courrèges, Hélène    75, 161
de Girolami, Marc O    168
Darwin, Charles    38
Davie, Grace    33
democracy
    defining    1
    equality as the foundation of    86
    importance of religious freedom for
          82–98
    pluralism, importance for    98–111
    pure    35
    religious freedom, democratic approach
          to    177–179
        assessment of religious claim
              179–180
        comparative demonstration    177–178
        consequences for the courts    179–184
        delegation to employers, argument
              against    180–181
        normative demonstration    1, 178–179
        nuanced deference to national
              traditions    181
        and pluralism    101
        proportionality considerations
              181–182
    self-restraint, democratic rule as    100
    substantive values    4
    theory    16–17
    usefulness of democratic approach    5
    *vivre ensemble*    4, 13, 14, 21, 80–118
    laïcité    27–57
Derrida, Jacques    12
dichotomous ideological discourses
    conflicting    52–53
    going beyond dichotomies    55–56
disaggregative approach
    defining    7
    potentially lesser protection of religious
          freedom under    7–8
    responses to    8–9
discrimination
    direct and indirect    119, 120, 122

against dissenters, abolition of in
          England    66–67
    justification test    120
    racial    84–85
dissenters, abolition of discrimination against
          (England)    66–67
'Divinitia' (fictional state)    63
Doe, Norman    68, 150
Doizy, Guillaume    41
Dorf, Michael C    17, 157
Dreyfus, Alfred/Dreyfus affair    40, 41
Drinkwater, Stephen    73
Duclert, Vincent    40, 41
Dworkin, Ronald    3, 61, 63, 65, 67, 69, 87,
          164

Eberle, Christopher    104, 106
*Ebrahimian v France* case (2015)
    compared with *Achbita*    144, 145
    deference to laïcité    140–144
    laïcité within remit    144–145
    rights of public agents to wear religious
          symbols    20
    ruling    173
    *see also* laïcité (French secularism)
Edge, Peter    69, 88, 134
education
    critical reading programme, conflict with
          religious upbringing (US *Mozert*
          case)    11, 13, 93, 95
    crucifixes on Italian state school classroom
          walls    65
    England
        and Church of England    71
        conflicts    77–78
        Education Act (1902)    71
        faith schools    71–73, 75
        *Jewish Free School (JFS)* case    84–85
        School Standards and Framework Act
              (1998)    71
        Teachers' Standards    76
        'Trojan Plot' scandal, Birmingham    73
    faith schools    71–73, 75
        *Jewish Free School (JFS)* case    84–85
    France
        French ideal    47
        Law banning display of religious symbols
              in schools (2004 Law)    23, 45–48
        religious freedom potentially hindering
              learning    23
*Egenberger v Evangelisches* case (2018)
    facts of case    146–147

rejection of church autonomy argument
in   147–152
autonomy not entailing
self-determination   147–148
comparison with British
position   150–151
connection independent of
employee's faith and impact on
followers   151–152
work religious ethos and the
employee's tasks, connection
requirement   148–149
religious organisations, rights to impose
adherence to religious ethos   20
ruling   174
**Eisgruber, Christopher**   5, 64, 87–88, 89
analogous-to-secular view   5, 6, 82, 83, 85
*Religious Freedom and the
Constitution*   86
response to critique of search for secular
comparators   90–91
**employment sector**
argument against delegation to
employers   180–181
argument against denying corporate
employers religious
freedoms   168–170
argument against denying employees vested
rights to equality   167–168
and ECHR   15–16
employer's prerogatives and secular
ethos   124–126
Equal Treatment Directive   15
genuine and determining occupational
requirement   120
lack of religious beliefs as reason to refuse
employment   146
reasons for research focus   15
refusal to work on Sundays   88
rights of religious organisations to impose
adherence to religious ethos   20
work religious ethos and the
employee's tasks, connection
requirement   148–149
independent of employee's faith and
impact on followers   151–152
*see also* consistency argument, religious
employees; religious symbols, right
to wear in workplace
**England**
and Brexit   182–184
British values and liberalism   25, 70–78

Church of England, independent from
politics   67–69
Common Law   59
compared with France   58–59, 79
educationand Church of England   71
conflicts   77–78
Education Act (1902)   71
faith schools   71–73, 75
*Jewish Free School (JFS)* case   84–85
School Standards and Framework Act
(1998)   71
Teachers' Standards   76
'Trojan Plot' scandal, Birmingham   73
ethno-religious groups, classifying   74
'extreme' religious views, targeting   24–25
faith schools   71–73, 75
*Jewish Free School (JFS)* case   84–85
freedom of conscience
protection independent of religious
views   75–76
protection independent of State views
on religion   76–78
fundamental British values (FBV)   76, 77,
78, 177
Houses of Parliament   68, 69
human rights legislation   15
Jewish people   70
Muslims in   70, 76–77
reasons for research focus   27–28
religious freedom   24–25
religious minorities in   71–74
*vivre ensemble*   58–79
*see also* establishment, church (England)
**epistemological problem**   5, 14, 83–85
accommodationist approach   11–13
*Jewish Free School (JFS)* case   84–85
**equality rights**
Equal Liberty   86
Equal Treatment Directive   15, 119,
122–123, 128
Equality Act (England)   150
establishment, equality objection to
62–63, 65
failure of equal regard   89
as foundation for democracy   86
and religious freedom   6, 157–173
*Ashers Baking* case (2018)   157,
171–172
balancing of private interests in legislative
ambiguous context   159–166
balancing of private interests in US
context   166–172

*Burwell v Hobby Lobby* case
(2014) 166, 167–170
commitment to equality not removing
religious freedom interests 162
*Masterpiece Cakeshop* case (2018) 166,
170–171
Waldron on 105
*see also Achbita (Samira) v G4S Secure
Solutions* case; *Bougnaoui v
Micropole* case (2017)
establishment, church (England) 19, 24–25,
60–70
Anglican Church 69
dissenters, abolition of discrimination
against 66–67
equality objection to 62–63, 65
forms 61
as inclusive form of secularism 60–70
compatibility with inclusive
socialism 60, 66, 67, 69, 70
inclusive secularism 66–69
independence between Church of England
and politics 67–69
majority/minority divide, beyond 63
mild 63
non-coercive 67
possibility of 61–65
Prevent duty 24, 78
stronger case for 63–65
tolerant model 60
*see also* Church of England; England
Enoch, David 108
Esbeck, Carl H 167, 168
European Convention on Human Rights
(ECHR) 15–16, 65, 141
European Court of Human Rights
(ECtHR) 2, 46, 65, 134, 145, 176
case law on proportionality versus
autonomy 152–156
comparative analysis of *Obst v
Schüth* 153–154
*Fernández Martínez v Spain* (2014),
analysis 152, 154–156
*Travaš v Croatia* (2016), analysis 152,
154–156
*Kokkinakis* decision (1993) 80, 81, 103
laïcité 39–42
overview of cases 152–153
religious freedom and equality 156, 159
religious freedom and pluralism 112, 118
*see also* Court of Justice of the European
Union (CJEU)

evolutionary theories 38
*Eweida v UK* (2013) 20*n*, 75, 130–132, 158,
163, 179
compared with *Achbita* 131, 134,
135–136
contracting out approach 134
facts and judgment 130–131

faith schools 71–73, 75
*Jewish Free School (JFS)* case 84–85
Fedtke, Jörg 18
Fergusson, James 73
Ferrari, Alessandro 18
Fish, Stanley 10–11, 92, 93, 97, 98
Fitzpatrick, Peter 18
Flake, Dallan 125
Fletcher, George P 18
Forest Service 90–91
Foyer, Jean 37
Fox, Jonathan 64
France
banning of display of religious symbols
in schools (2004 Law) 23, 45–48
banning of full covering of the face in
public places (2010 law) 7–8, 7*n*,
23–24, 48–49, 55, 56
Catholic Church 31–42, 155
cités 51
Civil Constitution of the Clergy 35
compared with England 58–59, 79
Conseil d'Etat 31, 42–45, 50, 128
*Demoiselle Marteaux* opinion 141
Muslim veil, wearing of 48
*Rapport* 38*n*, 39*n*, 40*n*, 43*n*, 49*n*
separatist/inclusive interpretation
of laïcité 45–48
Constitutional Council 43, 49, 55
Cour de cassation 124, 127, 129, 142
Dreyfus affair 40, 41
employment law 15, 116, 123–124
Goblet Law (1886) 38
inclusion principle 24
Jewish people 40
Law on Separation of Church and State
(1905) 38–42, 44, 57, 177
religious minorities 39–42
separatist laïcité 38–39
Law on the Deontology, Rights and Duties
of Public Agents (2016) 124, 141
legal position on right to wear religious
symbols in workplace 20,
123–124

living together with others while
　　also embracing core French
　　ideological commitments
　　*see vivre ensemble*
misplaced proportionality test    142–143
national identity    34–35
neutrality requirements    127
Parliament    46
political culture    30
public sphere    45, 128
reasons for research focus    27–28
Republican values    23, 24
riots of 2005    51–52
Second Empire    37–38
secularism *see* laïcité (French secularism)
social divides    23, 51–52
Third Republic    38
*see also* French Revolution
Frankenberg, Günter    18
freedom of speech    108
freedom of thought, conscience and
　　religion    176
　ECtHR on    81–82
　England
　　independent of doctrinal religious
　　　views    75–76
　　independent of State views on
　　　religion    76–78
　France
　　headscarf incidents    46
　　laïcité    38–39, 43
　liberalism and religion    94
Freeman, Michael    47
French Declaration of the Rights of Man and
　　the Citizen (1789)    31, 43
French Revolution    31, 32–38
　Catholic Church, hostility to    33, 34, 36,
　　37–38, 47
　class mobility    32
　heritage of    37–38
　ideals    32, 34–37, 55
　militant secularism    35
　political in    31, 34–35
　revolutionary heritage    37–38
　"The Terror" (September 1793 to
　　July 1794)    36
　Third Estate    32
　transcendence ideal    36, 37, 55
functionalist methods, comparative law    17
fundamental British values (FBV)    76, 77,
　　78, 177
Furet, François    31, 32, 34–36

gag rules    100–101
Garahan, Sabina    142
García Oliva, Javier    61, 154
Garnett, Richard W    168
Garvey, John H    14
Gaspard, Françoise    54
Gauchet, Marcel    44
Gaus, Gerald F    107
Gedicks, Frederick M    166
Gengembre, Gérard    33
Gerstenberg, Oliver    16, 123, 156
Gonzales, Gérard    56
Gordon, Michael    59
Greenawalt, Kent    15, 96, 104
Grimm, Dieter    28–31, 39, 43, 56, 59,
　　66, 81
Guesnet, François    76
Gunn, Jeremy T    58
Gutmann, Amy    1, 3

Haarscher, Guy    45, 56
Habermas, Jürgen,    1, 18, 81, 97
　on public reason    108, 109–110
Hall, Helen    61
Halpin, Andrew    17
Hambler, Andrew    119, 132, 133, 161
Hamburger, Philip A,    2
headscarf incidents (Islamic)    6, 45, 52, 132
　banning of headscarf    23, 45–48, 119
　case law    119–138
　coercion, evidence of    46
　complaints by patients in medical
　　context    141
　direct or indirect discrimination    119, 120,
　　122
　*see also Achbita (Samira) v G4S Secure
　　Solutions* case; religious symbols,
　　right to wear in workplace
Hennette, Stéphanie    124
Henry VIII of England    58
*hijab*
　compared with *burqa* or *niqab*    136
　compared with wearing cross
　　135–136
　customers' objections to    122, 123
　right to wear in workplace    131
*Hobby Lobby* case *see Burwell v Hobby Lobby
　　Stores* case (2014)
Hollingworth, Sumi    73
Holmes, Stephen    2, 29, 82
　and pluralism    82, 99, 100, 101
　and Rawls    103

homosexuality *see* same-sex couples,
   equality rights clashing with
   religious freedom
Horwitz, Morton J   168

immigration   28
impartiality concern, accommodationist
   approach   11–13
inclusion principle   3–4, 13, 15–20, 24,
   139
   rationale   110–111
inclusive secularism   32, 59
   English establishment   66–69
      dissenters, abolition of discrimination
         against   66–67
      independence between Church of
         England and politics   67–69
      non-coercive   67
      type three secularism   67
   laïcité   29–30
      moving closer to   80–81
integrity-protecting-commitment (IPC)
   8, 9
intolerance   13, 41
   intolerant religious citizen   10, 11,
      95, 98
   of liberalism, towards illiberal views
      92, 93–94, 97
   *see also* tolerance
intolerant view   11
Iser, Mattias   111
Islam
   fear of   19
   headscarf incidents *see* headscarf incidents
      (Islamic)
   integration into French Republic   47
   and laïcité   28–29, 44
      instrument for assimilation of
         Islam   53–54
   Quran   83
   terrorism   28
   visibility of   23
   *see also* Muslims
Islamophobia   52, 54

Ja'far, Zein   73
Jarnier, Jean-Luc   41
Jaurès, Jean   39, 41, 42
Jewish people   70
   antisemitism   40, 41
   *Jewish Free School (JFS)* case   84–85
   Joly, Bertrand   41

Kepel, Gilles (laïcité of)   44, 49–53
   conflicting ideological dichotomous
      discourses   52–53
      going beyond dichotomies   55–56
   critique of reasoning   54
   *La Fracture*   50
   link between religious radicalism
      and terrorism   49, 50–52, 57
   riots of 2005   51–52
   social divides   51–52
Khan, Mariam
Khattab, Nabil   73–74
Khosrokhavar, Farhad   54
King, Michael   77
Kintzler, Catherine   47
Knights, Samantha   15
*Kokkinakis v Greece* (1993)   2, 80, 103
Koppelman, Andrew   63, 166
Koussens, David   18, 48

Laborde, Cécile   5, 9, 61, 63–65, 87–88, 91
   *Liberalism's Religion*   63, 86
*Ladele v Islington BC* (2009)   20, 173
   clash of private interests   160, 161
   lack of procedural fairness in   162–163
   presentation of case   159–160
   religious freedom and equality   158,
      159–160
Laegaard, Sune   62
laïcité (French secularism)
   closed version   23, 45
   common values and liberalism   44–57
   communautarian   44
   communautarian vs inclusive   53–56
   conflicting ideological dichotomous
      discourses   52–53
      going beyond dichotomies   55–56
   constitutional principle   144
   contemporary form   36
   deference
      alleged, to constitutional laïcité
         context   126–129
      *Ebrahimian* case   140–144
      neutrality principle   141–142
      as opposed to delegation   140–146
   and democratic *vivre ensemble*   27–57
   endorsed by 2004 Law banning display
      of religious symbols in state
      schools   23, 45–48, 55
   extension of requirements to the purely
      private sphere   127–128
   and French Revolution   31, 32–38

of Gilles Kepel    49–53
historical analysis    31–44
inclusive type    29–30
    and English church establishment    60–70
    as ideal    30, 57, 59
instrument for assimilation of
        Islam    53–54
and Islam    28–29
whether a militant form of secularism    19,
        29, 31–36
misplaced deference to    128–129
national identity through universal
        ideals    34–35
private sphere    116
recent extensions of    45–49
religious minorities    39–42
secularisation and revolution    32–34
separatist
    with inclusive elements    42–43
    laïcité traditionally defined as    31
    Law on Separation of Church and State
        (1905)    38–42, 44, 57, 177
    separatist/militant conception endorsed
        by 2004 Law    23, 45–48
*see also* secularism
Larkin, Stuart    59
Larmore, Charles    104
*Lautsi v Italy* (2012)    65
Law Commission    67, 72
Law on Separation of Church and State
        (1905), France    38–42, 44, 57, 177
    religious minorities    39–42
    separatist laïcité    38–39
Lawson, Anna    157
Laycock, Douglas    169
Lee, Lois    76
Legrand, Pierre    18
legal norms    17
legitimacy principle    103–104
Leigh, Ian    33, 58, 61, 62, 67, 161
Leiken, Robert S    72
Letsas, George    87, 89
Lewis, Tom
liberalism
    and British values    70–78
    and common values, in laïcité    44–57
    contradictions    93–94
    criticisms    15
    intolerance towards illiberal views    92,
        93–94, 97
    of Laborde    64
    liberal democratic *vivre ensemble*    80–118

liberal public order as baseline    95–97
neutrality principle    93, 96
ordoliberal inspiration of *Achbita*
        123–124, 126
partiality, accusation of    11, 92–93, 97
and religion/religious freedom    15, 80–83,
        92, 93, 97, 98
substantive values    4
Liogier, Raphaël    38, 46
Long, Robert    70
Louis XIV of France    32
Lucas, John    58, 66, 68
Lund, Christopher C    90

McClure, Jennifer M    64
McColgan, Aileen    137
McConnell, Michael    10–13, 94–97
McCrea, Ronan    99, 161
McCrudden, Christopher    83, 85, 89, 109
    *Litigating Religions*    91
McFarlin, Jaimie K    168
McGoldrick    50, 51
Malik, Maleiha    132, 160
Mancini, Susanna    27
Markesinis, Basil    18
Marlière, Philippe    21
*Martínez (Fernández) v Spain* (2014),
        analysis    20, 154–156
    comparison with *Obst*    155
*Masterpiece Cakeshop* case (2018)    166, 167,
        173
    analogous-to-secular view    6–7
    compared with *Ashers Bakery*    172
    non-disparaging context    170–171
Mathiez, Albert    35
May, Theresa    183
Menski, Werner    16
method of avoidance *see* avoidance method
Michaels, Ralf    16
militant secularism (France)    19, 28, 29, 44
    laïcité classed as, whether    31–36
    separatist/militant conception endorsed
        by 2004 Law    23, 45–48
Miller, David    63–64
minorities, religious *see* religious minorities
Mirza, Munira    73
Modood, Tariq    62–63, 70, 73
Montgomery, Jonathan    2
Mormon Church    153
Morris, Bob    58, 62, 66, 68, 69
Morris, Lydia    73
Moyn, Samuel    9

*Mozert v Hawkins* (1987)   11, 13, 93, 95
Muir Watt, Horatia   14, 16
multiculturalism, versus secularism   28
Muslims
    assimilation of   23, 53–54
    banning of full covering of the face in
            public places   83, 136
        *burqa*   48–49, 55, 56, 83, 142
        France   7–8, 23–24, 48–49, 55
    customers' preferences regarding
            dress   119, 120, 122
    in England   70, 76–77
    fear of Islam   19
    headscarf incidents *see* headscarf incidents
            (Islamic)
    *hijab*, customers' objections to   122, 123,
            135–136
    immigration of families   28

*niqab*, ban on   8, 9, 48–49, 122
    Sunni   88
    veil, wearing of   8, 9, 48–49
    visibility of Islam   23
    *see also* Islam
Nadel, Sean   169
Nagel, Thomas   80, 91, 98
national constitutional sphere   121,
            126–129
natural justice principles   121
Nelson, James D   168
neutrality principle   6, 110, 141–142
    in France   127, 141–142
    liberalism   93, 96
    secularism   96
    unilateral policy, case law   119–123, 129
Newcombe, David G   58
*niqab*, ban on   8, 9, 48–49, 122
non-interference/non-intervention
    accommodationist approach   10–13
    avoidance method   24, 110
    free market economy   3–4
    inclusion principle   3
    ordoliberal baseline argument   122–126
    principle of   94–95
    religious symbols, right to wear in
            workplace   122–123
Norman, Edward R   61, 62, 68
norms   15, 117
    Catholic   155
    constitutional   147
    legal   17
Nussbaum, Martha   15, 21, 61, 62, 65

O'Cinneide, Colm   15, 182
Obin Report   46
*Obst v Germany* case (2010)   20
    comparison with *Martínez*   155
    comparison with *Schüth*   153–154
    Oleske, Jim Jr,   7
openness, attitude of   15
ordoliberal baseline argument,
            non-interventionist   122–126
    *Achbita* case   123–124, 126, 129, 180
overlapping consensus   105

Parisot, Valérie   75, 161
Pena-Ruiz, Henri   36
Perez, Nahshon   64
Petersen, Hanne   17
Picquart, Colonel   41
Pildes, Richard H   64
pluralism   14
    concept of religious freedom amenable
            to   17
    gag rules as protective of the public
            sphere   100–101
    Holmes on   99, 100, 101
    importance for democracy and religious
            freedom   98–111
    legal, theory of   16–17
    legitimacy principle   103–104
    and public reason *see* public reason
    public reason requirement   104
    and Rawls   99, 102–103
    and religious freedom   81, 82, 98–111
    and self-restraint   100
politics
    French political culture   30
    and French Revolution   31, 34–35
    independence from Church of
            England   67–69
    and public reason   107
Portier, Philipe   36
private interests, balancing
    *Burwell v Hobby Lobby Stores* case (2014)
        argument against denying
            corporate employers religious
            freedoms   168–170
        argument against denying employees
            vested rights to equality
            167–170
    clash of private interests   160, 161
    *Ladele* case (2009)   159–160
        lack of procedural fairness in
            162–163

in legislative ambiguous context   159–166
  *Bull v Hall* (2013)   163–165
  *Ladele* case (2009)   159–160, 162–163
  normative ambiguities, impact   164–166
in US context   166–171
  *Burwell v Hobby Lobby* (2014)   166,
    167–170
  *Masterpiece Cakeshop* (2018)   166,
    170–171
*see also* equality; religious freedom
**private sphere**   121, 124
contractual autonomy   121
laïcité   116
and public sphere   36n, 42, 57, 92, 101,
  103, 120
  public or private sector customers   120,
    126, 128n
religious symbols, right to wear in
  workplace   127–128
safeguarding from state interference   15, 91
strict form   47, 129
*see also* public sphere
**proportionality considerations**   139–140
*Achbita* case   120, 129
  critical analysis   136–137
autonomy versus proportionality
  146–157
  rejection of church autonomy argument
    in *Egenberger*   147–152
consistency over proportionality
  emphasis   130–137, 146
customer-facing role   121
lightness of sanction irrelevant in a
  proportionality test   143–144
misplaced test, France   142–143
reduction of proportionality test for
  procedural consistency   135–137
religious freedom, democratic approach
  to   181–182
scope for a revised reassessment   145–146
**public agents, right to wear religious
  symbols**   20, 43, 127
**public reason**   83
duty of civility argument   105, 107–108
Habermas on   109–110
improved political deliberation
  argument   105–106, 107
intelligibility argument   105, 106
and pluralism/religious freedom   104–110
and public forum   108–109
Rawls on   104–106, 108, 110
Waldron's critique of   105–106

**public sphere**   14, 28, 82
defining   127n
France   45, 128
full covering of face in   7n, 83, 128n, 136
  France   7–8, 23–24, 48–49, 52, 55
gag rules as protective of   100–101
'naked'   96
and private sphere   36n, 42, 57, 92, 101,
  103, 120
  public or private sector customers   120,
    126, 128n
*see also* private sphere

**Quinn, Philip L**   107
**Quong, Jonathan**   104, 107
**Quran**   83

**radicalism, religious, terrorism link**   49,
  50–52, 57, 77, 79, 177
**Rawls, John**   2, 3, 4, 14, 82, 96, 115, 139
citizenship ideal   104
and Holmes   103
and legitimacy principle   103–104
on overlapping consensus   105
on pluralism   99, 102–103
*Political Liberalism*   102, 103, 108
on public reason   104–106, 108, 110
reciprocity idea   104
**Raz, Joseph**   165
**Rehg, William**   109–110
**religion**
Christian and ethnocentric
  understanding   9
concept   12
defining in law and religion debates   82
diversity of voices   3, 5
epistemological problem   5, 11–13, 14, 83–85
and ethnicity   9, 84
lack of religious beliefs as reason to refuse
  employment   146
and liberalism   15, 80–83, 92, 93, 97, 98
regulation of   94
separation from state   38–42, 44, 57, 177
  *see also* Christianity; Islam; Jewish
    people; Muslims; religious
    autonomy; religious freedom;
    religious symbols; separatist
    secularism; Sikhs
**religious autonomy**   72
British position   150–151
  decline of autonomy in English
    law   74–78

*Egenberger* case, rejection of church
  autonomy argument in   147–152
  autonomy not entailing
    self-determination   147–148
  comparison with British
    position   150–151
  work religious ethos and the
    employee's tasks, connection
    requirement   148–152
German law   147–148
versus proportionality   146–157
  British position   150–151
  ECtHR guidelines   152–156
  rejection of church autonomy argument
    in *Egenberger*   147–152
  United States   155
*vivre ensemble* ideal   77
work religious ethos and the
  employee's tasks, connection
  requirement   148–149
  independent of employee's faith and
    impact on followers   151–152
**religious freedom**
analogous-to-secular view   5
democratic approach to   177–179
  comparative demonstration   177–178
  consequences for the courts   179–184
  delegation to employers, argument
    against   180–181
  normative demonstration   1, 178–179
  nuanced deference to national
    traditions   181
  and pluralism   101
  proportionality considerations
    181–182
dilution of   83–91
disaggregative approach   7–8
in England   24–25
epistemological problem   5, 11–13, 14,
  83–85
and equality rights   6, 157–173
  argument against denying
    corporate employers religious
    freedoms   168–170
  argument against denying employees
    vested rights to equality   167–168
  *Ashers Baking* case (2018)   157,
    171–172
  balancing of private interests in legislative
    ambiguous context   159–166
  balancing of private interests in US
    context   166–172

commitment to equality not removing
    religious freedom interests   162
as foundation for democracy   86
European frameworks and religious
    rights   15–16
as force for intolerance   13
importance for democracy   82–98
isolation of   92–97
and liberalism   15, 92
Muslim veil, wearing of   8, 9, 48–49
negative approach to   13
and pluralism   81, 82, 98–111
potentially hindering learning   23
practical importance of concept   83–84
and public reason *see* public reason
search for a secular comparator   87–88
  consequences for religious freedom   91
  critique of   89–91
  response of Eisgruber and Sager to
    critique   90–91
  secular analogies or equivalents,
    through   87
*see also* religion
*Religious Freedom in the Liberal State*
    (**Adhar and Leigh**)   62
**religious minorities**
courts' bias against   11–12
England   71–74
entrenched social divides   72–74
equality rights clashing with religious
    freedom of   20–21
Law on Separation of Church and State
    (1905)   39–42
Muslims   23
religious autonomy   72
rights   65
*see also* Muslims
**religious symbols**
banning of full covering of the face in
    public places   83, 128n, 136
France   7–8, 23–24, 48–49, 52, 55
Christian cross, right to wear over uniform
    (*Eweida*)   75, 130–131, 134–136,
    163, 179
consistency
  burdens of consistency argument for
    religious employees   132–135
  "contracting out" approach   134–135
  procedural   135–137
  as proof of sincerity and
    cogency   132–134
  versus proportionality   130–137

crucifixes on Italian state school classroom
walls　65
in France　20, 43
laïcité context, alleged deference
to　126–129
extension of requirements to purely
private sphere　127–128
misplaced deference　128–129
neutrality principle　6, 141–142
proportionality
versus consistency　135–137
critical analysis, in *Achbita*　136–137
factual divergence between *Eweida* and
*Achbita*　135–136
test reduced mainly for procedural
consistency　135–137
public agents, right to wear　20, 43, 127
right to wear in workplace　1, 119–138
Christian cross (*Eweida* case)　20n, 75,
130–131, 134–136, 158, 163, 179
contradiction between *Bougnaoui* and
*Achbita*　122–123
employer's prerogatives and secular
ethos　124–126
equality issues　86
moderate stance of French law　123–124
non-interventionist ordoliberal baseline
argument　122–126
in schools　23, 45–48, 65
spheres
contractual　122–126
national　126–129
and principles　121–129
private　127–128
*see also* headscarf incidents (Islamic)
revision principle　4–5, 13, 15–20, 110, 111,
139, 180
riots, France (2005)　51
Rivers, Julian　59, 71, 74
Rorty, Richard　20
Rosenfeld, Michel　27
Roughan, Nicole　17
Rousseau, Jean-Jacques　34–35
Roy, Olivier　28, 54
Rude-Antoine, Edwige　54

Sabel, Charles F　16, 17, 157
Sager, Lawrence　5, 64, 87–88, 89
analogous-to-secular view　5, 6, 82, 83, 85
*Religious Freedom and the Constitution*　86
response to critique of search for secular
comparators　90–91

same-sex couples, equality rights clashing
with religious freedom　20–21
refusal to provide services　157–173
bakers　6–7, 20, 84, 157, 171, 172
hoteliers　20, 163–164
weddings, in relation to　157, 158
*see also Ladele v Islington BC* (2009)
right to marry　164, 165
Sandberg, Russell　150
Sandel, Michael J　95
Sarkozy, Nicolas　48
*SAS v France* (2014)　55, 56
disaggregative approach　7–8
misplaced proportionality test　142–143
Schnapper, Dominique　18, 27, 45, 52, 56
schools *see* education
*Schüth v Germany* case (2011), comparison
with *Obst*　153–154
Schwartzman, Micah　5, 168
Scot, Jean-Paul　40
Scott, Craig　16
Scott, Joan W　53
'Secularia' (fictional state)　63, 64
secularism
constitutional states　29
liberal　43, 63
versus multiculturalism　28
neutrality principle　96
pluralism-friendly type　19
and positive constitutionalism　29
religious freedom through secular
analogies/equivalents　87
secularisation　32–34
'secular-to-analogous' view　178
type one (militant form)　19, 28, 29, 44
determining whether laïcité classed
as　31–36
separatist/militant conception endorsed
by 2004 Law　23, 45–48
type two (separatist)　2, 29, 31, 35
versus accommodationist　94
with inclusive elements　42–43
laïcité　38–39, 42–43, 45–48
state and religion, separation
between　2, 37–42
type three (inclusive)　29–30, 32, 59
and English church establishment
60–70
as ideal　30, 57, 59
moving closer to　80–81
*see also* laïcité (French secularism)
Seglow, Jonathan　165

self-restraint, democratic rule as    100
Senthilkumaran, Abi    73
separatist secularism (separation of Church
        and state)    2, 29, 35
    versus accommodationist secularism    94
    laïcité
        with inclusive elements    42–43
        separatist/militant conception endorsed
            by 2004 Law    23, 45–48
        traditionally defined as separatist    31
    Law on Separation of Church and State
        (1905)    38–39, 44, 57, 177
        religious minorities    39–42
        strict form    43
service providers, rights to refuse    6–7,
        157–173
    bakers    6–7, 20, 84, 157, 171, 172
    hoteliers    20, 163–164
    weddings, in relation to    157, 158
    *see also Ladele v Islington BC* (2009)
Shah, Prakash    12
Shiek, Dagmar    157
Sikhs
    refusal to wear motorcycle helmet    90
    turbans    131, 136
Simon, William H    17
Sinopoli, Richard C    65
Slaughter, Anne-Marie    17
Smith, Cyril    69
Smith, Steven D    93, 105
social divides
    England    72–74
    France    23, 51–52
Soboul, Albert    32
Solanke, Iyiola    134
Sorrel, Christian    38
Spalek, Basia    77
Spaventa, Eleanor    137
specific situation rule    134–135
spheres of competence    121–129
    contractual sphere    122–126
    national constitutional sphere    121,
        126–129
    private sphere *see* private sphere
    public sphere *see* public sphere
Stasi Report    46
state and religion, separation between
        *see* separatist secularism
Stout, Jeffrey    105
Struthers, Alison EC    76
Stychin, Carl    165
Sullivan, Kathleen    95–97

Sullivan, Winnifred Fallers    12–13
    *The Impossibility of Religious
        Freedom*    12

Tackett, Timothy    35, 36
Taylor, Charles    2
Tebbe, Nelson    15, 167, 168
terrorism
    Islamist    28
    link with religious radicalism    49, 50–52,
        57, 77, 79, 177
    and Prevent duty    24
Thomas, Oliver S    169
Thompson, Dennis    1, 3
Tocqueville, Alexis de    4, 32
tolerance    13, 28, 60, 93
    and democracy    60
    fundamental British values (FBV)    76
    and justice    41
    and liberalism    15*n*, 80, 92–95
    mutual    78*n*
    reason for    91, 98
    towards the intolerant or religious devout
        persons    11, 91
    *see also* intolerance
*Travaš v Croatia* case (2016), analysis    152,
        154–156
Tridimas, Takis    121
Trispiotis. Ilias    163
Tushnet, Mark    168
Twining, William    17

Unger, Roberto    1, 18, 111
United States    21*n*, 61*n*, 88
    Affordable Care Plan statute    167
    case law    20, 86, 88*n*, 89, 90*n*, 140, 156,
        157*n*, 158, 165*n*, 167
    Constitutional Clauses    96
    debates    140, 156–157, 166
    Declaration of Independence (1776)
        35*n*
    First Amendment    40, 96
    Free Exercise Clause    96
    private interests, balancing    166–172
    Religion Clause    96
    religious autonomy    155
    Religious Freedom Restoration Act
        (RFRA)    167–168, 169
    *see also Burwell v Hobby Lobby Stores*
        (2014); *Masterpiece Cakeshop*
        case (2018); *Mozert v Hawkins*
        (1987)

Van Tassell, Rebecca G   166
Valentin, Vincent   124, 125
Vallier, Kevin J   107
Vermeren, Pierre   53
Vickers, Lucy   15, 135, 137
Vincent, Carol   76
*vivre ensemble*   1, 7, 24, 77, 176
    breaking down of   23, 115
    common   178
    communautarian   177
    democratic   4, 6, 13, 14, 21,
        80–118
    and England   58–79
    interpretative notion   55–56
    marginal viewpoints   24
    mended   115–116
Volokh, Eugene   167, 168

Waldron, Jeremy   105–107
Walker, Neil   16
Walsh, Kevin C   168

Waltman, Jerold   150
Warhola, James W   33
Warnock, Mary   69
Weale, Albert   21
Weiler, Joseph HH   119, 132, 135
Wenar, Leif   104
Weil, Patrick   46
Weithman, Paul   105
West, Anne   73
Willaime, Jean-Paul   45
Williams, Katya   73
Williams, Kevin   47
Winock, Michel   41
Wintemute, Robert   183
Wolterstorff, Nicholas   83, 106, 107
workplace *see* employment sector; religious
        symbols

Zahle, Henrik   17
Zucca, L   18
Zumbansen, Peer C   16

www.ingramcontent.com/pod-product-compliance
Lightning Source LLC
Chambersburg PA
CBHW070241290326
41929CB00046B/2308